Outsourcing in European Emerging Economies

Drawing on a range of European cases, this edited volume analyses the offshoring and outsourcing of foreign companies, with a focus on territorial embeddedness.

The book opens by developing a theoretical framework and then presents a range of international case studies exploring the experiences of the service hub cities of Brno, Bratislava, Budapest, Krakow, and Prague. Attention is also given to internal and external determinants of embeddedness, with chapters on the employee perspective, the Fintech industry, corporate social responsibility, and the role of universities.

This volume will be of interest to advanced students and researchers in regional economics, economic geography, innovation studies, industrial economics, European economics, and international business.

Łukasz Mamica is an associate professor and the Head of Department of Public Economics, Cracow University of Economics, Poland. He is the coordinator of Research Area Industrial Policy and Development at the European Association for Evolutionary Political Economy (EAEPE). He has co-authored all the regional innovation strategies for the Malopolska region and has served as an expert in several projects funded by the OECD, the European Union, Polish government departments, and regional administration units.

Routledge Advances in Regional Economics, Science and Policy

Economic Clusters and Globalization
Diversity and Resilience
Edited by Francisco Puig and Berrbizne Urzelai

Transnational Regions in Historical Perspective
Edited by Marten Boon, Hein A.M. Klemann and Ben Wubs

Urban Development in China under the Institution of Land Rights
Jieming Zhu

The Geography of Mobility, Wellbeing and Development in China
Understanding Transformations Through Big Data
Edited by Wenjie Wu and Yiming Wang

Traveling Expertise and Regional Development
Andreas Öjehag-Pettersson and Tomas Mitander

Governing Cities
Asia's Urban Transformation
Edited by Kris Hartley, Glen Kuecker, Michael Waschak, Jun Jie Woo, and Charles Chao Rong Phua

Mental Health and Wellbeing in Rural Regions
International Perspectives
Edited by Sarah-Anne Munoz and Steve F. Bain

Family Business and Regional Development
Edited by Rodrigo Basco, Roger Stough and Lech Suwala

Outsourcing in European Emerging Economies
Territorial Embeddedness and Global Business Services
Edited by Łukasz Mamica

For more information about this series, please visit: www.routledge.com/series/RAIRESP

Outsourcing in European Emerging Economies

Territorial Embeddedness and Global Business Services

Edited by Łukasz Mamica

Routledge
Taylor & Francis Group
LONDON AND NEW YORK

First published 2021
by Routledge
2 Park Square, Milton Park, Abingdon, Oxon OX14 4RN

and by Routledge
605 Third Avenue, New York, NY 10017

First issued in paperback 2022

Routledge is an imprint of the Taylor & Francis Group, an informa business

Publisher's Note
The publisher has gone to great lengths to ensure the quality of this reprint but points out that some imperfections in the original copies may be apparent.

British Library Cataloguing-in-Publication Data
A catalogue record for this book is available from the British Library

Library of Congress Cataloging-in-Publication Data
A catalog record for this book has been requested

ISBN: 978-0-367-62168-1 (pbk)
ISBN: 978-0-367-89383-5 (hbk)
ISBN: 978-1-003-01888-9 (ebk)

DOI: 10.4324/9781003018889

Typeset in Times New Roman
by Apex CoVantage, LLC

Contents

Figures

Tables

Contributors

Paweł Białynicki-Birula – PhD; economist, lawyer, assistant professor, Department of Public Economy, Cracow University of Economics (Poland). His research interests focus on public management and administration, health economics, and public finance. Expert in several projects funded by domestic and foreign sources.

Zoltán Gál – PhD; full professor (Finance), University of Pécs (Hungary); senior researcher, Centre for Economic and Regional Research. President of the Hungarian Regional Science Association; regional ambassador of Global Network on Financial Geography and member of the European Organizing Committee of the European Regional Science Association (ERSA). Served as an invited expert at the European Commission DG Research, project manager of INTERREG, ESPON and in macro-financial FP7 projects. His research interests include regional finance, international finance, international economics, regional economics, financial and economic geography, and regional innovation. He has been a visiting scholar at the University of Oxford (UK), Trinity College, Dublin (Ireland), and others. He is a member of the editorial boards of several international journals.

Tomasz Geodecki – PhD (Economics); assistant professor, Department of Public Policy, Cracow University of Economics (Poland). His research interests include economics of innovation, political economy, and competitiveness in the context of globalisation of supply chains. He is an expert in European, national, and regional scientific projects and evaluation studies on innovation and economic competitiveness.

Jakub Głowacki – PhD (Economics); assistant professor, Department of Public Economics, Cracow University of Economics (Poland); member of the Board of the Malopolska Social Economy Fund (since 2009). His research interests include new technologies in the public sector, public policy analysis, local government, water policy, and renewable energy sources. He has authored and co-authored several dozen publications in these fields. He has served as an expert in numerous research and implementation projects funded by the European Union, Polish government departments, and regional administration units.

Janusz Górecki – PhD (Geography, Jagiellonian University) with a broad professional experience in analysing local and regional development and effects of foreign direct investments. Over the past nine years, he has worked as Head of Research at ABSL, a leading organisation representing business services in Poland.

Stanislav Klazar – PhD; associate professor, member of the Public Finance Department, University of Economics, Prague. He was coordinator of the international scientific conference, "Theoretical and Practical Aspects of Public Finance" (TPAPF). He has served as an expert in several projects financed by the Czech Ministry of Finance, the Czech Statistical Office, the Czech Chamber of Deputies, and the Czech Science Foundation.

Piotr Kopyciński – PhD (Economics); assistant professor, Department of Public Economics, Cracow University of Economics (Poland). He was Director of the Malopolska School of Public Administration, Cracow University of Economics (2014–2016). Research interests include public policy (particularly innovation policy and territorial policy), modes of governance (public governance, neo-Weberian state), and reforms in Central and Eastern Europe. He has served as an expert in numerous projects and authored/co-authored several dozen publications in these fields of study. Recently, he participated in the following projects: "Progress Assessment of the ESF Support to Public Administration" ("PAPA") (European Commission); "Decentralization Offering Better Results and Efficiency" ("DOBRE") on decentralization reforms in Ukraine (USAID); and "GOSPOSTRATEG-otoGOZ" on developing a system of indicators concerning circular economy (Ministry of Entrepreneurship and Technology, Poland).

Łukasz Mamica – PhD; associate professor. Currently, he is Head of Department of Public Economics, Cracow University of Economics. He is the coordinator of Research Area Industrial Policy and Development at European Association for Evolutionary Political Economy (EAEPE). He has co-authored all the regional innovation strategies for the Malopolska region and has served as an expert in several projects funded by OECD, the European Union, Polish government departments, and regional administration units.

Robert Marciniak – PhD; assistant professor, Department of Management Control, Institute of Management, Corvinus University of Budapest. As a senior academic lecturer, he teaches a number of management areas at various European universities. He is also a senior researcher and expert in global business services, supply-chain management, strategic management, IT management, and process management in Hungary.

Monika Mazur-Bubak – PhD (Political Science); Department of Public Economics, Faculty of Public Economy and Administration, Cracow University of Economics. She is a member of the board of the Polish Philosophical Society, member of the Polish Philosophical Society and Polish Karl Jaspers Society. Her main fields of interests include political philosophy, philosophy of war, social and political identities, business ethics, and free market ethics. She is currently working on a book on the modern paradigm of war based on modern theories of war and its anomalies.

František Ochrana – research professor, Centre for Social and Economic Studies, Faculty of Social Sciences, Charles University, Prague (Czech Republic). He has served as consultant to reform teams on the central level in the Czech Republic (Ministry of Finance, Ministry of Defence, Supreme Audit Office, Ministry of Foreign Affairs, and Ministry of the Interior) and as an expert in several projects funded by the European Union and the Grant Agency of the Czech Republic. He is the author of numerous scientific books and articles.

Agnieszka Pacut – PhD (Economics); assistant professor, Department of Management of Public Organisations, Cracow University of Economics (Poland). She completed a postgraduate course in Management of Non-governmental Organisations (Collegium Civitas, Poland) and Management in Public Administration (Cracow University of Economics, Poland). Her research interests include non-governmental organisations, social entrepreneurship, project management, and public policies. She has served as an expert in several projects funded by the European Union, OECD, Polish government departments, and regional administration units.

Michal Plaček – PhD; associate professor, Ambis, a.s., Prague (Czech Republic). His research focuses on public policy issues and public sector efficiency.

Oliver Rafaj – PhD; assistant professor (Economic Sciences), Department of Public Administration and Regional Development, Faculty of National Economy, University of Economics, Bratislava (Slovakia). He is a member of the Slovak section of ERSA. His research focuses on the determinants of city growth and the role of cities as centres of transmission of ideas.

Miroslav Šipikal – PhD; associate professor, University of Economics in Bratislava (Slovakia). Since 2005, he has been teaching at the Department of Public Administration and Regional Development. He is a member of the Slovak government advisory body for cohesion policy and closely works with several institutions on practical applications of policy measures. He was Director of the Business Innovation Centre in Banská Bystrica for more than 10 years and previously worked as General Director of the Slovak Investment and Trade Development Agency (SARIO). His main research interests include regional and innovation policy, evaluation of regional policy measures, regional innovation policies, and support of foreign direct investment.

Gabriela Vaceková – PhD; associate professor, Institute of Sociological Studies, Faculty of Social Sciences, Charles University, Prague (Czech Republic). She has been team leader and team member in numerous international and national research projects. She has authored a number of scientific papers and received Dean's awards for publications in 2015, 2016, 2017, and 2019.

Marcin Zawicki – PhD (Economics); habilitation in social and policy sciences; associate professor at Cracow University of Economics, Department of Public Policy; Director of the Institute of Public Policy and Administration, Collegium of Public Economy and Administration (since 2019); chairman of the Scientific Council of the Institute of Urban and Regional Development (since 2018); content editor of the Public Governance quarterly; Director of the Malopolska School of Public Administration CUE (2005–2008). He specialises in issues of public management and governance, public policy, and public administration and has authored over 100 publications on this subject as well as authored and co-authored over 120 reports, development programmes, and other commissioned expert reviews. He has participated in 70 research and implementation projects.

Preface

Nowadays, the outsourcing of business services is becoming increasingly important in the global economy. Due to intensifying international competition, business services and related processes are being transferred from firms operating in highly developed countries to locations where they are characterised by what is considered an optimal relationship between costs and quality. Offshoring and outsourcing pose real challenges to host countries because of their potential mobility and transience. It is relatively easy for outsourcing firms to change business partners and locations due to the fact that they are no longer obliged to bear considerable sunk costs. Another important factor in this regard is the fierce international competition for foreign investment. Consequently, from the perspective of host countries, the basic problem is how to create the right conditions for attracting offshore firms and offshored activities while at the same time preventing them from moving to other locations. In this context, the issue of embeddedness appears to be of key importance since it refers to the possibility of deepening relations and tightening ties between the existing partners and embedding the various dimensions of offshore firms' activities in local contexts.

In this book, we deal with the issue of territorial embeddedness of offshore firms in host countries. With regard to offshore sectors, the concept addresses the question of linkages between firms and their employees with their host cities/regions, which determine the opportunities for developing their respective businesses. The crisis caused by the 2020 pandemic will undoubtedly reveal the actual level of embeddedness of individual representatives of this sector in specific locations. We examine the factors that contribute to the qualitative transformation of the business process outsourcing sector in European emerging economies towards more advanced global business services and analyse the impact of this transformation on the level of embeddedness of its constituent firms in the region.

The first part of the monograph addresses the theoretical aspects of embeddedness of the outsourcing and offshoring sector. Its evolution towards global business services is discussed along with the foundations for its development as well as the globalisation trends in the service industries in the context of their consequences for the international division of labour. Next, the concept of territorial embeddedness of offshoring and outsourcing firms is defined, taking into account the numerous determinants of this phenomenon. This section is also devoted to issues of particular importance for the future of outsourcing and offshoring processes concerning the impact of new technologies for business development, especially automation and robotisation as the latter two trends generate demand for high qualifications in the broadly understood IT at the expense of simple repetitive processes. This part concludes with an analysis of European business services value chains from the perspective of emerging economies.

In the second part of the monograph, the authors discuss the dimensions of embeddedness in the outsourcing, offshoring, and global business services sector on the basis of international case studies conducted in Central and Eastern Europe. The transformation from a centrally planned to a market-driven economy and differences in labour costs triggered the development of this kind of economic activity in the region. Cities in the Visegrad countries, such as Budapest, Bratislava, Brno, Prague, and Krakow were selected for an in-depth analysis. The authors show the beginnings and development of this sector in individual agglomerations, highlighting the high standard of living offered by them to the demanding class of creative workers who are the most important resource of the outsourcing and offshoring sector and a key factor in promoting embeddedness in these locations.

The third part of the monograph is based on original research on the outsourcing and offshoring sector firms operating in Krakow. The choice of the city was influenced by the fact that according to the latest Tholons Services Globalization City Index 2019, it is the most attractive city in Central Europe and the second most attractive in Europe (after Dublin; in a previous edition of the survey, Krakow ranked first in Europe) and the eleventh worldwide location for such investment. Referring to the findings of the research conducted among all the levels of staff in Krakow's outsourcing and offshoring firms, the authors show the general trends and processes in this sector. Special attention is given to the consequences of the digital transformation, such as robotics, artificial intelligence, fintech, and big data. This section also discusses the role of universities in the sector studied from the viewpoint of firms and individual employees as well as the firms' actions and motivations in the area of corporate social responsibility. This part concludes with an analysis of the role of public authorities in the development of the offshoring and outsourcing sector and compares their opinions with the perspective of firm managers.

Łukasz Mamica

Acknowledgements

This book brings together research conducted by the Department of Public Economics, Faculty of Public Economy and Administration, Cracow University of Economics and its collaborators. The key part of the study on the business process outsourcing sector operating in Krakow was carried out as a commissioned research project.

This project has been financed by the Ministry of Science and Higher Education within the "Regional Initiative of Excellence" Programme for 2019–2022. Project no.: 021/RID/2018/19. Total funding: 11,897,131.40 PLN.

Such an extensive analysis of the determinants of embeddedness of the business process outsourcing sector in the Visegrad countries was possible thanks to the dedication of colleagues from research centres in Budapest, Bratislava, Pecs, Prague, and Krakow. As the editor of this book, I would like to acknowledge their contributions and thank them for their efforts. I also wish to thank Anna Chrabaszcz, who provided invaluable assistance in organisational and logistical matters, and Rafal Smietana, who proofread all the texts.

Part I

Theoretical aspects of the embeddedness of outsourcing and offshoring processes

1 The theory and evolution of outsourcing and offshoring processes

Piotr Kopyciński and Łukasz Mamica

Historical background

The theoretical foundations for the concept of outsourcing were laid by Adam Smith, who, in his *Wealth of Nations* (1776), discussed improvements in productivity possible owing to the division and specialisation of labour, such as breaking down the job to be done into simple operations, improving workers' skills, and providing adequate support equipment. In his view, the specialisation of labour favours cooperation amongst groups of employees and improves their individual productivity. In the wake of the 18th-century industrial revolution, Smith's views on the relocation of production began to be put into practice. David Ricardo's work *Principles of Political Economy and Taxation* (1817), in which he explained the main principles of a labour theory of value and theory of comparative advantage, was also important for the development of the theoretical foundations of outsourcing. In his view, free trade between two or more countries can be mutually beneficial, even when one country enjoys an absolute advantage over others in all areas of production. Friedman, when analysing the risks to American jobs as a result of their outsourcing to India due to wage differences, clearly states "Ricardo is still right" (2005, p. 264).

However, the practice of outsourcing by firms did not become widespread until the second half of the 19th century. This was essentially due to two developments: the spread of the railway network since 1830 and the invention of the telegraph in the same decade. Thanks to these innovations, the time of exchange of both information and goods among individual branches of enterprises was reduced. Further improvements in manufacturing technology, which permitted entrepreneurs to take advantage of economies of scale, also enabled them to operate more widely on regional and international markets (Porter, 1992). In the United States, the process of relocating production gained momentum after the Civil War, when the Massachusetts government imposed standards that came to be considered excessive and prompted northern textile factories to move production to southern states (Ouellette, 2013). The growth in outsourcing was fostered by lower tariffs, which fell from an average of 40% in the 1940s to about 5% in the early 21st century (Boudreaux, 2008). In the 20th century, the popularity of outsourcing-based business solutions was associated with the development of information technologies (IT).

They permitted a number of in-company processes to be automated; however, the latter eventually became so complicated that they had to be contracted out (Wiencek, 2004). Therefore, the main motive for outsourcing certain processes was not so much to lower the costs of their execution as the desire to focus on the key competences of a given firm, which led to a new division of labour (Factor, 2002). The precondition for any country to accept certain more advanced services from outside was always the availability of a suitably qualified workforce. Since training-up takes a fairly long time and, in most cases, requires the involvement of the public sphere, the capacity to absorb the processes in question depends on decisions taken a number of years previously. An example of such a policy of support for the higher education system, especially in the technical sphere, is India, where the University Grants Commission was established in 1952 and tasked with ensuring adequate teaching standards (I.N.C. for Cooperation with UNESCO, 1998). As a result, India eventually developed sufficient resources to become a key destination for the transfer of IT services.

However, outsourcing became formally seen as a legitimate business strategy only in 1989 (Mullin, 1996). The 1990s brought an increase in the interest of cost-saving measures by outsourcing more and more functions that were classified as not belonging to the core business.

The expansion of outsourcing was also supported by the systemic transformation that took place in Central and Eastern European countries in the early 1990s (Bookman, 1995). The collapse of communism and the centrally planned economy released significant reserves of skilled labour (partly by reducing artificial full-time employment and partly, unfortunately, by the collapse of a number of industries which were unable to survive the shock therapy). Moreover, the low wage levels in the post-socialist countries offered considerable rents to virtually any kind of outsourced production or services. The accession of Central and Eastern European countries to the European Union, the abolition of customs barriers, and the free movement of goods and services provided other impulses in favour of the advancement of outsourcing. The latter was supported on an international scale by the growing globalisation and the upward trend in international trade.

The concepts of outsourcing and offshoring

The starting point for the discussion of these concepts is Porter's value chain (Porter, 1985). In his approach, any firm's activities can be divided into: 1. primary ones, which are directly concerned with the manufacturing/creation and delivery of a product/service; and 2. back-office/support activities intended to ensure that the primary activities are as efficient and effective as possible. It should be emphasised that company core activities are generally not subject to transfer. The concepts of outsourcing and offshoring apply to the transfer of support services (back-office services), such as finance, HR, IT, supply chain management, help desk, information security, technology tools, and cloud platforms. This allows the firm to commit more of its resources to primary activities. Relocation occurs by consolidating and providing one or several support services from one central location rather than duplicating the roles in organisation within an in-house department or a local/overseas external third-party provider. The main aims of outsourcing and offshoring carried out in this manner are to reduce costs and to increase efficiency and effectiveness of company operations.

In the initial period of outsourcing, the prevailing motivation for moving production abroad to mainly southeastern Asian countries was to reduce manufacturing costs. A client that ordered products or services was considered as an owner of accumulated knowledge and experience, whereas the vendor as an entity whose main advantage was a lower-cost workforce; the latter being the crucial factor in deciding where to locate production. Over time, the concept of outsourcing evolved into strategic outsourcing based on the client's partnership with numerous vendors. The essence of such a change is well illustrated by the example of Dell (Power et al., 2006), which started cooperating with a number of parts suppliers, and decided to focus on IT systems. Its development model assumes that hardware suppliers have their own capacity to deliver progressively more technically advanced solutions and do not expect to be providing strictly defined parameters or specifying methods of manufacturing parts and components as long as they meet the required standards. The network of suppliers as well as the knowledge accumulated and developed by them become part of Dell's business strategy, which does not have sufficient resources to control and research new hardware solutions. The vendor that offers the lowest manufacturing cost becomes an equal business partner, whose development and research success also impacts on the competitive position of the customer. IBM also offers a good example of business strategy that involves creating new products or services through alliances and outsourcing arrangements (Ghemawat, 2007). The main mechanism regulating the relations between the suppliers and the recipients of outsourcing services are interfirm contracts, which provide the formal arrangements for this process and stabilise the entire sector (Anderson & Dekker, 2014).

The concept of outsourcing assumes greater budget flexibility due to the fact that services are purchased as and when the need arises. This flexibility of outsourcing reduces the costs resulting from the need to adapt one's own organisational structure to changing demand. Organisational inertia associated with both the recruitment and training processes, as well as the costs incurred due to the reduction of employment when the demand for a given service drops, makes outsourcing of selected aspects of a company's operations a more attractive option. Furthermore, large companies are the object of interest of the media and the public opinion; hence layoffs invariably attract negative publicity. Outsourcing therefore allows for a relatively straightforward employment reduction during an economic downturn or in the face of problems due to other reasons without unduly raising negative public emotions.

However, this kind of managerial approach to outsourcing has come under heavy criticism due to the unwillingness of companies with more capital to act as labour market stabilisers during a downturn, and thereby to take responsibility for the social dimension of their business decisions. The supporters of offshoring, i.e. business entities which order goods or services from more distant locations, are also accused of attempting to evade their domestic social security regulations or occupational safety standards. This approach was epitomised by the Dhaka garment factory collapse in Bangladesh in April 2013. As a result, more than 1100 people were killed and about 2500 were injured. The collapsed eight-story structure, originally erected as a commercial rather than industrial building, itself built in blatant violation of construction regulations, housed garment factories that manufactured clothes for many famous clothing brands worldwide. However, the criticism of outsourcing typically targets the loss of jobs caused by their relocation abroad (Dobbs, 2004). Such a perception of outsourcing is also fairly common in the eyes of public opinion in countries from which jobs are transferred. A survey conducted in the USA by the *New York Times* showed clearly that this process is responsible for the loss of jobs; moreover, two thirds of respondents expect firms to take greater responsibility for preserving manufacturing jobs (Conelly, 2012). The American experience shows that the process of outsourcing indeed involves job losses: a 10% increase in services and materials offshoring leads to a 2.6% reduction in the share of value added transferred to workers (Milberg & Winkler, 2013). Consequently, the sole beneficiaries of outsourcing are capital owners, a factor that increases the already high inequality levels in America. Even so, scepticism about offshoring is seen as a continuation of the anti-free trade sentiment rooted in the economic debate for many years (Irwin, 2005).

Definitions – an overview

The delegation of powers and instructions to perform certain activities by employees is an obvious task for managers in any firm. The latter's comprehensive strategy determines the ways and entities that handle its specific business processes and functional areas. Decisions in this area concern the transfer of tasks from one entity to another. At this stage, there are essentially two options – outsourcing and insourcing. The former involves separating certain functions and processes and entrusting them to external entities, while the latter consists in taking over the processes which so far have been contracted out. Managers are faced with the basic make-or-buy dilemma and each decision must be preceded by an integrated profit and loss analysis. Choosing the buy option means engaging in outsourcing. The rationale for outsourcing is perhaps best illustrated by the following quote: "because there are others who can do it cheaper, faster, better and because we have other, more important, demands on our resources" (Power et al., 2006, p. 1).

The definitional issues associated with offshoring and outsourcing are widely discussed both in the literature (cf. Oshri et al., 2015) and in various manuals that purport to provide practical knowledge on this issue (Swientozielskyj, 2015). For this reason, only the most important concepts will be mapped out in this chapter. The starting point for all the considerations is the location of the entity that takes over the implementation of the tasks in question, namely:

1 Keeping the tasks in question within the existing company, but in a specially designated unit, or entrusting these tasks to an external entity.
2 Geographical reallocation of tasks: leaving their implementation in this country or transferring them abroad.

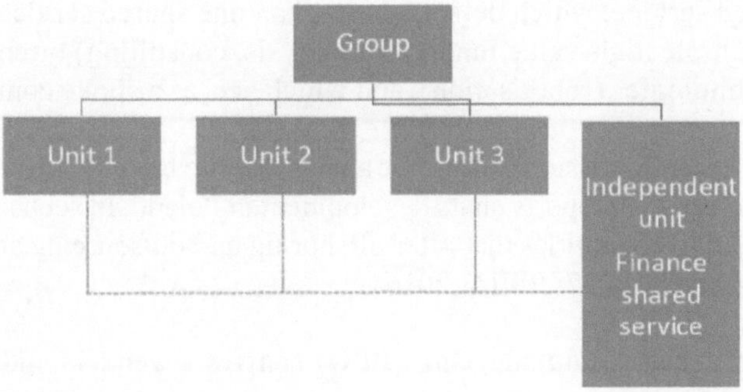

Figure 1.1 Shared services – an example of relocation of a company's accounting services
Source: Based on Swientozielskyj (2015).

In the case of entrusting these tasks to a specially established unit within a given company, its distinguishing feature as compared to other forms of intra-corporate transformation is that it constitutes a separate and autonomous unit, providing services to other units perceived as clients (as opposed to centralised services, where a new unit, e.g. dealing with financial matters, is controlled centrally and viewed as a support centre, and also in opposition to decentralised services, where each unit has its own department, e.g. dealing with financial matters) (Swientozielskyj, 2015).

The starting point for further consideration is the term **sourcing**. According to Oshri et al. (2015, p. 3),

> sourcing is the act through which work is contracted or delegated to an external or internal entity that could be physically located anywhere. It encompasses various insourcing (keeping work in-house) and outsourcing arrangements such as offshore outsourcing, captive offshoring, nearshoring and onshoring.

It thus consists in transferring selected processes, which have so far taken place within a specific corporate structure – in another unit within the organisation – to an external domestic or international entity. In this context, **outsourcing** is understood as entrusting to an external entity the responsibility to discharge specific tasks performed so far within the purchasing firm (Oshri et al., 2015). Conversely, **offshoring** refers to "the relocation of organisational activities (e.g. information technology, finance and accounting, back office and human resources) to a wholly owned subsidiary or an independent service provider in another country" (Oshri et al., 2015, p. 8). In this context, the following arrangements are possible: the **captive model** (tasks are delegated to a subsidiary: a. located in the same country: **shared service,** or b. abroad: **captive centre/captive shared services**); **offshore outsourcing** (work is taken over by an independent entity abroad); and **nearshoring** (the target entity is located in a neighbouring country) (Oshri et al., 2015).

Global business services (GBS) is an entity perceived as a further evolved form of shared service, which delivers more than one shared service, is characterised by multiple high-value functions (analysis, consulting) often associated with new technologies (robotisation), and which acts as a spoke connected with the hub.

The sector under discussion can also be analysed more broadly, as is the case, for example, in subsequent reports on its development in Poland. In such an approach, the following kinds of entities that offer offshoring and outsourcing activities can be identified (ABSL, 2017; PIFIA, 2016):

- **Business processes outsourcing (BPO) centres** – vendors and third-party providers of services to external customers (e.g. accounting, customer service, finance, HR);
- **Shared services centres** (SSC) – operate within a specific company and provide services to its various branches in a given region of the world or globally, primarily in the following areas: finance and accounting (F&A), HR, internal clients' needs, IT support, marketing, procurement;
- **IT centres (IT)** – vendors and providers providing IT solutions for external customers (e.g. system, application or infrastructure maintenance, and technical support), as well as developing and implementing software; and
- **Research & development centres (R&D)** – conduct research, as well as work on product or software development.

The outsourcing and offshoring sector as discussed in this book has various definitions in the literature. The term business process outsourcing (BPO) appears to be the most frequently used to refer to the entire sector in broad terms. In the USA, the acronym BPO denotes business process offshoring; in our book, however, we shall use it in the above-mentioned broad sense.

Advantages and disadvantages of outsourcing

The concepts of outsourcing and offshoring are based on the expectation to generate a number of benefits for the company. The most obvious is the reduction of the running costs of certain processes, including those due to savings as a result of diminished oversight and control activities. In this context, Shah (1998) mentions not only technology and audit costs but also the reduction in clerical and management levels, reduction in working capital exposure and tax compliance liabilities, as well as the release of resources that can be committed to core firm operations. The firm's own resources freed up in this way can be more effectively deployed to develop its key competencies or to avoid a costly process of hiring employees needed to handle these processes. The reduction of costs of the outsourced processes results from the fact that they can be more effectively carried out by a specialised entity. In this case, there is an effect of scale, which is accompanied by greater specialisation and a better use of employees' time while accumulating relevant experience. The problem of ownership of resources and knowledge becomes secondary; instead, the key issue is having access to them. Being self-sufficient is becoming economically unprofitable due to a range of more advantageous possibilities to deploy the available resources. In some cases, entering into cooperation in the field of outsourcing is also seen as a way to seek innovation (Aubert et al., 2015). The crucial characteristics of successful outsourcing contracts include low uncertainty and measurability (Lacity et al., 2010).

Process transfers are not without their shortcomings, as Swientozielskyj (2015) points out in his work. In his view, they include the following:

- The need to have sufficient funds to establish a new location and recruit and train staff;
- The time needed to start up in a new location – up to 18 months (staff training, testing new IT systems, lack of leadership);
- The loss of face-to-face contacts (important e.g. for HR);
- Technical issues (e.g. differences in accounting practices between countries);
- Strain on IT resources;
- Costs of consolidating data;
- Withdrawal of recourses from current units;
- Cultural differences.

The decision to transfer certain processes, apart from the unquestionable benefits due to the reduction in a firm's operating costs as well as improving the efficiency and effectiveness of its operations, is also fraught with certain disadvantages. The latter include the often high kick-off costs, time needed to transfer the target processes, cultural differences, and difficulty with maintaining direct contact. Firms that outsource to multiple vendors tend to fare better since it allows them to increase their bargaining power and enhance performance (Koo et al., 2017).

Conclusions

The concept of contracting out back-office activities in order to better deploy one's resources to core business areas was already discussed by the representatives of classical economics. These functions can be delegated to subsidiaries, which allows the parent firm to retain control over them; on the other hand, such a unit is likely to morph into a kind of island within an organisation characterised by an inbuilt cultural resistance to change (Swientozielskyj, 2015). Another solution involves outsourcing to external providers, which marks a clear boundary between the company's core business and its back-office serviced by an external entity. In the latter case, however, there is a risk that the quality of services provided by such an entity may not be up to the standards expected by the outsourcing firm. Other problems may involve reintegrating back-office operations into the firm's structure (Swientozielskyj, 2015). This does not alter the fact, however, that the outsourcing and offshoring sector is likely to continue to develop intensively, which can be attested to by the history of its market value and the growing number of employees.

References

ABSL. (2017). *Business Services Sector in Poland 2017*. Warsaw: ABSL.

Anderson, S.W., & Dekker, H.C. (2014). The role of management controls in transforming firm boundaries and sustaining hybrid organizational forms. *FNT in Accounting*, *8*(2), pp. 75–141. https://doi.org/10.1561/1400000032.

Aubert, B.A., Kishore, R., & Iriyama, A. (2015). Exploring and managing the "innovation through outsourcing" paradox. *The Journal of Strategic Information Systems*, *24*(4), pp. 255–269. https://doi.org/10.1016/j.jsis.2015.10.003.

Bookman, M.Z. (1995). The transformation of East-Central Europe. *Orbis*, *39*(4), pp. 604–622. https://doi.org/10.1016/0030-4387(95)90013-6.

Boudreaux, D.J. (2008). *Globalization: Greenwood Guides to Business and Economics*. Westport, CT and London: Greenwood Press [accessed from: http://site.ebrary.com/lib/alltitles/docDetail.action?docID=10213994].

Conelly, M. (2012). Poll finds consumers confusion on where Apple devices are made. *The New York Times*, Janaury 25, 2012.

Dobbs, L. (2004). *Exporting America: Why Corporate Greed is Shipping American Jobs Overseas* (1st ed.). New York: Warner Books.

Factor, A. (2002). *Analyzing Application Service Providers*. Palo Alto, CA: Sun Microsystems [accessed from: http://proquest.tech.safaribooksonline.de/0130894257].

Friedman, T.L. (2005). *The World is Flat: A Brief History of the Twenty-first Century* (1st ed.). New York, NY: Farrar Straus and Giroux [accessed from: www.loc.gov/catdir/enhancements/fy0617/2004028685-b.html].

Ghemawat, P. (2007). Managing differences: The central challenge of global strategy. *Harvard Business Review*, *85*, pp. 58–68.

I.N.C. for Cooperation with UNESCO. (1998). *Higher Education in India: Vision and Action; Country Paper*. World Conference on Higher Education in the Twenty-first Century: Vision and Action. New Delhi: Indian National Commission for Cooperation with UNESCO.

Irwin, D. (2005). *Free Trade Under Fire*. Princeton: Princeton University Press.

Koo, Y., Lee, J.-N., Heng, Ch.S., & Park, J. (2017). Effect of multi-vendor outsourcing on organizational learning: A social relation perspective. *Information & Management*, *54*(3), pp. 396–413. https://doi.org/10.1016/j.im.2016.09.007.

Lacity, M.C., Khan, S., Yan, A., & Willcocks, L.P. (2010). A review of the IT outsourcing empirical literature and future research directions. *Journal of Information Technology*, *25*(4), pp. 395–433. https://doi.org/10.1057/jit.2010.21.

Milberg, W.S., & Winkler, D. (2013). *Outsourcing Economics: Global Value Chains in Capitalist Development*. Cambridge: Cambridge University Press.

Mullin, R. (1996). Managing the outsourced enterprise. *Journal of Business Strategy*, *17*(4), pp. 28–36. https://doi.org/10.1108/eb039792.

Oshri, I., Kotlarsky, J., & Willcocks, L.P. (2015). *The Handbook of Global Outsourcing and Offshoring* (3rd ed.). London: Palgrave Macmillan.

Ouellette, S. (2013). *US Textile Production in Historical Perspective: A Case Study from Massachusetts*. London: Routledge.

PIFIA. (2016). *Business Services Sector in Poland* 2016. Warsaw: The Polish Information and Foreign Investment Agency.

Porter, G. (1992). *The Rise of Big Business: 1860–1920* (2nd ed.). Wheeling, IL: Harlan Davidson.

Porter, M.E. (1985). *Competitive Advantage: Creating and Sustaining Superior Performance*. New York: Simon and Schuster.

Power, M.J., Desouza, K.C., & Bonifazi, C. (2006). *The Outsourcing Handbook: How to Implement a Successful Outsourcing Process*. London: Kogan Page [accessed from: www.loc.gov/catdir/enhancements/fy0715/2005031046-d.html].

Ricardo, D. (1817). *Principles of Political Economy and Taxation*. London: John Murray.

Shah, B. (1998). Shared services. *Industrial Management*, *40*(5), pp. 4–8.

Smith, A. (1776). *An Inquiry into the Nature and Causes of the Wealth of Nations*. London: W. Strahan and T. Cadell.

Swientozielskyj, S. (2015). *Certificate in Global Business Services*. London: The Hackett Group.

Wiencek, D. (2004). Ethical challanges of information systems. The carnage of outsourcing and other technology-enabled organizational imperatives. In L.L. Brennan & V.E. Johnson (Eds.), *Social, Ethical, and Policy Implications of Information Technology*. Hershey, PA: IGI Global, pp. 141–158.

2 Globalisation trends in the service industries

Consequences for the international division of labour

Tomasz Geodecki

Introduction

Traditionally, the main criterion for assessing the position of an economy in the international division of labour was mostly whether it exported raw materials or highly processed goods (Smith & White, 1992; Mittelman, 1995). The way to overcome this division was to industrialise and in newer approaches, to acquire competencies needed to produce high added-value goods (Amsden, 2001; Lin & Chang, 2009). Nowadays, in the era of globalisation, transnational corporations have organised production systems in which developing economies are also included in the provision of sophisticated products. They are characterised by low wages, hence labour-intensive production stages tend to be transferred to them, which leads to their industrialisation (Mittelman, 1995; Jones & Kierzkowski, 2005; Baldwin, 2006; Baldwin & Lopez-Gonzalez, 2013). Thus, the term *global international division of labour* was coined (Mittelman, 1995) to emphasize its association with globalisation. Subsequent sections of this chapter are devoted to a brief overview of the causes and scope of the globalisation of business services; reviewing the theory of offshoring with an emphasis on trends in the business services sector; identifying the mechanisms of upgrading in international value chains; and considering their impact on the international division of labour.

The causes and scope of business service globalisation

Globalisation involves a progressive separation of the different production stages, resulting in the final product being created by combining semi-finished inputs manufactured in a number of locations managed by the head office. It is known as offshoring, fragmentation, or slicing-up of the value chain (Baldwin, 2006). The overriding rationale for the separation of individual production stages is cost (Mallampally & Zimny, 2000; Baldwin, 2012), but this would have been unfeasible had it not been for the progress in communication technologies that have made it possible to trade in services traditionally considered as non-tradable. Other factors that contribute to increasing the firms' propensity to offshore services include access to expertise/skills, flexibility improvement, focus on core capabilities, and access to global markets (Lacity et al., 2017). The factors associated with the business environment include the competitive pressure and the response of firms to accepted industry practice (Hutzschenreuter et al., 2011; Milberg & Winkler, 2013). The choice of location is usually determined by political and economic stability, infrastructure, the quality of education and language skills, government incentives, and cultural compatibility (Fernandez-Stark & Gereffi, 2010; Lacity et al., 2017).

In view of India's success as an important location for the offshore services industry, international reviews of the sector's research highlight the need for more studies of sourcing destinations besides that country (Lacity et al., 2017). Fernandez-Stark and Gereffi (2010) propose to focus on three emerging offshore service locations: Central and Eastern European countries (CEE), [In this chapter, the acronym CEE refers to the 11 economies of the region that belong to the European Union: Bulgaria, Croatia, Czech Republic, Estonia, Hungary, Latvia, Lithuania, Poland, Romania, Slovakia, Slovenia. (cf. Chapter 6)], India, and Ireland. In our search for answers to the question of a new international division of labour, we shall focus on analysing trends in these three locations, comparing them to changes taking place in two developed countries, Germany and the USA. The focus is on global business information technology (IT) services and professional services, which tend to be offshored most often.

The propensity to offshore them is linked to technical progress in the field of remote information transmission. A review of the motives and circumstances of the development of the offshore services industry leads to the conclusion that "ICT made it possible, wage differences made it profitable" (cf. R. Baldwin, 2012, p. 2).

The term *offshoring* refers to the geographical criterion (home vs. abroad), while from the point of view of a firm's boundaries, internalised vs. externalised (outsourced) activities can be identified (UNCTAD, 2004; Radło, 2016). However, from the perspective of the evolution of the international division of labour, offshoring plays a crucial role. Fernandez-Stark and Gereffi (2010) use the term *offshore services industry* (OSI) as "referring to services conducted in one country and consumed in another" (p. 7).

In order to specify the contents of the term *business services*, we shall use Eurostat's definition (2013), according to which it includes technical, computer, and other professional services performed by an enterprise for another enterprise and/or the public administration and covered by Statistical Classification of Economic Activities in the European Community – from the French, Nomenclature Statistique des activités économiques dans la Communauté européenne (NACE) Rev. 2 divisions 62, 69, 71, 73, and 78 and groups 58.2, 63.1, and 70.2. We shall also adopt the observation made by Wölfl (2005) and Wirtz et al. (2015) that input-output statistics with a distinction between intermediate and final use may be helpful in capturing outsourcing.

The World Input-Output Database (WIOD – Timmer, 2015) makes it possible to identify five sectors/branches that entirely or largely cover business services. Indeed, compared to other services, they are characterised, on average, by a larger and growing share of exports in total output of the global economy (see Table 2.1).

Table 2.1 Share of exports in total output of business services in 2014

NACE Rev. 2 code	*NACE description*	*Exports/total output*	
		2004	*2014*
J58	Publishing activities	12.0%	17.5%
J62_J63	Computer programming, consultancy, and related activities; information service activities	9.6%	18.1%
M69_M70	Legal and accounting activities; activities of head offices; management consultancy activities	6.0%	8.8%
M71	Architectural and engineering activities; technical testing and analysis	9.9%	12.2%
M73	Advertising and market research	8.0%	11.4%
G-N	Services of the business economy	7.2%	8.8%

Source: Own calculations based on WIOD.

Since the full scope of WIOD data for India includes sectors of IT (J62_J63) and professional business services (M69_M70, and M71), we shall focus on them when outlining the basic trends in this chapter.

Offshoring services industry in economic theory

The phenomenon of offshoring is analysed by a number of economic theories. Markusen (2005), in his exploration of the causes of offshoring white-collar jobs, focuses on trade and foreign direct investment theories, while Wirtz et al. (2015), in their analysis of the causes of the emergence of the global business services sector, focus on the motives of outsourcing services from the perspective of the theory of firm and its boundaries. In the following short overview, both perspectives shall be combined.

Offshoring services in the theory of firm

Among the theories of outsourcing and offshoring based on the neoclassical enterprise models, the one devised by Jones and Kierzkowski (1988) occupies a special place. It explains how the growing economies of scale and progressive specialisation of production factors within the firm lead to the division of the production process into fragmented blocks linked by services. Individual bundles of such services include coordination, administration, transport, and financial services. The new role of services studied by Jones and Kierzkowski involves coordinating the activities of production blocks across national borders. Technological progress in ICT reduces the costs of remote communication and production coordination, resulting in a growing demand for international ICT services.

Figure 2.1, which supports these assumptions, shows an increased share of coordination services in total value added as the world economy becomes

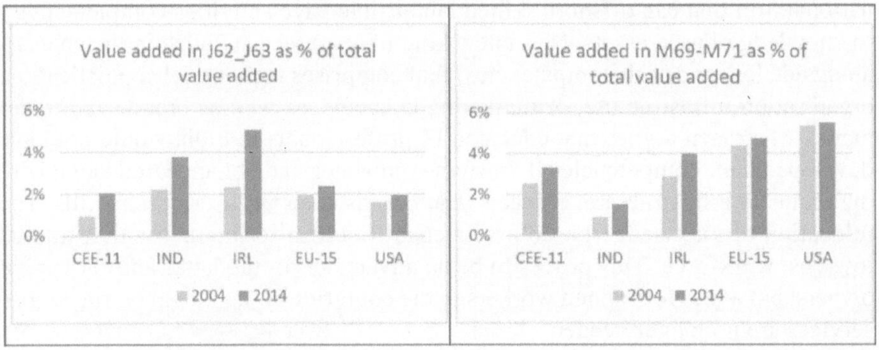

Figure 2.1 Share of value added of NACE 2 sectors J62, J63 and M69, M70, and M71 in total value added of national economies

Source: Own study based on WIOD.

internationalised. Between 2004 and 2014, the total share of services, including information and communication technology (ICT) and professional business services, increased by 1/5 and 1/20, respectively, in developed countries. In some offshore services locations (CEE, IRL, IND), this share had even doubled.

Theories of firm also explain different motives for offshore insourcing (by establishing a foreign affiliate) and offshore outsourcing (by trading with independent contractors) (see Radło, 2016). In the case of foreign direct investment (FDI), a firm has an opportunity to save on production costs and reduce its marginal costs. This increases the volume of production and increases profits. Outsourcing, on the other hand, reduces the scale of a firm's operations, giving it the opportunity to reduce fixed costs, which, under certain circumstances, may also increase profits, especially when it focuses on its core competencies. In a resource-based view, the latter are profit-generating knowledge resources that offer access to multiple markets, increase the benefits to consumers of final products, and are difficult for competitors to follow (Hamel & Prahalad, 1990, pp. 83–84).

Outsourcing and offshoring of services in foreign trade theories

In trade theories, offshoring acts as a mechanism to improve the allocation of resources in the global economy in line with Ricardo's comparative advantages and factor abundance theory. Markusen (2005) proposes new models for analysing this phenomenon on the basis of white-collar services offshoring, including the emergence of new kinds of services, the specificity of trade in intermediate goods, and the transfer of service centres to skilled-labour-scarce economies. This trend reverses the traditional flow of knowledge-based services: they are beginning to be provided by developing countries and imported by developed ones. This theory is particularly useful in analysing the performance of an international firm that can offshore skilled labour-intensive activities complementary to knowledge-based assets. It is a new kind of resource (included in the analysis alongside low and high competencies) that comprises managerial sophistication, organisation infrastructure, or marketing channels, as well as brands and trademarks. Markusen argues that educated IT professionals in India would not have developed their competencies if Western companies had not appeared along with the requisite infrastructure, contacts, and brands keen to absorb their skills. The relocation of knowledge-based assets enables a firm to interact with a trained low-cost workforce. This proves to be an advantage for the latter and for capital owners, but a loss for trained workers in the countries of the global North, whose services are no longer needed.

Figure 2.2 shows the share of selected economies in global exports of business services. The share of developed countries decreased (Germany and the USA), whereas the share of economies – target locations of offshored services – increased (CEE, India, and Ireland).

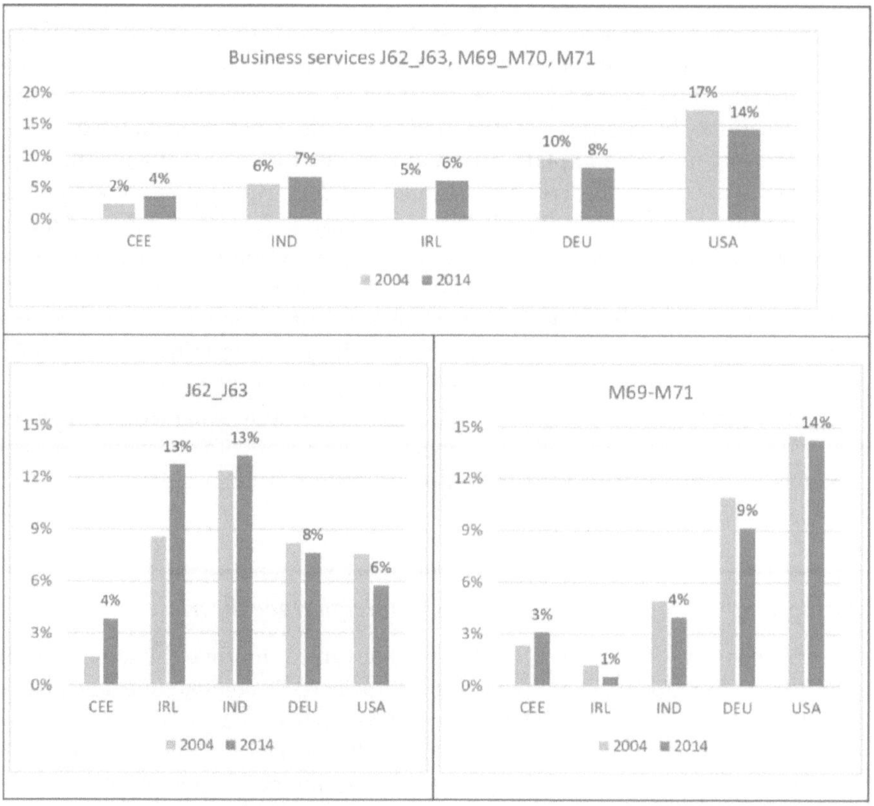

Figure 2.2 Share of selected economies in global services exports

Source: Own study based on WIOD.

The phenomena under discussion cause a growing concern amongst employees in developed countries (Amiti & Wei, 2004; Milberg & Winkler, 2013). Offshoring white-collar jobs is considered as a special case of job loss, since it was hoped that business services would represent a sustainable comparative advantage of these economies. Baldwin (2006, 2019) notes that these hopes proved to be vain – globalisation also affects office-based work. Tasks that were previously considered to be non-tradable turned out to be offshorable when telephone and internet connection costs dropped nearly to zero. We are no longer dealing with trade in goods and services as products of a factory that integrates a number of tasks (e.g. design, assembly, and accounting), but with an exchange of tasks. Employees in different countries undertaking the same task (e.g. accounting) compete with one another. In this way, the design of jet engines may become an export specialty of a developed country, while the more common accounting processes is carried out by firms in countries with lower labour costs. We no longer analyse the traditional exchange of cloth for wine; instead, economies increasingly specialise in specific production stages of a given good (trade in tasks, cf. Grossman & Rossi-Hansberg, 2006). This makes it impossible to predict to what extent and where new task combinations achieved via computerisation and decreasing communication costs will become effective. Moreover, the complexity of interactions among factories and offices means that in an instant, a new management method may dramatically change cost proportions. Previous permanent commercial advantages are becoming "kaleidoscopic" (Baldwin, 2006; Deardorff & Haveman, 1995).

Offshoring in foreign direct investment theories

Offshoring from the perspective of FDI theories is analysed with respect to the three advantages of ownership, location, and internalisation (the so-called OLI model, cf. Dunning, 1993), all of which must be possessed by a firm in order to undertake FDI.

Ownership advantages are based either on monopolistic power resulting from barriers to entry in a developed country and on the possession of scarce resources or competencies. They increasingly rely on the ability to find and integrate globally dispersed knowledge-based resources (Dunning, 2000). Therefore, low-cost firms based in developing countries do not usually provide services directly to demanding customers (Fernandez-Stark et al., 2011).

Location advantages make it possible to identify two distinct kinds of foreign investment: resource- versus market-seeking (Narula & Pineli, 2017). The behaviour of a given multinational enterprise is explained by the factor-proportion (or the vertical model) if investment profitability is based on factor price differences, particularly the price of labour. In this model, different, geographically scattered branches of a firm produce different goods or services, as is the case, e.g. with services offshoring due to wage differences.

The existence or absence of advantages in terms of internalisation determines whether a firm pursues FDI offshore insourcing or whether it prefers to rely on market relations by (offshore) outsourcing.

According to transaction costs theory (Williamson, 1985), internalisation occurs when the transaction costs of an outsourced good or service are higher than those supplied in-house. Therefore, as the efficiency of markets (technology and legal aspects of cooperation) improves, the motivation to externalise increases. When analysing the emerging global business services (GBS) model, Wirtz et al. (2015) point out that the most important motives for outsourcing to specialised service providers are savings on ownership costs, a focus on key competencies, and the opportunity to engage firms that specialise in international labour and skills cost arbitrage. Milberg and Winkler (2013) argue that as competencies and infrastructure improve, more and more developing countries offer specialised services at a decent quality level. Offshore outsourcing makes it possible to rely on competing suppliers, and thereby keep the prices of intermediate inputs lower.

Nevertheless, many firms prefer FDI, which enables them to maintain capital control over the offshored process, especially in terms of ownership of rent-generating assets. These reasons were identified by Gupta et al. (2006) when surveying entrepreneurs who offshore in the financial sector. Entrepreneurs willing to undertake FDI are more likely to achieve a larger scale of operations and have greater advantage over local suppliers in terms of experience or technological superiority. Maintaining control over the processes was also considered important from the perspective of brand perception. The propensity to rely on market relations is especially reduced if the process transferred is considered to be a 'world class' one and if there is a risk that competitors would gain access to the knowledge essential to the creation of value by a given firm (Dunning, 1993; UNCTAD, 2004).

Table 2.2 presents the number of domestic firms in the top 25 in the three most globalised business services sectors. Apart from the size of the economy, an important variable that implies an advantage of multinational enterprises (MNEs) on local markets seems to be the level of economic development of a given country closely associated with its technological advancement. This confirms that the advantage of MNEs over local firms is a characteristic feature of the host economies.

Table 2.2 Number of domestic firms in the most globalised services industries (global ultimate owners by headquarter country) in the top 25 firms by revenues in 2018*, **

	CEE11	*IND*	*IRL*	*DEU*	*USA*
J62	8	12	0	17	25
M69	7	15	3	25	25
M71	14	17	9	11	23
M73	3	11	5	16	21

* Or the latest available.

** Only those operators for which data on the global ultimate owner are available were taken into account.

Source: Orbis database, Bureau Van Dyke.

Upgrading in global value chains

In order to describe the structural framework of offshoring processes, researchers refer to global value chains. The term *value chain* was proposed by Porter (1985) and refers to the entire range of a firm's activities – from concept through manufacturing to end use, including all technologically and economically distinct activities that a firm performs to do business. The adjective *global* was added to reflect the trend that value chain activities tend to disperse across the world (OECD, 2013). Business services are not exempt from this trend – more and more international operators engage subcontractors from low-cost developing countries in ICT and other non-core activities.[1]

Two currents of global value chain research can be identified (Bair, 2005). The older one, based on world-systems (Wallerstein, 2004), emphasises the core–periphery division between economic processes: the core processes with high added value usually take place in developed countries, whereas the peripheral ones in developing countries. The central issue here is "the fact of unequal exchange . . . that continually reproduces the basic core-periphery division of labour itself" (Hopkins & Wallerstein, 1977, p. 117, cited in Bair, 2005). This process has continued since the inception of modern capitalism and results in the division of the world into core, semi-peripheral, and peripheral areas. In the first group, based on technological and competence advantages, advanced economic processes are organised. Due to the difficulty inherent in copying, they are carried out only by a handful of entities worldwide and protected by strong countries; that is why they are mostly located within the latter. The core–periphery relation, therefore, has its geographical and political consequences. The modern globalisation phase involves locating central processes in developing countries as well, which does not imply, however, that they control most of the value generated during their execution. A frequently cited example of analysis in this spirit was provided by Linden et al. (2009) and concerns the iPhone. In its market price ($299), less than one-half constituted what the Chinese factory was paid, but in the latter, 85% was generated by intermediate goods purchased from other Far Eastern and American electronics manufacturers. Shih (1996), who studied the distribution of added value between the different stages of production in the electronics industry, demonstrated that its largest proportion occurs in the initial stages – product development and design – and in the final stages – customer service and after-sales service. Due to the U-shaped dependence of the share of added value on the production stage, it came to be called a smiling curve.

The newer *global commodity chain camp* is being developed by Gary Gereffi and his associates. Researchers associated with this current theory often attempt to answer the question whether, and if so, how participation in global value chains (GVCs) is conducive to industrial upgrading understood as "a process of improving the ability of a firm or an economy to move to more profitable and/or technologically sophisticated capital and skill-intensive economic niches" (Gereffi, 1999, pp. 51–2). Globalisation enables exporters from emerging economies to develop technological competence in a given production stage because improving the quality of products and the efficiency of processes to meet the requirements of the chain is a precondition for joining it (Baldwin & Lopez-Gonzalez, 2013; Pietrobelli & Rabellotti, 2011). Nevertheless, value chains contain structural barriers that make it difficult or prevent weaker actors from advancing to higher value-added links. The ability to capture value added, according to a study by Gereffi et al. (2005), is based on three factors: complexity, ability to codify transactions, and capabilities of potential suppliers. Dicken (2015) focuses on three intermediate modes of governance in GVC:

- Captive value chains, where smaller suppliers are dependent on large buyers and deprived of opportunities to work for others;
- Relational value chains, where suppliers and customers are dependent on each other due to the complexity of the transactions and lack of ability to standardise them;
- Modular value chains, where the supplier takes over a larger portion of the added value because transactions can be standardised and coded; tasks outsourced by lead firms are sold to a wide range of customers because they are not customer-specific (accounting, IT, logistics).

Fernandez-Stark et al. (2011) analysed the upgrading processes in the OSI sector and identified three major kinds of lead firms:

- Shared services centres identified with the captive mode of governance – usually foreign subsidiaries of lead firms from developing countries;
- Third-party providers from developed countries with branches in developing countries – their popularity is strengthened by their brand. Moreover, buyers from developing countries prefer to buy from well-known firms with an established international reputation;
- Third-party providers from India which specialise in IT services.

An important achievement by Fernandez-Stark et al. (2011) was the mapping of the kinds of offshore services and their division according to their added value potential based on firm-level analysis. The shift to more value-added activities involves traditional mechanisms (product and process advancement), but the authors also identified functional advancement based on improving one's position in a given value chain or joining another (Fernandez-Stark et al., 2011; OECD, 2013).

The cited study findings show that sector-specific case studies are the right method to study upgrading processes. Quantitative data provide only a general outline of trends in the international division of labour, but with the help of international input-output tables, they can be followed at sectoral level. Figures 2.3 and 2.4. show three dimensions of upgrading:

1 The extent to which actors in developing and developed countries, respectively, are involved in exporting business services that provide intermediate

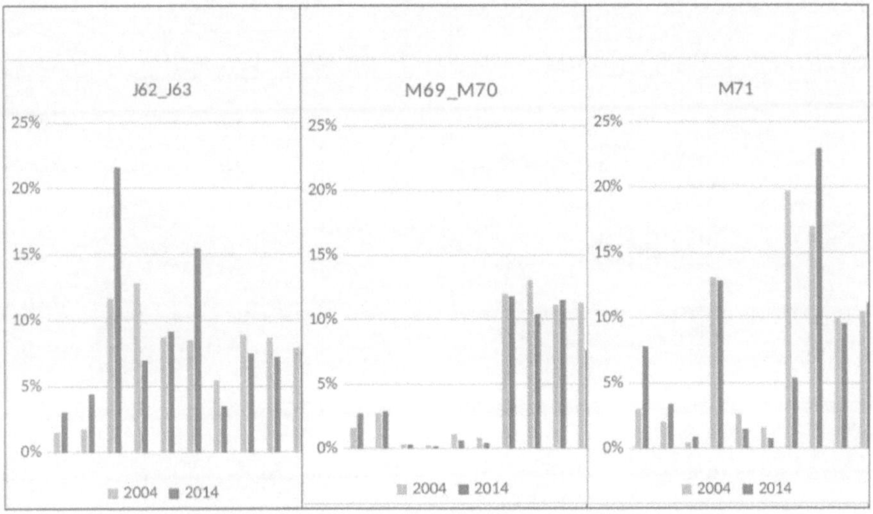

Figure 2.3 Shares of selected economies in global exports of final and intermediate goods in business services sector

Source: Own study based on WIOD.

inputs vs. final goods that generate more added value (see Figure 2.3). In the case of IT_BS, the growing capacity of developing countries to export final services can be seen (with India as the leader). This kind of service is outsourced by developed countries. In the professional services sector M69_M70, upgrading seems to be more difficult – operators based in developed countries tend to offshore intermediate stages (in Germany and the USA, the share of intermediate inputs in world exports is reduced by about 25%) – but they do not relinquish the profitable final links in the value chains. Yet another offshoring model is seen in architectural and engineering activities (M71). In this area, not only developing countries but also developed ones are building their advantages in exports of intermediate inputs, such as the engine design services proposed as an example by Baldwin (2006).

2 The ability to create added value, which is represented here by GVC Income (added value obtained by selling final goods to domestic and foreign customers directly or through other operators – cf. Timmer et al., 2013; Grodzicki & Geodecki, 2016). GVC Income (GVCI), presented in radar charts (Figure 2.4.), is presented in much the same way as the revealed comparative advantages (RCA), i.e. by analysing whether the GVCI share of a given sector in the total GVCI for all branches in a given country is greater than the same share calculated for the whole world. An RCA GVCI above one represents an advantage in obtaining added value. In OSI-located economies, higher GVCI values can be observed in 2014 than in 2004, which represents upgrading,

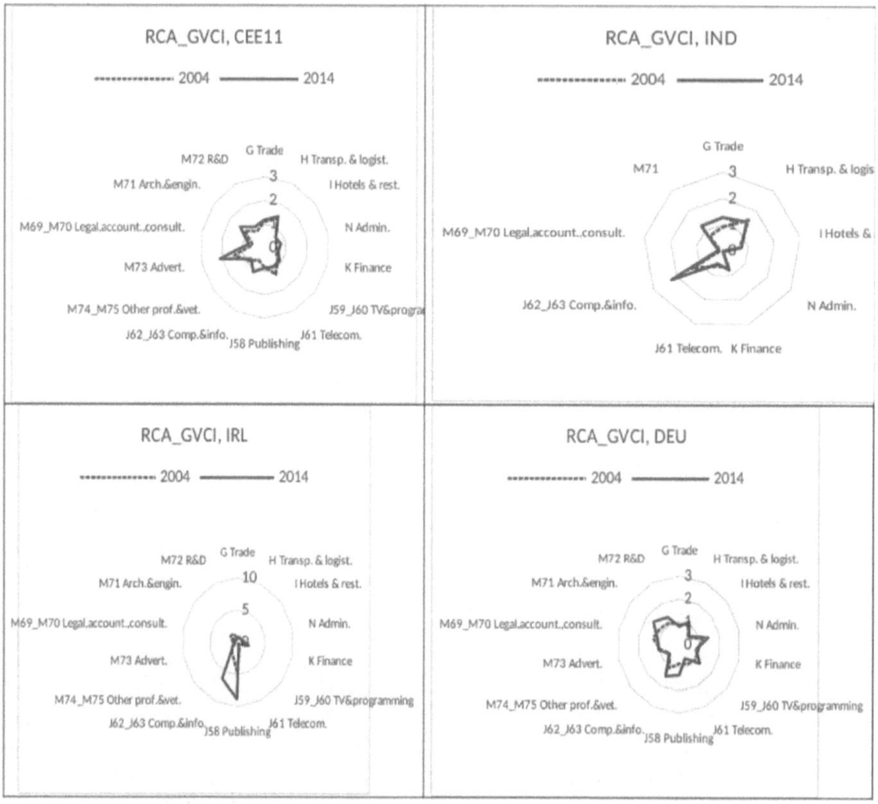

Figure 2.4 Revealed comparative advantages in GVC Income in selected economies

The service sectors are ranked clockwise from the least knowledge-intensive:

G – Wholesale and retail trade, repair of motor vehicles and motorcycles
H – Transportation and storage
I – Accommodation and food service activities
N – Administrative and support service activities
K – Financial and insurance activities
J59_J60 – Motion picture, video, television programme production; programming and broadcasting activities
J61 – Telecommunications
J58 – Publishing activities
J62_J63 – Computer programming, consultancy and related activities; Information service activities
M74_M75 – Other professional, scientific and technical activities; veterinary activities
M73 – Advertising and market research
M69_M70 – Computer programming, consultancy and related activities; information service activities
M71 – Architectural and engineering activities; technical testing and analysis
M72 – Scientific research and development

Source: Own study based on WIOD.

i.e. the ability to obtain higher added value. Ireland, which lost its share in revenues from the sale of advanced business services focusing on ICT and financial services, is an exception.

3 The extent to which GVCI is achieved in knowledge-intensive business services. The service sectors are ranked clockwise (cf. Figure 2.4.) from the least knowledge-intensive (trade [G]) to the most knowledge-intensive (R&D [72]). Gaining an advantage in value added in knowledge-intensive sectors means specialising in them. Between 2004 and 2014, CEE increased its comparative advantages to more than one in virtually all professional and IT divisions, which are the most knowledge-intensive service sectors. On the other hand, India and Ireland are examples of success in ICT. The analysis of GVCI growth in the German economy reveals increased comparative advantages in the most knowledge-intensive services (M71, M72, and J62). In the M69_M70 sector, although RCA still exceeds one, it was reduced, which suggests that these tasks (legal and accounting activities, among others) are offshored.

Implications of offshoring services for the international division of labour

Several conclusions can be drawn from the foregoing review of theories and observed trends in the development of the offshore services industry about the changing map of the international division of labour between 2004 and 2014.

- Developments in communication technologies and the removal of barriers to trade and foreign investment have led to the integration of a number of developing countries into the global production system. This has resulted, among other things, in their rapid industrialisation. Their growing presence in services value chains and their share in global services exports have also been observed.
- International corporations that wish to retain control over rent-generating assets tend to offshore via FDI. If they decide to outsource business services, they tend to entrust them to large operators from developed countries that often pursue FDI in low-cost locations. In the most globalised branches of business services in developing countries, most operators use capital coming from developed countries. MNEs from India are also active in the information technology outsourcing segment.
- The analysed locations for offshoring services – the CEE countries, India, and Ireland – each have respectable shares in the exports of intermediate inputs in the IT sector. However, they have also been successful in increasing their shares in final exports, which may signify a functional upgrading of economic operators in these countries. Firms in the largest developed countries tend to offshore such services, which supports the observation made by Gereffi et al. (2005) that suppliers in chains where knowledge can

be more easily codified are likely to capture a greater share of added value. In contrast, in the professional services sector, the CEE, India, and Ireland have relatively modest shares, with the share of CEE increasing. The shares of developed countries in exports of intermediate services in this sector are decreasing but remain stable in final services.

- The analysed offshored services locations have been gaining the capacity to derive more value added in certain knowledge-intensive business services (KIBS), which may suggest upgrading their position in the chain. India and Ireland expanded mostly in technology-based KIBS, while the CEE countries captured more added value in the professional and creative services segments alongside IT (see Chapter 4). The growing specialisation in the provision of business services would not have been possible without the existence of a large pool of suitable human capital (Fernandez-Stark, 2011; OECD, 2013).
- Even though the large share of FDI along with the rapid growth of added value suggests that knowledge transfer and learning processes are taking place, it implies that a proportion of this value is being repatriated, which may reduce investment in the development of local potential (Kalecki, 1985; Milberg & Winkler, 2013). The issue of local benefits resulting from territorial embeddedness of the offshore services industry will be addressed in more detail in Chapter 6.

For developing countries, becoming involved in international trade in business services is a challenge and an opportunity at the same time. Outsourced services rarely involve those in which the target firms have core competencies to create the highest added value (Schwörer, 2013). Furthermore, sectors with lower barriers to entry may have a less permanent competitive advantage (Milberg & Winkler, 2013). Conversely, an increasing part of the world's added value is being generated in services where the offshored white-collar jobs are fairly well paid. Above all, however, there are smaller capital barriers to entry in services than in manufacturing as the competence base is easier to build than a manufacturing one (Baldwin & Lopez-Gonzalez, 2013; Jones & Kierzkowski, 2005). And although this makes these competitive advantages less sustainable than in manufacturing, developing countries in the early catching-up stages find it easier to join the global economic cycle.

Note

1 The global production networks (GPN) approach differs from that of GVC and its predecessor – global commodity chains (GCCs). The patterns of uneven economic development seen in the global economy are understood here as arising from global network configurations and are reflected in regional development (Coe & Yeung, 2015; Dicken, 2015). Thus, GPN research methods are derived from economic geography and international political economy. The interrelations of production networks, local institutions, and regional assets as well as their impact on territorial development are analysed (Coe & Yeung, 2015, p. 19). In this approach, a sub-national region is a key economic development locus. Hence, besides value and power, an important conceptual category is embeddedness in its societal, networking, and territorial dimensions. We will examine this issue in more detail in Chapter 6.

References

Amiti, M., & Wei, S.-J. (2004). *Fear of Oursourcing: Is it Justified*? NBER Working Paper, No. 10808.

Amsden, A.H. (2001). *The Rise of "The Rest": Challenges to the West From Late-Industrializing Economies*. Oxford: Oxford University Press.

Bair, J. (2005). Global capitalism and commodity chains: Looking back, going forward. *Competition & Change*, *9*(2), pp. 153–180. https://doi.org/10.1179/102452905X45382 30.

Baldwin, R.E. (2006). *Globalisation: The Great Unbundling(s)*. Economic Council of Finland.

Baldwin, R.E. (2012). *Global Supply Chains: Why They Emerged, Why They Matter, and Where They are Going*. CEPR Discussion Papers, No. 9103.

Baldwin, R.E. (2019). *The globotics Upheaval: Globalization, Robotics, and the Future of Work*. Oxford: Oxford University Press.

Baldwin, R.E., & Lopez-Gonzalez, J. (2013). *Supply Chain Trade: A Portrait of Global Patterns and Several Testable Hypotheses*. NBER Working Paper, No. 18957.

Coe, N.M., & Yeung, H.W.-C. (2015). *Global Production Networks: Theorizing Economic Development in an Interconnected World*. Oxford: Oxford University Press.

Deardorff, A.V., & Haveman, J.D. (1995). The effects of US trade laws on poverty in America. *Journal of Human Resources*, *30*(4), pp. 807–825.

Dicken, P. (2015). *Global Shift: Mapping the Changing Contours of the World Economy*. New York: The Guilford Press.

Dunning, J.H. (1993). *Multinational Enterprises and the Global Economy*. Boston, MA: Addison-Wesley.

Dunning, J.H. (2000). The eclectic paradigm as an envelope for economic and business theories of MNE activity. *International Business Review*, *9*(2), pp. 163–190.

Eurostat. (2013). *Structural Business Statistics Glossary* [accessed from: https://ec.europa.eu/eurostat/statistics-explained/index.php?title=Glossary:Business_services, 4 February 2020].

Fernandez-Stark, K., Bamber, P., & Gereffi, G. (2011). The offshore services value chain: Upgrading trajectories in developing countries. *International Journal of Technological Learning, Innovation and Development*, *4*(1–3), pp. 206–234. https://doi.org/10.1504/IJTLID.2011.041905.

Fernandez-Stark, K., & Gereffi, G. (Eds.). (2010). *The Offshore Services Global Value Chain*. Durham, NC: Center on Globalization, Governance & Competitiveness, Duke University.

Gereffi, G. (1999). International trade and industrial upgrading in the apparel commodity chain. *Journal of International Economics*, *48*(1), pp. 37–70.

Gereffi, G., Humphrey, J., & Sturgeon, T. (2005). The governance of global value chains. *Review of International Political Economy*, *12*(1), pp. 78–104.

Grodzicki, M.J., & Geodecki, T. (2016). New dimensions of core-periphery relations in an economically integrated Europe: The role of global value chains. *Eastern European Economics*, *54*(5), pp. 377–404.

Grossman, G.M., & Rossi-Hansberg, E. (2006). *The Rise of Offshoring: It's Not Wine for Cloth Anymore*. Proceedings – Economic Policy Symposium – Jackson Hole, Federal Reserve Bank of Kansas City, pp. 59–102.

Gupta, S., Puranam, P., & Srikanth, K. (2006). *Services Sourcing in the Banking and Financial Services Industries: Exploding Myths and Describing Emerging Best Practice*. London: London Business School and Capco Institute.

Hamel, G., & Prahalad, C.K. (1990). The core competence of the corporation. *Harvard Business Review*, *68*(3), pp. 79–91.
Hopkins, T., & Wallerstein, I. (1977). Patterns of development of the modern world-system. *Review*, *1*(2), pp. 11–145.
Hutzschenreuter, T., Lewin, A.Y., & Dresel, S. (2011). Governance modes for offshoring activities: A comparison of US and German firms. *International Business Review*, *20*(3), pp. 291–313. https://doi.org/10.1016/j.ibusrev.2011.01.007.
Jones, R.W., & Kierzkowski, H. (1988). *The Role of Services in Production and International Trade: A Theoretical Framework*. Working Paper, No. 145. Rochester Center for Economic Research, University of Rochester.
Jones, R.W., & Kierzkowski, H. (2005). International fragmentation and the new economic geography. *The North American Journal of Economics and Finance*, *16*(1), pp. 1–10.
Kalecki, M. (1985). Formy pomocy zagranicznej. In J. Osiatyński (Ed.), *Michał Kalecki; Dzieła* (Vol. 5). Warszawa: Państwowe Wydawnictwo Ekonomiczne.
Lacity, M.C., Khan, S.A., & Yan, A. (2017). Review of the empirical business services sourcing literature: An update and future directions. In L.P. Willcocks, M.C. Lacity, & C. Sauer (Eds.), *Outsourcing and Offshoring Business Services* (pp. 499–651). London: Palgrave Macmillan.
Lin, J., & Chang, H.J. (2009). Should Industrial Policy in developing countries conform to comparative advantage or defy it? A debate between Justin Lin and Ha-Joon Chang. *Development Policy Review*, *27*(5), pp. 483–502.
Linden, G., Kraemer, K.L., & Dedrick, J. (2009). Who captures value in a global innovation network? The case of Apple's iPod. *Communications of the ACM*, *52*(3), pp. 140–144.
Mallampally, P., & Zimny, Z. (2000). Foreign direct investment in services. In Y. Aharoni & L. Nachum (Eds.), *Globalization of Services: Some Implications for Theory and Practice*. London: Routledge, pp. 25–49.
Markusen, J. (2005). *Modelling the Offshoring of White-Collar Services: From Comparative Advantage to the New Theories of Trade and FDI*. Working Paper, No. 11827. National Bureau of Economic Research.
Milberg, W., & Winkler, D. (2013). *Outsourcing Economics: Global Value Chains in Capitalist Development*. Cambridge: Cambridge University Press.
Mittelman, J.H. (1995). Rethinking the international division of labour in the context of globalisation. *Third World Quarterly*, *16*(2), pp. 273–296.
Narula, R., & Pineli, A. (2017). Multinational enterprises and economic development in host countries: What we know and what we don't know. In G. Giorgioni (Ed.), *Development Finance*. London: Palgrave Macmillan, pp. 147–188.
OECD. (2013). *Interconnected Economies: Benefiting from Global Value Chains*. OECD Publishing.
Pietrobelli, C., & Rabellotti, R. (2011). Global value chains meet innovation systems: Are there learning opportunities for developing countries? *World Development*, *39*(7), pp. 1261–1269. https://doi.org/10.1016/j.worlddev.2010.05.013.
Porter, M.E. (1985). *Competitive Advantage: Creating and Sustaining Superior Performance*. New York: Free Press.
Radło, M.-J. (2016). *Offshoring, Outsourcing and Production Fragmentation: Linking Macroeconomic and Micro-/Business Perspectives*. London: Palgrave Macmillan.
Schwörer, T. (2013). Offshoring, domestic outsourcing and productivity: Evidence for a number of European countries. *Review of World Economics*, *149*(1), pp. 131–149. https://doi.org/10.1007/s10290-012-0139-9.
Shih, S. (1996). *Me-Too is Not My Style* (No. 136). Taipei: Acer Foundation.

Smith, D.A., & White, D.R. (1992). Structure and dynamics of the global economy: Network analysis of international trade 1965–1980. *Social Forces*, *70*(4), pp. 857–893.

Timmer, M.P., Dietzenbacher, E., Los, B., Stehrer, R., & de Vries, G.J. (2015). An illustrated user guide to the world input–output database: The case of global automotive production. *Review of International Economics*, *23*(3), pp. 575–605. https://doi.org/10.1111/roie.12178.

Timmer, M.P., Los, B., Stehrer, R., & De Vries, G.J. (2013). Fragmentation, incomes and jobs: An analysis of European competitiveness. *Economic Policy*, *28*(76), pp. 613–661. https://doi.org/10.1111/1468-0327.12018.

UNCTAD. (2004). *World Investment Report 2004: The Shift Towards Services*. United Nations Geneva.

Wallerstein, I.M. (2004). *World-Systems Analysis: An Introduction*. Durham, NC: Duke University Press.

Williamson, O.E. (1985). *The Economic Institutions of Capitalism: Firms, Markets, Relational Contracting*. New York: Free Press.

Wirtz, J., Tuzovic, S., & Ehret, M. (2015). Global business services. *Journal of Service Management*, *26*(4), pp. 565–587. https://doi.org/10.1108/JOSM-01-2015-0024.

Wölfl, A. (2005). *The Service Economy in OECD Countries*. Paris: OECD.

3 The determinants of territorial embeddedness of offshoring and outsourcing firms

A conceptualisation of the problem

Paweł Białynicki-Birula and Agnieszka Pacut

Introduction

The concept of embeddedness straddles the boundary between economics and sociology, being one of the central research issues of such sub-disciplines as the new economic sociology and the new economic geography. It was popularised in the literature in the second half of the 1980s and offered a new perspective on how economic problems are approached (Krippner & Alvarez, 2007). Over time, the concept of embeddedness was also adopted to explain a range of other social issues (Dacin et al., 1999). By showing the inseparable links between economic organisations and their environment, it refers to interpersonal relations and the social, cultural, political, and cognitive context of decisions taken by actors in various aspects of economic and social life (Adaman & Divine, 2001; Beckert, 2003).

One of the fundamental dimensions of embeddedness involves the spatial aspects of actors/economic operators, making this concept useful for analysing territorial factors (Dicken & Malmberg, 2001; Hess, 2004). Owing to its explanatory power when applied to socio-economic phenomena which occur in the relationships with the environment (Beckert, 2003, pp. 792–795), particularly that between economic activity and spaces or places (Jones, 2008), the concept has also been adapted to research on offshoring and outsourcing firms (multinational companies, transnational corporations) (Heidenreich, 2012; Heidenreich & Mattes, 2012). It helps to explain the incentives, behaviours, and performance of multinational corporations, and their economic links in the form of production networks analysed from a spatial – global, national, regional, and local – perspective. Embeddedness also contributes to the innovativeness of multinational firms by facilitating access to external resources and competencies as well as coordination with internal and external actors (Heidenreich, 2012). Through various links, offshoring and outsourcing firms are not only globally embedded but also nationally and locally embedded (Ratajczak-Mrozek, 2014; Halinen & Törnroos, 1998; Heidenreich et al., 2012). This explains the impact of this group of firms on the socio-economic development of a given territory (Dicken et al., 1994).

Origins of the concept

K. Polanyi (1944) is considered to be the inventor of the concept of embeddedness – he created it to express his opposition to the dominance of the tendency to absolutise the market in social sciences (Barber, 1995). The author perceived embeddedness in terms of relations between the economy and society, and, contrary to classical economic theories, emphasised the fact that the former was determined by the latter. Accordingly, he considered the idea of autonomy of the economy to be fundamentally false, proving that the processes that characterise it are shaped by phenomena which occur in social life. At the same time, he advocated the idea of treating these links in institutional terms owing to the role played by historical, political, social, and cultural factors. It should be underscored that in Polanyi's view, embeddedness is clearly depersonalised, as it concerns not so much economic entities or their interactions as the exchange that represents their activities (Hess, 2004).

A major contribution to the popularity of the concept was made in the mid-1980s by M. Granovetter (1985), whose work belongs to economic sociology. The concept in question was used by this researcher to refute the 'atomised' vision of man proffered by both the economic and sociological mainstream (Swedberg, 1991). His approach is distinguished by defining embeddedness in terms of the activity of economic entities by on-going personal relations and network structures. Unlike Polanyi, who places this concept in the macro sphere (i.e. abstractly conceived economy and society), Granovetter redirected his attention to the meso level (i.e. the specific personal connections among the entities that engage in economic activity).

The concept of embeddedness as understood by Granovetter has become very popular in the social sciences and has led to redefining a number of research problems. At the same time, it has provoked a lively debate and elicited a lot of vocal criticism. In particular, the concept in question was condemned for its indeterminacy and lack of explanation of the mechanism via which social structures influence economic activity (Pike et al., 2000; Uzzi, 1997) as well as the adoption of too narrow a viewpoint due to the non-inclusion of the role of social or cultural systems larger than networks, such as kinship, gender, polity, education, or communication (Barber, 1995). It has also been argued that networks are only one of many possible sets of social relationships, and that due to its abstractness, the approach fails to take into consideration the specificity of collective entities or recognise the importance of the market (Krippner, 2001).

Such criticism did not prevent the spread or thwart the popularity of the concept of embeddedness in the social sciences starting with the 1990s. In this context, the following fields of research should be mentioned: theory of organisation and institutions (Halinen & Törnroos, 1998; Dacin et al., 1999); economic sociology (Lie, 1997; Murdoch et al., 2000); networks and organisations (Uzzi, 1996, 1997); network theory and cultural sociology (Emirbayer & Goodwin, 1994); and economic geography (Dicken et al., 1994; Dicken & Malmberg, 2001). It should be noted that in these areas, it is not uncommon to adopt a special understanding of embeddedness associated with the modified Granovetter's approach. In this context, the division proposed by S. Zukin and P. DiMaggio (1990) is the main point of reference for many researchers (Hess, 2004).

The essence and types of embeddedness

Despite its ambiguity and indefiniteness, embeddedness is now a very popular concept in the social sciences (Jessop, 2001; Uzzi, 1997). In the literature, depending on research specialty, different ways of understanding it have a negative impact on both the possibility to agree on its universal meaning or to maintain analytical precision. Therefore, in order to capture the essence of the concept under consideration, at least an attempt should be made to identify the elements that constitute the common denominator of most approaches. For this purpose, it makes sense to refer to Zukin and DiMaggio's approach, which is particularly appreciated by researchers. As it is considered to be an extension of Granovetter's approach, it seems reasonable to start with the latter author.

Granovetter (1985, p. 504) defined embeddedness in terms of the overarching influence of interpersonal relationship networks of on the activity of economic operators. In this perspective, the concept shows a twofold characteristic, namely the immersion of economic actors in social relations and the creation by the latter of social structures with an individual history (Halinen & Törnroos, 1998). As a result, embeddedness has been identified with influencing economic activity by a social structure (network) understood as regularly recurring interpersonal relationship patterns (Hess, 2004). Accordingly, it denotes a kind of contextualisation of economic activity due to ongoing interactions and accentuates the fact that market exchange is determined by complex social processes (Dacin et al., 1999). In the course of his research work, Granovetter (1992) identified two types of embeddedness, namely relational embeddedness, based on the dyadic relations that bind the individual pairs of actors, and structural embeddedness, which involves the entire network, which permitted him to cover the aspect of agency at both individual and collective levels.

Zukin and DiMaggio's (1990) contribution consists primarily in broadening the scope of the concept in order to take account of the impact of broad social systems on economic agents . These researchers together have thus proposed a total of four types of embeddedness: cognitive, cultural, political, and Granovetter's original structural (network) embeddness. The cognitive aspect concerns the regularity of thought processes at the individual level that determine the reasoning of economic operators. Cultural embeddedness refers to the fact that certain general patterns of thinking and attitudes resulting from culture and tradition profoundly affect decision-makers. And finally, political embeddedness refers to the institutional framework of activity and underscores the struggle for dominance and power between economic actors and 'non-market' entities/institutions.

It should be noted that the popularity of embeddedness resulted in the emergence of various typologies based on the approaches proposed by Granovetter or Zukin and DiMaggio, which identify more or fewer determinants of economic

Table 3.1 Types, dimensions, and perspective of embeddedness

Author	*Taxonomy of embeddedness*
Types of embeddedness	
Granovetter (1985, 1992)	structural, relational
Zukin and DiMaggio (1990)	structural, cognitive, political, cultural
Uzzi (1996)	structural
Halinen and Törnroos (1998)	temporal, spatial, social, political, market, technological
Brinton and Kariya (1998)	institutional
Dequech (2003)	cognitive, cultural
Hagedoorn (2006)	environmental, inter-organisational
Hess (2004)	territorial, network, societal
Dimensions of embeddedness	
Halinen and Törnroos (1998)	vertical, horizontal
Perspective of embeddedness	
Halinen and Törnroos (1998)	micro, macro

Source: Own study.

activity (or types of embeddedness). One of the most comprehensive systematisations was proposed by A. Halinen and J. Törnroos (1998), who identified a total of six types of embeddedness: temporal, spatial, technological, market, political, and social. In the literature, there are also more fragmentary approaches that focus on single determinants of economic activity, e.g. positional, corporate, institutional, or environmental embeddedness (Gulati & Gargiulo, 1999; Hagedoorn, 2006).

Apart from the typologies mentioned above, for analytical purposes, researchers also employ the following features of the concept in question: dimensions (vertical, horizontal) and perspectives (micro and macro) (Halinen & Törnroos, 1998; Fletcher & Barrett, 2001; Gulati & Gargiulo, 1999). Vertical embeddedness focuses on the relations between different levels of geographically defined networks in the channel structure or a specific industry based on the distinct qualities of individuals and firms. On the other hand, horizontal embeddedness refers to the relations among actors at a certain level in the network, e.g. between firms in a given sector or area.

Territorial embeddedness

The identification of the territorial dimension/type of embeddedness is based on the observation that systems of social relations have an essentially spatial nature and, as a consequence, economic interactions embedded in them also demonstrate such properties (Hess, 2004). Hence, the concept of embeddedness has come to describe and explain the relations between economic entities and their environment with reference to a variety of geographical scales (Pike et al., 2000). The literature employs various terms (spatial, territorial, and local) and definitions to circumscribe the denotations of space and geography for the actors' activity. At the same time, researchers emphasise the networked nature of relations among the economic actors and certain intrinsic similarities or complementarities manifest in their "proximity of physical and socio-cultural characteristics" (Lewis et al., 2002, p. 438).

Generally speaking, territorial embeddedness refers to the way economic activity is organised in a given area (Halinen & Törnroos, 1998). It describes how actors are anchored in a particular area in the sense of absorbing the benefits or being subject to restrictions by economic processes or social dynamics existing in these places (Hess, 2004). Embeddedness understood in this way is clearly associated with the recognition of the importance of location in firms' activities (Ratajczak-Mrozek, 2014). It should be noted, however, that the main point of reference is not so much the territory as the relations and socio-economic processes located in a specific place. Consequently, territorial embeddedness by necessity integrates aspects of other types of embeddedness to the extent that the relations they describe occur in the area in question.

Territorial embeddedness comprises a variety of determinants of economic activity in the spatial dimension. In particular, it is associated with research on specific areas in terms of such factors or aspects as local/regional economic and social structures; infrastructure development level; availability of capital; entrepreneurial spirit; innovativeness; or level of organisational culture (Domański, 2005). It is assumed in the literature that an important factor affecting territorial embeddedness is the density and intensity of links between economic entities located in a given area, especially those that manufacture goods and engage in R&D.

More recent literature shows a clear tendency to emphasise the multi-level nature of territorial embeddedness (cf. Pike et al., 2000). For this reason, the concept refers not only to the international level but also to the national, regional, and local ones. At the micro level, territorial embeddedness is clearly cognitive due to the inclusion of mental models (Halinen & Törnroos, 1998). Research at the local and regional level focuses on three groups of issues, namely the importance of external economies for local production systems, the formation of local cultures and institutional structures, and the role of spatial proximity in creating trust between business partners (Lewis et al., 2002). In general, local/regional embeddedness tends to be explained in terms of "a company's efforts to interact and build relationships with local actors in order to exchange resources, knowledge and information" (Wright, 2010, p. 127). At the international level, researchers examine the issue of building links by foreign actors/multinational firms with actors in given locations.

The idea of territorial embeddedness is particularly popular in economic geography, where it constitutes a central part of an intellectual tradition that emphasises the social side of economic processes and their spatial dimension. It is combined with the adoption of evolutionary and institutional viewpoints in the analysis of economic development while emphasising the benefits of diversity/institutional thickness. Due to the growing importance of global production/services networks, there is now a tendency to focus on the issue of translocal linkages, which entails moving away from analysing territorial embeddedness exclusively in terms of spatial logic (Hess, 2004).

Embeddedness of offshore services firms

The activity of offshore services firms is a part of wider phenomena of international economic activity, and therefore their embeddedness should be considered first of all in the context of multinational enterprises (MNEs) or global production networks (GPNs). As with other kinds of MNEs, outsourcing and offshoring was initially triggered mainly by the mounting internal and external pressures to adapt and reduce costs, but now more strategic benefits, such as the potential to improve quality or increase market share, are gaining in significance (Tate et al., 2009). In general, MNEs' activities are associated with the globalisation processes, but in the literature, opinions on their impacts are divided. On the one hand, globalisation is seen as an equalising force, which causes disembedding, while on the other, empirical research clearly shows that the local context is still relevant and local knowledge and embeddedness rank among the key success factors (Meyer et al., 2011).

As regards GPNs, territorial embeddedness purports to explain local economic development in that it concerns the 'anchoring' of global firms in specific locations, which affects the latter's broader development prospects (Kleibert, 2014). In this context, the following positive outcomes of embeddedness are mentioned: access to valuable resources, economies of localisation and urbanisation, access to knowledge, innovation, opportunities, and improved performance. On the other hand, negative territorial embeddedness outcomes include: lock-in, relational and operational risk, and inferior performance (Ratajczak-Mrozek, 2017).

The local context plays a key role in international business research. Special attention is paid to two dimensions, namely the institutional frameworks and the provision of resources. It is pointed out that the former is not internationally mobile, which forces MNEs to adapt their organisation and management accordingly. The costs and benefits of these adjustments to a certain extent determine the international attractiveness of a given location. Early research attributed a crucial role to local resources or those of the economy as a whole in the MNEs' location decisions. Recent studies, however, discriminate between 'natural' and 'created' assets, which make up the location-specific advantages of individual countries and thus attract foreign multinationals (Meyer et al., 2011).

According to a widely held view, the capacity of firms to compete internationally is based on interrelated location advantages in their home country (Ferraris, 2014). Multinational corporations usually build primary resources in their country, and those subsequently drive their international development. At the same time, it is pointed out that MNEs are increasingly dependent on knowledge, as competition forces them to seek and develop their knowledge advantages wherever possible. This is the main factor in cultivating knowledge resources in less developed countries that affects the formation of various industry clusters. Once an MNE subsidiary has gained access to knowledge, it may choose to transfer it to other units in the MNE network or integrate it with its own knowledge to create new competencies.

The network approach proves that a subsidiary is simultaneously embedded in two business contexts: the internal MNE and the external one (the host country). The roles of subsidiaries are therefore shaped and influenced by these two contexts. These interactions enable subsidiaries to access assets from different sources and to influence their internal and external business partners. The quintessence of foreign direct investment is therefore a combination of company-specific assets (ownership advantages) with assets specific to the location of its foreign branches (location advantages). This combination of resources is particularly evident when multinational corporations take over firms in other countries in order to increase their asset portfolio and, thus, their capacity to compete both locally and globally (Meyer et al., 2011).

In this context, the territorial embeddedness of offshore outsourcing firms is best described in terms of the relational approach as applied to MNEs and referred to as multiple embeddedness (Dicken & Malmberg, 2001). This approach considers the multiscalarity of embeddedness as well as its development over time. It recognises that firms are not only legally limited entities and owners of both tangible and intangible property but also institutions with permeable and unclear boundaries. In other words, MNEs are conceived as networks within networks or systems within systems (Dicken & Malmberg, 2001). This concept also involves analysing the activities of subsidiaries on two levels, namely their interactions with entities operating in local contexts and at subsidiary level. To take full advantage of the opportunities offered by each local context, it is assumed that subsidiaries must be externally embedded in each local context and, at the same time, must be sufficiently internally embedded in the MNE network for external benefits to be potentially available to other MNE organisational units (Meyer et al., 2011).

Dicken and Malmberg's (2001) conceptual model of firm-territory relationships takes into account the different dimensions of the complex set of relations in which firms operate. This model includes the nexus of three major dimensions – firms, industrial systems, and territories – which are embedded in the overall macro dimension of governance systems. In this perspective, location (territory) is not the only spatial logic of embeddedness. Other elements that affect the latter are the industrial system (contact network across which firms interact, i.e. firms interacting in various ways form a system), the arena (i.e. firms active within the same market, regulatory, or institutional framework form a system), as well as the firm itself (defined as a dense network of relationships, networks within networks). Both firms and governance elements operate at a range of geographic scales (both local and global). This underscores the multiscalarity of embeddedness as well as its development over time, linked across space by relations among embedded actors, which change in shape and scope over time.

Multiscalar approach seems to be offering an apt and at the same time an inspiring perspective for analyzing territorial embeddedness of offshore outsourcing firms. Nonetheless it needs to be emphasized that considering the concept in question from the perspective of host countries, above all the spatial optics seems to present the most paramount importance. This is way due to the fact that such firms are relatively easy to relocate and the degree of their territorial embeddedness can be considered as a set of factors that determine the alternative costs of doing business elsewhere. These factors and costs are multi-faceted and involve both strictly economic and social conditions of carrying on an activity. Moreover, they affect not only the firms themselves but also their employees and their family members. Territorial embeddedness framed that way provide the only potential space for the activity of public actors of host countries, both national and local level.

Conclusion

The concept of embeddedness draws on the assumption about the defining influence of the social structure on economic activity and, in consequence, leads to the recognition of the social nature of economic processes. Contrary to Granovetter's view, identifying various types of embeddedness means that a variety of social systems are at play, not only those based on personal relationships or ties. Thus, for analytical purposes, the recognition of a number of distinct types of embeddedness is linked to the breakdown of the different aspects of these 'social' influences into different groups of mechanisms. This results in a significant expansion and enrichment of the conceptualisation of economic phenomena, particularly the role of a wider range of factors than those which have so far qualified as endogenous in economics. An unquestionable advantage of the concept of embeddedness is the possibility to adopt an institutional point of view, in which economic processes are described through the prism of the impact of a range of factors known as 'the rules of the social game.'

The concept of territorial embeddedness analysed in relation to the offshore services industry highlights the way in which business activity is organised in a given area. It is expressed in the efforts of this group of firms to establish contacts with local actors in order to exchange resources, knowledge, and information. In other words, the main subject of the analysis concerns the broad spectrum of socio-economic relations established by the offshoring and outsourcing firms with their environment. Owing to the multidimensional and multifaceted nature of territorial embeddedness, it makes sense to consider this concept in relation to the firms themselves, their employees, and their families. Only by adopting this broader, dual approach will it be possible to fully assess the benefits and costs of doing business in a given location.

References

Adaman, F., & Divine, P. (Ed.). (2001). *The Socially Embedded Economy*. Montreal: Black Rose Books.

Barber, B. (1995). All economies are "embedded": The career of a concept, and beyond. *Social Research*, *62*(2), pp. 387–413.

Beckert, J. (2003). Economic sociology and embeddedness: How shall we conceptualize economic action? *Journal of Economic Issues*, *37*(3), pp. 769–787. https://doi.org/10.1080/00213624.2003.11506613.

Brinton, M.C., & Kariya, T. (1998). Institutional embeddedness in Japanese labor markets. In M.C. Brinton & V. Nee (Eds.), *The New Institutionalism in Sociology*. New York: Russell Sage Foundation, pp. 181–207.

Dacin, M.T., Ventresca, M.J., & Beal, B.D. (1999). The embeddedness of organizations: Dialogue & directions. *Journal of Management*, *25*(3), pp. 317–356. https://doi.org/10.1177/014920639902500304.

Dequech, D. (2003). Cognitive and cultural embeddedness: Combining institutional economics and economic sociology. *Journal of Economic Issues*, *37*(2), pp. 461–470. https://doi.org/10.1080/00213624.2003.11506594.

Dicken, P., Forsgren, M., & Malmberg, A. (1994). The local embeddedness of transnational corporations. In A. Amin & N. Thrift (Eds.), *Globalisation, Institutions and Regional Development in Europe*. Oxford: Oxford University Press, pp. 23–45.

Dicken, P., & Malmberg, A. (2001). Firms in territories: A relational perspective. *Economic Geography*, *77*(4), pp. 345–363. https://doi.org/10.2307/3594105.

Domański, B. (2005). Korporacje ponadnarodowe a miejsce (region). In T. Czyż & H. Rogacki (Eds.), *Koncepcje teoretyczne badań przestrzenno-ekonomicznych*. Biuletyn KPZK PAN, 219, Warszawa: PWN, pp. 130–145.

Emirbayer, M., & Goodwin, J. (1994). Network analysis, culture, and the problem of agency. *American Journal of Sociology*, *99*(6), pp. 1411–1454.

Ferraris, A. (2014). Rethinking the literature on "multiple embeddedness" and subsidiary-specific advantages. *Multinational Business Review*, *22*(1), pp. 15–33.

Fletcher, R., & Barrett, N. (2001). Embeddedness and the evolution of global networks: An Australian case study. *Industrial Marketing Management*, *30*(7), pp. 561–573. https://doi.org/10.1016/S0019-8501(99)00120-0.

Granovetter, M. (1985). Economic action and social structure: The problem of embeddedness. *American Journal of Sociology*, *91*(3), pp. 481–510. https://doi.org/10.1086/228311.

Granovetter, M. (1992). Problems and explanation in economic sociology. In N. Nohria & R.G. Eccles (Ed.), *Networks and Organizations: Structure, Form and Action* (pp. 25–56). Boston: Harvard Business School Press.

Gulati, R., & Gargiulo, M. (1999). Where do interorganizational networks come from? *American Journal of Sociology*, *104*(5), pp. 1439–1493. https://doi.org/10.1086/210179.

Hagedoorn, J. (2006). Understanding the cross-level embeddedness of interfirm partnership formation. *Academy of Management Review*, *31*(3), pp. 670–680. https://doi.org/10.5465/amr.2006.21318924.

Halinen, A., & Törnroos, J.-Å. (1998). The role of embeddedness in the evolution of business networks. *Scandinavian Journal of Management*, *14*(3), pp. 187–205. https://doi.org/10.1016/S0956-5221(98)80009-2.

Heidenreich, M. (2012). The social embeddedness of multinational companies: A literature review. *Socio-Economic Review*, *10*(3), pp. 549–579. https://doi.org/10.1093/ser/mws010.

Heidenreich, M., Barmeyer, C., Koschatzky, K., Mattes, J., Baier, E., & Krüth, K. (2012). *Multinational Enterprises and Innovation: Regional Learning in Networks*. London: Routledge.

Heidenreich, M., & Mattes, J. (2012). Regional embeddedness of multinational companies and their limits. A typology. In M. Heidenreich (Ed.), *Institutional Embeddedness of Multinational Companies*. London: Edward Elgar, pp. 29–58.

Hess, M. (2004). 'Spatial' relationships? Towards a reconceptualization of embedded ness. *Progress in Human Geography*, *28*(2), pp. 165–186. https://doi.org/10.1191/0309132504ph479oa.

Jessop, B. (2001). Regulationist and autopoieticist reflections on Polanyi's account of market economies and the market society. *New Political Economy*, *6*(2), pp. 213–232.

Jones, A. (2008). Beyond embeddedness: Economic practices and the invisible dimensions of transnational business activity. *Progress in Human Geography*, *32*(1), pp. 71–88. https://doi.org/10.1177/0309132507084817.

Kleibert, J.M. (2014). Strategic coupling in "next wave cities": Local institutional actors and the offshore service sector in the Philippines. *Singapore Journal of Tropical Geography*, *35*(2), pp. 245–260.

Krippner, G.R. (2001). The elusive market: Embeddedness and the paradigm of economic sociology. *Theory and Society*, *30*(6), pp. 775–810.

Krippner, G.R., & Alvarez, A.S. (2007). Embeddedness and the intellectual projects of economic sociology. *Annual Review of Sociology*, *33*(1), pp. 219–240. https://doi.org/10.1146/annurev.soc.33.040406.131647.

Lewis, N., Moran, W., Perrier-Cornet, P., & Barker, J. (2002). Territoriality, enterprise and réglementation in industry governance. *Progress in Human Geography*, *26*(4), pp. 433–462.

Lie, J. (1997). Sociology of markets. *Annual Review of Sociology*, *23*, pp. 341–360.

Meyer, K.E., Mudambi, R., & Narula, R. (2011). Multinational enterprises and local contexts: The opportunities and challenges of multiple embeddedness. *Journal of Management Studies*, *48*(2), pp. 235–252.

Murdoch, J., Marsden, T., & Banks, J. (2000). Quality, nature, and embeddedness: Some theoretical considerations in the context of the food sector. *Economic Geography*, *76*(2), pp. 107–125.

Pike, A., Lagendijk, A., & Vale, M. (2000). Critical reflections on 'embeddedness' in economic geography: Labour market governance in the North East region of England. In A. Giunta, A. Lagendijk, & A. Pike (Eds.), *Restructuring Industry and Territory: The Experience of Europe's Regions*. London: TSO, pp. 59–82.

Polanyi, K. (1944). *The Great Transformation: The Political and Economic Origins of Our Time*. New York: Rinehart.

Ratajczak-Mrozek, M. (2014). Companies' simultaneous embeddedness in local, international and global networks: A conceptualisation from the perspective of local enterprises and their degree of internationalisation. *Poznan University of Economics Review*, *14*, pp. 31–47.

Ratajczak-Mrozek, M. (2017). *Network Embeddness: Examining the Effect on Business Performance and Internationalization*. Cham: Palgrave McMillan.

Swedberg, R. (1991). Major traditions of economic sociology. *Annual Review of Sociology*, *17*, pp. 251–276.

Tate, W.L., Ellram, L.M., Bals, L., & Hartmann, E. (2009). Offshore outsourcing of services: An evolutionary perspective. *International Journal of Production Economics*, *120*(2), pp. 512–524.

Uzzi, B. (1996). The sources and consequences of embeddedness for the economic performance of organizations: The network effect. *American Sociological Review*, *61*(4), pp. 674–698.

Uzzi, B. (1997). Social structure and competition in interfirm networks: The paradox of embeddedness. *Administrative Science Quarterly*, *42*, pp. 35–67.

Wright, R. (2010). Competitiveness and changing patterns of embeddedness in Romania. *Competitiveness Review: An International Business Journal*, *20*(2), pp. 126–138. https://doi.org/10.1108/10595421011029848.

Zukin, S., & DiMaggio, P. (1990). *Structures of Capital: The Social Organization of the Economy*. Cambridge: Cambridge University Press.

4 The importance of new technologies for business development

Automation and robotisation in the services industry

Tomasz Geodecki and Jakub Głowacki

Introduction

As early as in the 19th century, mechanisation made it possible to eliminate the most onerous and repetitive work in agriculture, whereas the automation of manufacturing redirected employees to the services sector. But technical progress did not stop, and before our very eyes algorithms are replacing people in the services sector, which seemed to be the last bastion of hired labour. Are we, then, facing an "end of work", as Jeremy Rifkin proclaimed a quarter of a century ago? The aim of this chapter is to present outsourcing and offshoring from the perspective of innovative solutions and, thus, lay the groundwork for further analysis. Based on the literature, it discusses the importance of technology for the development of firms and the entire economy, the role of innovation in the services sector, and outlines the development trends characteristic of this sector triggered by the advent of the fourth industrial revolution.

The importance of new technologies for the development of firms

J. Schumpeter's *Theory of Economic Development* (1912/1982) is considered to be the first systematic study on the role of innovation and new technologies in economic processes. He opposed the perception of innovation as gradual change in otherwise circular economic processes. In his view, breakthrough innovations constitute a massive disruption of an existing balance. The train destroyed the horse-drawn postal carriage market just as text messages replaced telegrams and pagers. An innovator that increases consumer utility or reduces manufacturing costs is rewarded by society with profit. The latter is temporarily monopolistic in nature, and thus the innovator avoids having to operate under perfect competition, in which all manufacturers have identical technology at their disposal. Even a small price premium attracts new producers to the industry, which results in increased supply and reduced prices to eventually eliminate profit. A satisfactory profit is therefore achieved only as a reward for innovation – for doing something better. It is earned by pioneers who have the motivation, idea, and energy to borrow

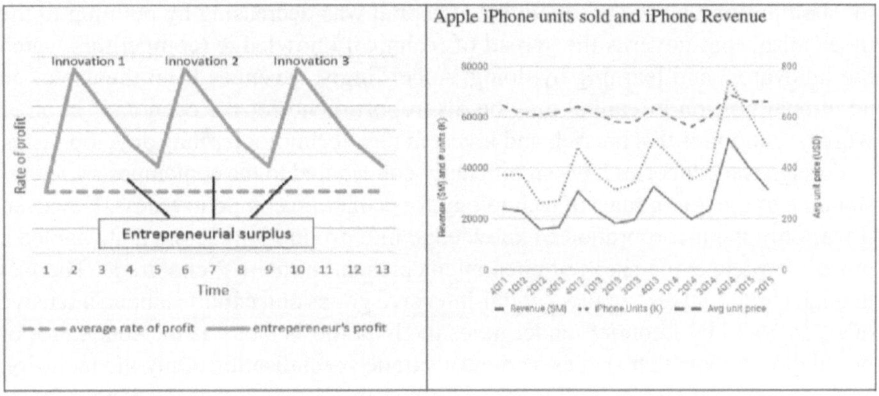

Figure 4.1 The generation and dissipation of entrepreneurial surplus

Source: Own study based on Kaplinsky and Morris (2002, p. 26) and Rusiecki (2015).

money and start new production. The success of a new undertaking destroys old enterprises that fail to adjust, attracts followers, and helps spread the new way of production. This process of 'creative destruction', triggered by new technological solutions, underlies competition among firms to a much greater extent than low prices.

The findings of studies carried out by business practitioners (Porter, 1979; Kaplinsky & Morris, 2002) confirm that the source of economic rents lies in technological and organisational capabilities, skills, and marketing capabilities (such as brand names) that increase factor productivity and create entry barriers which are difficult to overcome for competitors. Thus, the focus on maintaining innovative capabilities and the capacity to continually improve products as well as the methods of manufacturing and delivering them is a prerequisite for keeping the profit rate above average, as illustrated by the left side of Figure 4.1.

Technological determinants of economic development

R. Solow, whose model of growth became the dominant mode of perceiving development processes in the following decades, contributed significantly to the recognition of the importance of new technologies for economic growth. Technical change is understood as any kind of shift in the production function which ensures that a larger output is obtained from the same input of labour and capital (Solow, 1957). Why and how entrepreneurs introduce new technologies remained outside the scope of inquiry at the time (cf. Blaug, 1997). For developing countries, the most important consequence of this was to be the expected convergence of income levels – there, the return on investment was to be higher given the relative scarcity of capital. The inconsistency of this conclusion with even superficial observations – i.e. the absence of equalisation of development levels – became one of the reasons why the Solow model was challenged. P. Romer (1986) disproved the assumption that the productivity of capital was decreasing by pointing to the mechanism that governs the spread of technical knowledge (competitors watch the innovator) and learning by doing. Accordingly, revenues from the use of an additional portion of capital may be disproportionate for the economy; in other words, economies that are rich and invest in new technologies may develop faster.

Foreign trade theories have significantly contributed to the contemporary understanding of the importance of technology for economic competitiveness. However, it was only the incorporation of knowledge into production factors that enabled a more complete explanation of phenomena present in international trade. The fact that the United States imports capital-intensive goods and exports labour-intensive ones, as noted by Leontief, undermines the hypothesis that it is the abundance of production factors that shapes a country's trade specialisation. Only the inclusion of human capital and technology made it possible to show that this labour intensity is only ostensible. Labour equipped with knowledge and technology becomes embodied in exported goods and determines the shape of American foreign trade (Obstfeld & Krugman, 2003, pp. 102–104). Likewise, taking into account the fact that products exported by some economies have a quality advantage, which is primarily technological, resolves the paradox observed by Kaldor (1978) that countries where labour costs increased the fastest in the post-war period also increased their shares in world exports.

The imperative to increase an economy's exports in order to improve its competitiveness was criticised by Krugman (1996). Attempts to adopt a strategic approach to trade invariably leads to the advocacy of mercantilist methods, which were found to be wrong already 200 years ago. Nevertheless, as Krugman himself points out in his work, imperfect competition and path dependence cause companies and countries to seek technological advantage (Krugman, 1996; Milberg & Winkler, 2013). In fact, economists from developing countries have always been suspicious of the argument that worldwide prosperity is maximised when the existing international division of labour is accepted (Evans, 1995), with lower efficiency of production factors in developing countries resulting from their lesser capacity to assimilate free knowledge. On the contrary, as Amsden (2001) argues, technological knowledge is a fiercely guarded resource because it generates economic rents. Therefore, nations that have achieved manufacturing competencies in learning-prone industries and economies of scale "are rich and others stay poor" (Reinert, 2007). If developing countries are to be competitive, they must acquire competencies in the most advanced sectors of the economy, which are susceptible to the introduction of new technologies (Fagerberg & Godinho, 2004; Lin& Chang, 2009).

Referring to reflections on the competitiveness of the national economy, Porter (1990) argues that it is true that nations will export those goods that make most use of the factors with which they are relatively well endowed, but the most important ones are rarely inherited. Today, the skilled human resources and the scientific base that determine technological superiority must be produced independently and constantly reproduced. These observations are based on Porter's previous research (1979) on competitiveness factors at the industry level. He found that the profitability of operators in an industry is determined, among other things, by the threat posed by the emergence of substitutes and barriers to entry, in other words, factors resulting directly from the technology used by the manufacturer and its competitors. Specialisation makes it possible to maintain competitive advantages, but only in certain sectors – and it is in relation to them that the concept of competitiveness makes sense. In the long run, the only way to maintain a competitive advantage in a given sector is to produce and provide increasingly sophisticated products and services.

Innovation and new technologies in service industries

Individual branches of the economy are not evenly equipped to generate new useful knowledge to build barriers to entry. Initially, they were mainly associated with manufacturing, so the first classifications of high-tech branches included the processing industry. The classification of industries by technology level (i.e. high-tech and low-tech) reflects the research and development (R&D) intensity in an industry's turnover. It is recognised that high-tech companies are more likely to undertake research that generates positive externalities in the economy, embark on more innovative activities, create more added value, and contribute to the overall competitiveness of the economy (Godin, 2004).

In services, innovation is of a different nature than in manufacturing due to the specific characteristics of the former, which include intangibility, heterogeneity, inseparability, and perishability (the so called IHIP criteria) (Morrar, 2014; Wirtz et al., 2015; Panasiuk & Tokarz, 2012). Intangibility means, among other things, that a potential purchaser cannot assess the service before it has been provided. Heterogeneity means that the characteristics of a service are shaped by both the provider and the recipient, with restrictions applicable to the standardisation of services as products. The inseparability of service provision and consumption processes implies restrictions on the possibility of increasing scale and maintaining confidentiality. Therefore, in this context, contracts tend to be used more often than patent protection (Arundel & Kabla, 1998; Miles et al., 2000). It is also difficult to separate the product from the process, so the traditional division into product and process innovations fails (Morrar, 2014). Perishability is associated with the inability to produce services for storage, and therefore the sale of such services is often limited by the human potential available to the service provider; that is why services are sometimes outsourced and located in places where human capital is abundant (Fernandez-Stark, 2011; Morrar, 2014). Since the provision of a service often does not require capital-intensive production techniques, from the perspective of building barriers to entry, maintaining an advantage over competitors nonetheless requires the latest technologies to be rapidly implemented and is to a much greater extent based on competencies and human capital (Sirilli & Evangelista, 1998).

Due to the lower intensity of formalised R&D, the services sector was initially perceived as innovation-poor. As the theory of innovation developed, however, the services sector became considered so distinct in nature that attempts were made to extend the notion of innovation known from the manufacturing sector (Kanerva et al., 2006). The latest edition of the Oslo Manual (2018), an international methodology for measuring innovation, updated the ways in which data is measured and interpreted compared to the 2005 edition, adapting it to the services sector and including innovation "across the entire business sector, including services sector firms specialised in providing knowledge-based services" (p. 22).

Classification of services by technology and knowledge intensity

With the services sector becoming the most important source of wealth in developed countries, the OECD and Eurostat included services in the classification of technological intensity in the mid-1990s. The current NACE Rev. 2 contains Section J (Information and communication) in order to account for Information Society industries (Miles et al., 2018). Thus, four groups of knowledge-intensive business services(KIBS)[1] can be identified:

- High-tech knowledge-intensive services, which include divisions in this section (excluding publishing activities [58]) and R&D activities (72);
- Knowledge intensive financial services (divisions 64–66);
- Knowledge-intensive market services (excluding financial intermediation and high-tech services): which includes section M (without the above-mentioned R&D and veterinary activities [75]), and water and air transport (50&51) and employment, security, and investigation activities (78&80);
- Other knowledge-intensive services (NACE 2 divisions 58, 75, 84 to 88, and 90 to 93).

For the business services of interest to us, Miles et al. (2018) devised a helpful classification based on different knowledge areas and, thus, identified three kinds of knowledge-intensive business services:

1 P-KIBS (as in professional) covering a large number of activities grouped under NACE Rev. 2 divisions legal and accounting activities and management consultancy activities (69 and 70);
2 T-KIBS (as in technology) covering a large proportion of activities of computer programming, consultancy, and related activities (62), architectural and engineering activities, technical testing, and analysis (71), and scientific research and development (72);
3 C-KIBS (as in creative): grouping together certain activities of two NACE Rev. 2 divisions: advertising and market research, (73) and other professional, scientific, and technical activities (74).[2]

Figure 4.2 shows the share of the KIBS sector broken down by type according to Miles et al. (2018) in the value added generated by the European Union member

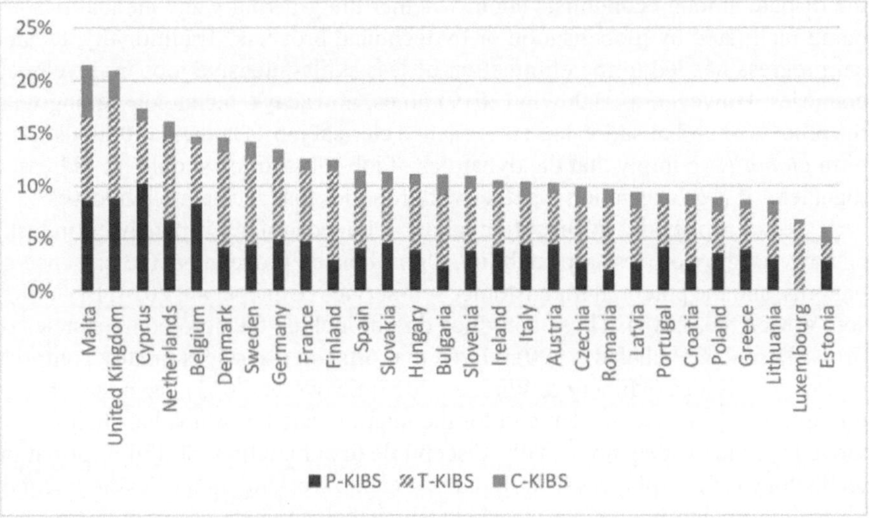

Figure 4.2 Share of KIBS in the added value generated by European economies in 2017

* Total business economy except financial and insurance activities.

Source: Own study based on Eurostat.

states, which implies that it is strongly linked to the ranking of economies in terms of GDP per capita.

Based on firm-level research, Fernandez-Stark et al. (2011) devised a very useful taxonomy of offshore services industries (OSI), classifying them by sector and by their capacity to create added value (see Chapter 2). Its limited usefulness for our purposes is due to its incompatibility with the applied classifications of economic activities (e.g. NACE).

Automating service provision

As the processing power of computers increases, progress is also being made in the areas of machine control, algorithm development, information processing, and transfer. The processing of large sets of unstructured data facilitates the creation of a more comprehensive picture of certain phenomena by capturing relationships not previously perceived due to human cognitive limitations. The digitalisation of knowledge can be costly, but using it in large-scale processes reduces its marginal cost to zero (Bitner et al., 2014), which makes some of the human analytical competencies redundant. Furthermore, universal access to information eliminates information asymmetry and makes some intermediary services forfeit their raison d'être.

Empirical research demonstrates that technical change is more than 90% likely to soon eliminate administrative and secretarial staff, money handlers, and customer information staff (Bitner et al., 2014). Milberg and Winkler (2013) remind us of the dispute among economists about whether the growing wage inequalities are being facilitated by globalisation or by technical progress. Traditionally, technical progress has led to the elimination of less skills-intensive jobs in developed countries. However, as Baldwin (2019) notes, nowadays, technology along with the process of globalisation has also reached clerical jobs. Baldwin (2019) uses the term *globotics* to imply that the dynamics of job substitution should be addressed together – it is globalisation together with robotics that accelerate job losses.

A greater propensity to substitute labour with technology is perceived in tasks characterised by process repeatability, algorithmised procedures, the presence of patterns, and the potential for customer self-service (Bitner et al., 2014; Brynjolfsson & McAfee, 2014). These activities do not include the core-competencies of firms (Hamel & Prahalad, 1990). Given that offshored services mainly comprise non-core activities (Milberg & Winkler, 2013; Schwörer, 2013), technical change will ultimately reduce the demand for the intermediate links in value chains to be moved abroad, as they are usually susceptible to automation. Skilful information technology (IT) employees from India or Ireland, working on the development of algorithms, themselves create a world in which their competencies will be replaced by artificial intelligence. A greater demand for human labour will remain in the final links of value chains characterised by the highest added value. Serving a demanding customer will require a direct contact between human beings for a long time to come.

The fourth industrial revolution

The fourth industrial revolution, also known as Industry 4.0, is a paradigm that aims to improve the productivity and efficiency of manufacturing firms by implementing advanced systems based on modern communication systems. The so-called *intelligent manufacturing* integrates the operation of equipment, hardware, and technology in order to optimise the production process, reduce costs and risks, as well as maximise profits (Tesch da Silva et al., 2020). The concept of Industry 4.0 (Industrie 4.0) was formulated by a German team working under the aegis of the Ministry of Education and Research and consisting of scientists from technical higher education institutions and universities together with leading representatives of major firms (ThyssenKrupp AG, Deutsche Telekom AG, BMW AG, Deutsche Post DHL AG, Software AG, TRUMPF GmbH & Co. KG, Infineon Technologies AG, Hewlett-Packard GmbH, Daimler AG, Festo AG & Co. KG, ABB Ltd). (Kagermann et al., 2013).

The idea of Industry 4.0 also had important political ramifications. It was devised to a large extent in response to the ever-deepening economic crisis in Europe, and its main objective was to secure the future of German manufacturing and to secure its leading position in the production engineering sector. In its original form, Industry 4.0 primarily involved the use of the Internet of Things and Services in the production process. The Internet of Things (IoT) includes smart energy networks, smart products, and smart buildings, whereas the Internet

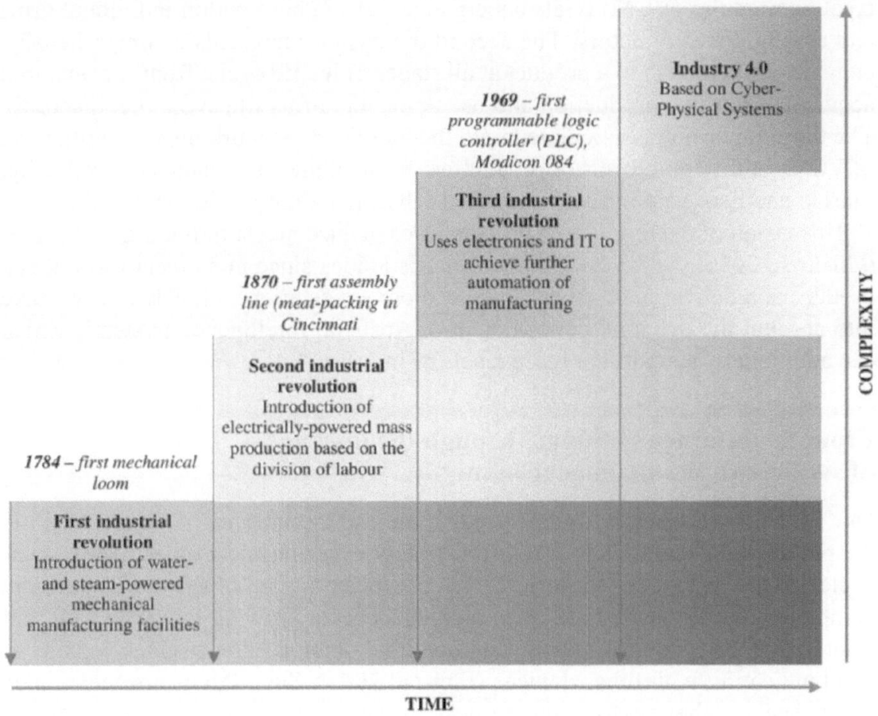

Figure 4.3 From the first to the fourth industrial revolution

Source: Own study based on (Kagermann et al., 2013, p. 13).

of Services (IoS) comprises smart mobility and smart logistics. It is worth noting that Industry 4.0 was one of the first concepts to combine the IoT with the IoS.

Industry 4.0 met with great international interest and marked the beginning of discussions on the so-called fourth industrial revolution. Thus, the number of publications dealing with this subject increased, both in the academic community and in the private sector (Beier et al., 2020). Apart from further development of the concept itself and the assessment of its impact on socio-economic development, attempts have been made to create a vision of the development of this trend in the literature (Lee et al., 2014). It has also attracted a fair amount of criticism, which mainly concerns the lack of a precise definition of this phenomenon (Heng, 2014; Lasi et al., 2014). One of the attempts to define a precise framework for Industry 4.0 was made by Stock and Seliger (2016). They identified three dimensions characteristic of this paradigm:

- Horizontal integration across the entire value creation network;
- End-to-end engineering across the entire product life cycle;
- Vertical integration and networked manufacturing systems.

The first dimension describes the intelligent networking and digitalisation of value creation modules (VCM) (Halstenberg et al., 2017) both within individual firms and among different actors. The second dimension represents a comprehensive engineering approach to a product at all stages of its life cycle: from raw material acquisition through production and use to the end of its life cycle (i.e. disposal). The third dimension is associated with the intelligent networking and digitisation of VCMs at different levels of production, from all the components of production lines to ancillary value-chain functions such as marketing, sales, and R&D.

This vision of the production process leads to the concept of Intelligent Factory (Gilchrist, 2016), which is an almost futuristic idea since in its ideal form, it can produce and deliver goods that far exceed our expectations, especially if we take into account the dynamic development of Artificial Intelligence Systems, which can additionally support the basic tenets of Industry 4.0.

From the internet of things through the internet of services to the sharing economy

One of the basic tenets of Industry 4.0 is the use the Internet of Things (IoT) in the production process. The idea is that nearly every physical object can be connected to the Internet. Naturally, it does not mean that all of them will turn into computers, but for some time now, there has been a growing tendency to install in pieces of everyday equipment (but not only) small computer chips capable of communicating with other devices (Fleisch, 2007). Such things are then called smart, because they perform the purpose for which they were made in a slightly better way. Let us take as an example the simple electric kettle: all it needs is a temperature sensor and a Bluetooth module. Thanks to its capacity to communicate with a smartphone, it becomes capable of boiling water at a given time and up to a specified temperature. The smart home or the smart car are being developed according to the same principles.

Apart from the IoT phenomenon, the Internet of Services (IoS) trend was being developed. Initially, it was rather an underdefined theoretical concept in telecommunications and Internet services (Soriano et al., 2013) or used to describe the transformation of the financial sector (Black et al., 2001), which, due to highly standardised procedures and large capital resources, has moved a significant proportion of its activity to the virtual world. The popularisation of the Industry 4.0 concept not only in the production area and the development of the IoT permitted a broader view of the IoS. New services that previously could not be provided or were ineffectively provided began to emerge.

Thus, with properly equipped components of the system, firms were able to offer services more efficiently and at a lower cost. Popular vehicle rental networks that charge fees by the minute are but one example. In order to launch such a service, in principle one needs only a smartphone, a car equipped with a GPS tracker, and a universal broadband access to the Internet. This made it possible to rent cars by the minute without incurring staff costs, as is the case with traditional firms. Although the depreciation of vehicles in such systems is slightly higher than in

Table 4.1 Analytic perspectives on the sharing economy

		Platform orientation	
		For-profit	*Non-profit*
Type of provider	*Peer-to-Peer*	Airbnb, Relay Rides	Food Swaps, Time Banks
	Business-to-Peer	Zipcar	Makerspaces

Source: Own study based on (Schor, 2016, p. 4).

the case of traditional rentals, savings resulting from the automation of the entire process exceed the extra costs.

This approach has given rise to the dynamic development of the sharing economy sector, which has become very popular thanks to the IoT and IoS not only in the commercial sector but also in the non-profit one (Heinrichs, 2013; Richardson, 2015). A synthetic picture of the sharing economy is shown in Table 4.1 (Schor, 2016), where two analytic perspectives on this trend are illustrated: the market orientation (for profit/non-profit) and the service provider orientation (peer-to-peer/business-to-peer).

Both the IoS and the sharing economy have fundamentally changed the face of sales of many goods and services, which is due to the fact that more and more often we do not have to purchase certain items in order to use them. The actual owner of the goods is the entrepreneur, whereas the user only buys the right to use them for a certain period of time.

Robotic process automation

Robotic process automation (RPA) is an example of the fourth industrial revolution's forays into the services sector. Networking and automation no longer apply to the production line, but to administrative and business processes carried out by people. Not so long ago, people seemed irreplaceable in these types of activities, but the development of data science, machine learning, and artificial intelligence make the processes more accurate, more efficient and effective, and permit the monitoring processes to be improved.

RPA is a fairly new information technology involving the creation of software agents (also known as bots), which, using a number of computer apps, reproduce the activities performed by people in certain business processes. The tasks performed quite efficiently by bots are usually based on well-structured and repetitive rules (Syed et al., 2020). RPA has evolved from desktop automation (DA), relatively simple software programmes that performed single tasks using structured data. Unlike DA, however, RPA bots can interact with multiple systems, work autonomously, and perform routine tasks. The more sophisticated RPA bots combine into cognitive or intelligent automation (IA), which is capable of performing unusual tasks that require evaluation based on unstructured data (Kokina & Blanchette,2019).

Table 4.2 Comparison of workforce arbitrage characteristics and automated workforce characteristics

Workforce arbitrage characteristics	*Automated workforce characteristics*
15–30% cost take out	**40–75%** cost take out for relevant functions
Model is scalable to the extent that you can scale work	Model is scalable and is **largely independent of work growth**
Custom/complex, legacy: "Your mess for less"	**Transformative** – new way of doing business
Access to **low cost workers** **Necessary** to provide continuous value	Access to **'rocket scientists'** who can codify manual processes
Revenue/profit correlated to people	Revenue/profit **NOT** correlated to people

Source: Own study based on (KPMG, 2016, p. 4).

However, RPA will undoubtedly have a significant impact on the business process outsourcing (BPO) market worldwide. In its report, KPMG (2016) presented the findings of a study involving buyers, consultants, and outsourcing service providers, which shows that the demand for this type of services fell in 2015 with the value of outsourcing contracts in India rapidly decreasing. In the four quarters to June 2015, Indian IT service providers reduced employment by 100,000 people. On the other hand, Tata Consultancy Services recorded a $3 billion increase in productivity as a result of the drop in the number of employees while the Infosys Automation Platform pilot reported a 37% improvement in productivity and 17% savings due to employment reduction. Faced with rising global labour costs, KPMG considers RPA to be a destructive force for the development of the BPO industry, which maintains a strong presence in Central Europe.

Conclusion

New technologies provide the foundation for the development of competitive firms and entire economies. The competitiveness of an economy is defined as the sum of the successes of individual operators whose development is affected by conditions prevalent at the industry level. Innovative sectors constitute the cornerstones of competitive economies and have long been identified in manufacturing, while the services sector was perceived as less innovative. The development of innovation theory led to the recognition that the latter does innovate, albeit differently from manufacturing in that it relies much more on human capital. However, automation and robotisation processes can eliminate human labour, especially in easily algorithmised tasks that can be handled by the clients themselves. This can pose a serious challenge for developing economies, which are taking over the intermediate links in the services value chains. Automation and robotisation, which are primarily identified with the manufacturing sector, began to expand into the services sector with the advent of the fourth industrial revolution and are manifested in such phenomena as the Internet of Things, the sharing economy, and robotic process automation. All of these have had a considerable impact on the outsourcing and offshoring sector, which is subject to an in-depth analysis in the following chapters of this book.

Notes

1 https://ec.europa.eu/eurostat/statistics-explained/index.php/Glossary:Knowledge-intensive_services_(KIS) (accessed on 4 February 2020).
2 Schnabl and Zenker (2013) and Micek (2015) do not consider division (74) as KIBS.

References

Amsden, A. (2001). *The Rise of "the Rest": Challenges to the West From Late-Industrializing Economies*. Oxford: Oxford University Press.

Arundel, A., & Kabla, I. (1998). What percentage of innovations are patented? Empirical estimates for European firms. *Research Policy*, *27*(2), pp. 127–141.

Baldwin, R. (2019). *The Globotics Upheaval: Globalization, Robotics, and the Future of Work*. Oxford: Oxford University Press.

Beier, G., Ullrich, A., Niehoff, S., Reißig, M., & Habich, M. (2020). Industry 4.0: How it is defined from a sociotechnical perspective and how much sustainability it includes: A literature review. *Journal of Cleaner Production*, *259*. https://doi.org/10.1016/j.jclepro.2020.120856.

Bitner, M., Starościk, R., & Szczerba P. (2014). *Czy robot zabierze pracę?* WISE Working Paper.

Black, N.J., Lockett, A., Winklhofer, H., & Ennew, C. (2001). The adoption of Internet financial services: A qualitative study. *International Journal of Retail & Distribution Management*, *29*(8), pp. 390–398. https://doi.org/10.1108/09590550110397033.

Blaug, M. (1997). *Economic Theory in Retrospect*. Cambridge: Cambridge University Press.

Brynjolfsson, E., & McAfee, A. (2014). *The Second Machine Age: Work, Progress, and Prosperity in a Time of Brilliant Technologies*. New York: W.W. Norton & Company.

Evans, P. (1995). *Embedded Autonomy: States and Industrial Transformation*. Princeton: Princeton University Press.

Fagerberg, J., & Godinho, M.M. (2004). Innovation and Catching Up. In J. Fagerberg, D. Mowery, & R.R. Nelson (Eds.), *The Oxford Handbook of Innovation*. Oxford: Oxford University Press.

Fernandez-Stark, K., Bamber, P., & Gereffi, G. (2011). The offshore services value chain: Upgrading trajectories in developing countries. *International Journal of Technological Learning, Innovation and Development*, *4*(1–3), pp. 206–234.

Fleisch, E. (2007). *What is the Internet of Things? An Economic Perspective*. Auto-ID White Paper [accessed from: www.Alexandria.Unisg.Ch/Publikationen/68983].

Gilchrist, A. (2016). *Industry 4.0: The Industrial Internet of Things*. Apress; Distributed by Springer Science+Business Media, New York [accessed from: http://proquest.tech.safaribooksonline.de/9781484220474].

Godin, B. (2004). The obsession for competitiveness and its impact on statistics: The construction of high-technology indicators. *Research Policy*, *33*(8), pp. 1217–1229.

Halstenberg, F.A., Steingrímsson, J.G., & Stark, R. (2017). Material reutilization cycles across industries and production lines. In R. Stark, G. Seliger, & J. Bonvoisin (Eds.), *Sustainable Production, Life Cycle Engineering and Management. Sustainable Manufacturing:*

Challenges, Solutions and Implementation Perspectives (Vol. 29). SpringerOpen, pp. 163–173 [accessed from: https://doi.org/10.1007/978-3-319-48514-0_11].

Hamel, G., & Prahalad, C.K. (1990). The core competence of the corporation. *Harvard Business Review*, *68*(3), pp. 79–91.

Heinrichs, H. (2013). Sharing economy: A potential new pathway to sustainability. *GAIA – Ecological Perspectives for Science and Society*, *22*(4), pp. 228–231. https://doi.org/10.14512/gaia.22.4.5.

Heng, S. (2014). *Industry 4.0: Upgrading of Germany's Industrial Capabilities on the Horizon* [accessed from: SSRN 2656608].

Kagermann, H., Helbig, J., Hellinger, A., & Wahlster, W. (2013). *Recommendations for Implementing the Strategic Initiative INDUSTRIE 4.0: Securing the Future of German Manufacturing Industry; Final Report of the Industrie 4.0 Working Group*. Forschungsunion [accessed from: https://books.google.pl/books?id=AsfOoAEACAAJ].

Kaldor, N. (1978). *Further Essays on Applied Economics*. London: Duckworth London.

Kanerva, M., Hollanders, H., & Arundel, A. (2006). *2006 TrendChart report: Can We Measure and Compare Innovation in Services*. Maastricht: MERIT.

Kaplinsky, R., & Morris, M. (2002). *A Handbook for Value Chain Research*. Institute of Development Studies [accessed from: www.ids.ac.uk/ids/global/pdfs/VchNov01.pdf].

Kokina, J., & Blanchette, S. (2019). Early evidence of digital labor in accounting: Innovation with robotic process automation. *International Journal of Accounting Information Systems*, *35*, p. 100431. https://doi.org/10.1016/j.accinf.2019.100431.

KPMG. (2016). *Bots in the Back Office: The Coming Wave of Digital Workers* [accessed from: https://assets.kpmg/content/dam/kpmg/pdf/2016/02/bots-in-the-back-office.pdf].

Krugman, P.R. (1996). Making sense of the competitiveness debate. *Oxford Review of Economic Policy*, *12*(3), pp. 17–25.

Lasi, H., Fettke, P., Kemper, H.-G., Feld, T., & Hoffmann, M. (2014). Industry 4.0. *Business & Information Systems Engineering*, *6*(4), pp. 239–242.

Lee, J., Kao, H.-A., & Yang, S. (2014). Service innovation and smart analytics for industry 4.0 and big data environment. *Procedia Cirp*, *16*(1), pp. 3–8.

Lin, J., & Chang, H.-J. (2009). Should industrial policy in developing countries conform to comparative advantage or defy it? A debate between Justin Lin and Ha-Joon Chang. *Development Policy Review*, *27*(5), pp. 483–502.

Micek, G. (2015). FDI trends in the business services sector: The case of Poland. In B. Galgóczi, J. Drahokoupil, & M. Bernaciak (Eds.), *Foreign Investment in Eastern and Southern Europe After 2008: Still a Lever of Growth*. Brussels: European Trade Union Institute (ETUI), pp. 297–318.

Milberg, W., & Winkler, D. (2013). *Outsourcing Economics: Global Value Chains in Capitalist Development*. Cambridge: Cambridge University Press.

Miles, I., Andersen, B., Boden, M., & Howells, J. (2000). Service production and intellectual property. *International Journal of Technology Management*, *20*(1/2), pp. 95–115.

Miles, I.D., Belousova, V., & Chichkanov, N. (2018). Knowledge intensive business services: Ambiguities and continuities. *Foresight*, *20*(1), pp. 1–26.

Morrar, R. (2014). Innovation in services: A literature review. *Technology Innovation Management Review*, *4*(4).

Obstfeld, M., & Krugman, P.R. (2003). *International Economics: Theory and Policy*. Boston: Pearson Education, Inc.

Oslo Manual. (2018). *Oslo Manual 2018: Guidelines for collecting, Reporting and Using Data on Innovation*. Organisation for Economic Co-operation and Development, & Statistical Office of the European Communities. OECD Publishing.

Panasiuk, A., & Tokarz, A. (2012). *Specyfika i klasyfikacja usług. Współczesna Ekonomika Usług*. Warszawa: Wyd. Nauk. PWN.

Porter, M.E. (1979). How Competitive Forces Shape Strategy. *Harvard Business Review*, March/April Issue [accessed from: https://hbr.org/1979/03/how-competitive-forces-shape-strategy].

Porter, M.E. (1990). *The Competitive Advantage of Nations: With a New Introduction*. New York: Free Press.

Reinert, E.S. (2007). *How Rich Countries Got Rich . . . and Why Poor Countries Stay Poor*. London: Constable & Robinson.

Richardson, L. (2015). Performing the sharing economy. *Geoforum*, *67*, pp. 121–129. https://doi.org/10.1016/j.geoforum.2015.11.004.

Romer, P.M. (1986). Increasing returns and long-run growth. *Journal of Political Economy*, *94*(5), pp. 1002–1037.

Rusiecki, P. (2015). *Strategic Price Management: Case Study: Smartphone Companies Pricing Strategies*. Kraków: Uniwersytet Ekonomiczny w Krakowie.

Schnabl, E., & Zenker, A. (2013). *Statistical Classification of Knowledge-intensive Business Services (KIBS) with NACE Rev. 2*. Fraunhofer ISI Karlsruhe.

Schor, J. (2016). Debating the sharing economy. *Journal of Self-Governance and Management Economics*, *4*(3), pp. 7–22.

Schumpeter, J.A. (1982). *The Theory of Economic Development: An Inquiry into Profits, Capital, Credit, Interest, and the Business Cycle (1912/1934)*. New Brunswick and London: Transaction Publishers, p. 244.

Schwörer, T. (2013). Offshoring, domestic outsourcing and productivity: Evidence for a number of European countries. *Review of World Economics*, *149*(1), pp. 131–149.

Sirilli, G., & Evangelista, R. (1998). Technological innovation in services and manufacturing: Results from Italian surveys. *Research Policy*, *27*(9), pp. 881–899.

Solow, R.M. (1957). Technical change and the aggregate production function. *The Review of Economics and Statistics*, *39*(3), pp. 312–320.

Soriano, J., Heitz, C., Hutter, H.-P., Fernández, R., Hierro, J.J., Vogel, J., Edmonds, A., & Bohnert, T.M. (2013). Internet of services. In E. Bertin, N. Crespi, & T. Magedanz (Eds.), *LNCS Sublibrary: SL 3 – Information Systems and Applications, incl. Internet/Web and HCI. Evolution of Telecommunication Services: The Convergence of Telecom and Internet: Technologies and Ecosystems* (Vol. 7768). Springer, pp. 283–325. https://doi.org/10.1007/978-3-642-41569-2_14.

Stock, T., & Seliger, G. (2016). Opportunities of sustainable manufacturing in industry 4.0. *Procedia Cirp*, *40*, pp. 536–541. https://doi.org/10.1016/j.procir.2016.01.129.

Syed, R., Suriadi, S., Adams, M., Bandara, W., Leemans, S.J.J., Ouyang, C., ter Hofstede, A.H.M., van de Weerd, I., Wynn, M.T., & Reijers, H.A. (2020). Robotic process automation: Contemporary themes and challenges. *Computers in Industry*, *115*, p. 103162. https://doi.org/10.1016/j.compind.2019.103162.

Tesch da Silva, F.S., da Costa, C.A., Paredes Crovato, C.D., & Rosa Righi, R. (2020). Looking at energy through the lens of industry 4.0: A systematic literature review of concerns and challenges. *Computers & Industrial Engineering*, p. 106426. https://doi.org/10.1016/j.cie.2020.106426.

Wirtz, J., Tuzovic, S., & Ehret, M. (2015). Global business services. *Journal of Service Management*, *26*(4), pp. 565–587.

5 Impact sourcing

Theoretical analysis in relation to corporate social responsibility in a globalised market

Monika Mazur-Bubak

Introduction

Outsourcing has become one of the modern pillars of a globalised economy. Thanks to the availability and capacity to accurately profile the services to be outsourced to an organisation or company, it has largely contributed to their rapid development. It is considered to be of crucial importance for the growth and economic success of both the United States and European economies (Corbett, 2004, p. 3). Outsourcing is practised by international giants, such as IBM, Xerox, General Electric, or Delphi, firms with a much smaller scope of operation, as well as small and medium-sized enterprises. In fact, in today's economic conditions, it is hard to find an organisation or a company that does not take advantage of outsourcing at all. However, a number of direct disadvantages of outsourcing affect the distribution of global wealth and the standard of living in the poorest regions of the world since this model of organisation supports the largest and most efficient logistics centres, excluding entire employee groups from possible training-up in a given stage of the process. The second charge faced by contracting firms, whether they order products or services, is the lack of oversight and control over their supply chains, which leads to individual employees not being treated in a fair and dignified manner. As a result of the recognition of the profound problem of welfare inequality, sustainable business development models, such as corporate social responsibility (CSR) and creating shared values (CSV), have emerged. At the same time, outsourcing in a global context relies heavily on business relations based on mutual trust. These relations cannot be limited to the buyer and the provider of services or products; on the contrary, it is now recognised that the trust that firms gain from the communities in which they operate and their ensuing responsibility must also be taken into account. This has resulted in projects generally referred to as socially responsible sourcing. The aim of these initiatives is to take into account the responsibility of organisations and firms both towards local communities and towards the global human community by advocating for the most economically disadvantaged people. This is done in recognition of the fact that outsourcing services and their development should be considered as a component of the global market.

Another important argument for the recognition of this issue as important is provided by theories referring to the concept of *capabilities*, which focuses on the need to improve the living conditions of the most economically and socially disadvantaged people in different communities worldwide. This is particularly true of Martha Nussbaum and Amartya Sen. The former believes that every person should be provided with a so-called *list of capabilities*, which goes far beyond Maslow's classic pyramid of needs and builds upon John Rawls' theory of political justice (Nussbaum, 2003). Amartya Sen, in turn, apart from numerous works devoted to promoting appropriate and effective ways of equalising opportunities in the global context, formulated the widely commented upon and still extremely popular Human Development Index (Sen, 1999).

Responsible outsourcing involves practices designated to at least partially overcome problems resulting from social and economic inequalities through the activation of social groups at a high risk of professional exclusion. This chapter discusses solutions adopted by non-governmental organizations (NGOs) and the social enterprise Digital Divide Data as well as the extent to which they draw on the concepts of CSR and CSV. In the last section, the main advantages and emerging difficulties in achieving the basic objectives of value sourcing projects are identified. The aim of this paper is to emphasise the need for modern firms and organisations to take into account the context of social responsibility in their supply chain management and outsourcing procedures.

Trust – the need to strengthen mutual trust and responsibility

Social trust affects numerous aspects of human functioning in society; as such, it is directly reflected in the number and range of commitments made in individual national markets while the stability of governments directly affects the willingness of investors to use their resources in a given region of the world. The most important companion of trust – no matter what area of life it affects – is responsibility. If we trust someone, we are willing to assume responsibility for the relationship. In entrepreneurship, trust is a dimension that significantly affects business relations and the achievement of the intended goals (Morgan & Hunt, 1994). Today, models of the process of building trust are being developed based on understanding the dynamics of this relationship over time (Huang & Wilkinson, 2013). Trust, however, should not be identified with profitability indicators or findings of a prospective partner's credibility analysis. On the contrary, it is expressed as a certain positive attitude, based (especially in business) on the belief that both parties will benefit from a given exchange. "Ring (1996) proposes that trust is of two types, one being fragile and the other resilient. Whereas fragile trust is more calculative, resilient trust is said to be based on a perception of goodwill" (Das & Teng, 2001, p. 255). Most definitions include an aspect of good faith and uncertainty, which is where trust differs from any reliability check, such as that proposed by Ganesan: "a belief, sentiment, or an expectation about an exchange partner that results from the partner's expertise, reliability, and intentionality" (1994).

In outsourcing, the relationship of trust binds the buyer and the provider of a given service or product. Accordingly, trust is key to the success of a transaction:

- When the uncertainty (e.g. complexity and ambiguity) of unmet expectations is high;
- When the vulnerability of control (e.g. failure of formal contract) is high;
- When the stakes (e.g. financial loss) of unmet expectation or control failure are high;
- When long-term interdependence (e.g. reciprocal relationship) is high (Li, 2012).

Peter Ping Li goes on to add that trust is most important when it is understood as a certain choice; in other words, when its presence or absence triggers a certain action, and when it is expressed in something more than only a calculated credibility of the other party (Li, 2012).

Anticipating the effects and designing the success of outsourcing was based in particular on a management control system (MCS), which collected information and evaluated and formulated organisational strategies, and eventually on projects to extend the MCS directly to issues associated with trust – primarily in the so-called strategic alliances in which an organisation's core activities are being outsourced (Das & Teng, 2001). Trust usually emerges between two entities – the principal and the contractor, or rather the buyer and the provider of a given service. A number of strategies and techniques for minimising risk and building trust and control systems were proposed, among them Laurie Kirsch's concept of social control, which, however, applies on a micro-scale, namely to the control of an organisation's members in terms of organisational culture and values considered to be crucial, rather than in the context of controlling local communities.

This third entity, the local community, or simply the human community, appears in the outsourcing relationship and distorts the simple relationship of trust between two firms. The procedure of outsourcing specific services or products attracts heavy criticism on the part of civil societies.

One of the most serious charges levelled against outsourcing firms is their drive to reduce operating costs by refusing to secure financial sustenance to its employees. Most employees of the outside company work on temporary contracts, which do not provide sufficient social or legal protection. Thus, outsourcing a given product or service allows for cost-cutting, which takes place to the disadvantage of the employees who are tasked with manufacturing or delivering it. Quite often, the latter have no alternative employment opportunities and, hence, find themselves forced to work without benefits or safeguards. In the face of the COVID-19 pandemic, the entire sector of temporary workers, self-employed or independent contractors, whose social security contributions are not paid, is extremely difficult, if not outright dramatic. According to research carried out by the US Bureau of Labour Statistics, the reduction in job opportunities has largely hit the self-employed and those on contracts without social security contributions (Thomson-DeVeaux, 2020). The protracted threat of COVID-19 is bound to exacerbate social inequalities and drastically reduce the standard of living of those deprived of social protection, which, in turn, is bound to further increase economic inequalities.

The use of outsourcing on a macroeconomic scale may also have a direct impact on humankind's main problems associated with political stability and international order. A good example of unexpected negative consequences of outsourcing was the US government's decision to use private military forces to protect the facilities and sensitive areas where the regular army was previously deployed. Michael Corbett points out that in the 1990s, the US Department of Defence generated savings of 30%, and subsequently even 40% after the Cold War. Unfortunately, he chose not to mention that reassigning part of the budget to the activities of paramilitary organisations resulted in some of them (e.g. Blackwater) becoming monopolists in the protected areas at a huge cost to the US budget. Another important issue is geopolitical in scope in that it includes the serious consequences of underwriting the activities of such organisations (Mazur-Bubak, in press; Scahill, 2008) and the transformation of war into a service provided by private entities (Uesseler, 2008). With the outsourcing of private military services, political problems resulting from accountability and the obligation to report on the activities of the military to citizens and international public opinion have been removed. In other words, the outsourcing of military services has definitely violated the relationship of trust of both US citizens and international opinion in the legitimacy, intentions, and means used by private military forces on behalf of the US Army.

Another area of criticism of outsourcing (related to inadequate remuneration of employees in terms of benefits and insurance) is the lack of control over supply chains, including that over the working conditions of those employed in different links in these chains. One of the most famous protests, in which the process of offshoring (together with the artificially high margins imposed by multinationals) was roundly condemned, took place in New York City in 1997. Young people from a poor district in New York strongly objected to the way in which the American multinational corporation Nike organised its supply chain. It was revealed that factory floor workers in Indonesia were earning \$2 a day, whereas a pair of shoes sold for \$100–180 cost the company \$5 to produce. The excessive margin compounded by the awareness of unfairly low wages for workers was the cause of young people's protests (Roberts et al., 2011, pp. 486–487). During the meeting of Nike representatives with the Edenwald Gun Hill Neighborhood Centre, the protesters directly formulated three demands against Nike:

1 Those who work for Nike overseas should be paid a living wage, with independent monitoring to ensure that it is happening.
2 Nike sneakers should be sold less expensively in America with no concessions to American workforce (i.e. no downsizing, or loss of benefits).
3 Nice should seriously re-invest in the inner city in America, especially New York City since it has been the subject of much of their advertising (Roberts et al., 2011, p. 486).

This and other protests have shown that any outsourcing relations beyond the buyer and the seller must also take into consideration other entities, namely communities directly affected by their activity. A backlash usually occurs when these communities find out that they can no longer trust the manufacturer. As a result, they demand that, specifically, the entire manufacturing process involving supply chains is carried out in an ethically sound manner, subcontractors and employees are treated with dignity, and consumers are being charged a fair price. As Steve Reicher and Cliff Stott commented, the initial anti-cuts protest in London in September 2011 quickly escalated into a class war. A sense of justice or injustice of a given practice has a direct impact on people's actions, regardless of whether the grievance itself has affected an individual or a group.

"The sense of illegitimacy is at its most potent when it relates to our group memberships. For when illegitimacy is a collective experience, it gives rise to a collective grievance. And that grievance is felt not only when an individual is personally treated unfairly but when any member of his or her group is so treated. This phenomenon, above all, lies at the root of collective disorder" (Stott & Reicher, 2011, p. 35).

Ignoring public opinion or simply the communities concerned in running a business, including the way in which work is managed, does not seem to be a good solution. Moreover, pressure from international public opinion has led to the establishment of business rules that require oversight and monitoring of the entire supply chain. Sources of these regulations include: the *Guiding Principles on Business and Human Rights: Implementing the United Nations 'Protect, Respect and Remedy' Framework* formulated by UN Special Representative John Ruggie (2011); *The Bribery Act* (2011); and the *Foreign Corrupt Practices Act* (FCPA). Currently, companies operating in the European Union are bound by the European Commission Communication of 25.10.2011 on a renewed EU strategy for 2011–2014 on corporate responsibility. The document contains important information for the European private sector on the current directions of EU policy in the field of CSR. Contrary to expectations, the Communication does not stipulate new regulatory mechanisms, it only signposts further work by the Commission on the promotion of CSR in Europe, specifies its expectations towards enterprises operating in the EU, and defines how the Commission understands social responsibility.

The Communication calls for the following:

- A still voluntary reporting obligation (on the impact on communities and the environment);
- A recommendation to comply with OECD guidelines, ISO 26 000 standards and UN programmes;
- The requirement to respect human rights and labour standards throughout the supply chain;
- The obligation to inform customers about the implementation of the ESG (Environmental, Social, Governance) criteria;
- Active opposition to practices such as greenwashing; and
- Recommendation to draw up national plans for the implementation of the UN Guidelines on Human Rights and national plans for the promotion of CSR.

Corporate social responsibility vs. inequality

With the emergence of global sourcing opportunities, reservations have arisen regarding whether such a management model can meet the requirements of sustainable development and its basic tenets of social responsibility, taking into account both social and environmental factors (Nicholson et al., 2017, p. 1). As a result, a theory of socially responsible sourcing was formulated, with a view to rethinking the ways in which firms operate in terms of their impact on communities. This theory showed the possibilities of enacting the so-called win-win scenarios (Porter & Kramer, 2006; Porter & Kramer, 2011). The concept of CSR has a number of variants. Howard Bowen was one of the first to point out the need to take into account the good of society in doing business in his work *Social responsibilities of the businessman* (1953). Other major proponents of this concept include Keith Davis (1960), Joseph W. McGuire (1963), Harold Johnson (1971), and Edward Freeman (2010). The last two researchers emphasised the participation of stakeholders defined as all those affected by a business activity – from employees to the local community. This latter concept was introduced in contrast to a model in which managers were accountable only to shareholders. Accordingly, apart from shareholder profit, business activities began to be assessed in terms of the values that they contribute to the functioning of all the entities they influence, on the assumption that corporations and firms use public goods or resources resulting from the order in which political communities operate – from using public roads to the principles dictating that agreements should be respected.

The theory of creating shared values (CSV) takes the CSR concept further. Michael Porter and Mark Kramer (2006, 2011), when analysing the activities of firms within the CSR framework, noticed that decisions on investing in this area are made too arbitrarily and often overlook the genuine needs of local communities and/or other stakeholders. They pointed out that CSV is not about charity, but it is supposed to underlie all the activities of organisations and firms. In other words, the main aim of their operation should be to satisfy a certain need of a given community, among others by sourcing products and markets, redefining productivity in supply chains, and contributing to a local development cluster (Porter & Kramer, 2011).

The concept of CSV thus emphasises the need to implement supply chain standards, which are not so much about maximising profit as about achieving sustainable profit for all stakeholders. It is a model that aims to hold firms and organisations accountable for unfair business practices and strategies, such as the unfairly high margins for their products, greenwashing, and others. In general, the CSV concept was supposed to answer the question: How to fix capitalism? As a result, a model based on sustainable development was proposed, which is expected to minimise the risks associated with an unprecedented accumulation of capital and help remedy unequal access to goods. As Oxfam International's calculations show, one of the major global problems today is the extent to which social inequalities are growing: Economic inequality is out of control. In 2019, the world's billionaires, only 2,153 people, had more wealth than 4.6 billion people.

The richest 22 men in the world own more wealth than all the women in Africa. These extremes of wealth exist alongside great poverty. New World Bank estimates show that almost half of the world's population lives on less than $5.50 a day, and the rate of poverty reduction has halved since 2013 (Lawson et al., 2020).

The rate at which social inequalities intensify should therefore be taken into account in the entire process of production and distribution of a given product or in the provision of services. Outsourcing thus appears to be one of the mechanisms that influence wealth distribution. The lack of transparency in supply chains and arbitrary price manipulations do not constitute or lead to market self-regulation as envisaged by Adam Smith.

Inspired by the concepts of CSR and CSV, a new model of outsourcing was developed, known as *impact sourcing.*

Impact sourcing – outsourcing that fosters equal opportunities for the least privileged

Impact sourcing (ImS) is a term that applies to IT service procurement models that focus not so much on shareholder profit as on social mission and social value creation (Madon & Sharanappa, 2013; Sandeep et al., 2013; Heeks & Arun, 2010; Lacity & Willcocks, 2014). According to Sandeep and Ravishankar, the idea that ImS can play a role in providing sustainable livelihoods to marginalised individuals in the global south is steadily gaining credence among academics and practitioners. The claims of ImS ventures of positively impacting lives of marginalised individuals through employment have been supported by recent empirical inquiries (Sandeep & Ravishankar, 2016b).

Thanks to the research by authors such as Heeks and Arun (2010), ImS became considered as worthy of attention. Social outsourcing is a hybrid form of impact sourcing that involves social enterprises. "When used by government, it can be seen as a hybrid of the workfare outsourcing found in wage employment schemes, and the commercial outsourcing of government activities to the private sector" (Heeks & Arun, 2010, p. 441). Thus, social outsourcing relies on outsourcing the production of goods or the provision of services to social enterprises. The principal in this case may be local government, central government, or the private entrepreneur.

"Such models are now being collectively referred to as impact sourcing. Carmel et al. (2013, p. 5) define ImS as the practice of training and hiring marginalised individuals to provide information technology, business process, or other digitally-enabled services. The ImS business model consciously provides employment opportunities to communities and groups whose life chances are deemed poor" (Sandeep et al., 2013).

ImS primarily occurs in contexts where services are outsourced by private entrepreneurs. On the one hand, it involves maximising a firm's the socio-economic potential while recognising profit and strengthening of market competitiveness through the provision of high-quality services to be important objectives; whereas on the other, it promotes supporting the most socially and economically vulnerable groups. As the Rockefeller Foundation's report indicates, this model can be profitably applied by entrepreneurs (Bulloch & Long, 2012).

An example of a successful social enterprise is Digital Divide Data (DDD), which operates, among other places, in Laos, Cambodia, and Kenya. The DDD programme recruits local secondary school students who have moved from rural to urban areas or live in the poorest districts of cities and suburbs; are low-paid employees of the 'informal sector'; and are women and/or people with disabilities. All those eligible and willing are offered two development opportunities. First, they participate in intensive training in business skills, English, soft-skills, and technology. One they have passed the courses, they are employed as assistants for 6–8 hours per day. The assistants receive continuous support in choosing further education. Part of the tuition costs are covered by the assistants from their own salaries and the balance is provided by DDD as loans or study grants. At their next career level, assistants are either supported in finding a job outside DDD, or some of the best ones are promoted to managerial positions.

Limitations of impact sourcing

According to Heeks and Arun (2010), apart from the numerous advantages in terms of supporting the creation of micro-firms providing IT services, the model is not without certain limitations. The original Kudumbashree project was based on a loan and subsidy mechanism of about US$5,500 with the necessary US$30 of own contribution to the creation of local small IT businesses for women in Kerala, India, identified as living below the poverty line. Half of the grant amount was refundable. This model has led to the founding of 232 IT social enterprises since 1999. The impact assessment showed significant improvements in such areas as human capital (skills, attitude, health, knowledge); social capital (networks, relationships); physical capital (producer goods, infrastructure); financial capital (earnings, savings); and political capital (empowerment, status, gender, relations) (Heeks & Arun, 2010, p. 445). The main problem faced by the founders of these IT firms was that they had to wait for payment for the goods or services provided (from 3–12 months). For this reason, in order to maintain liquidity and repay the loan instalment, these women were forced to sell or pledge their property. Moreover, Kerala is distinct from other India regions in that its residents are fairly well educated, are highly politically aware, and involved in social and political activity, even as their earnings remain low.[1] The model under discussion may thus produce different results in communities with a poor network of social structures and low social mobilisation. Moreover, the training up of Kerala's women did not pose a big problem as the level of education of local residents was higher than that of better-off citizens from other parts of India. Apart from skills directly relevant to IT projects, a certain challenge was to acquire entrepreneurial skills (Heeks & Arun, 2010, p. 451).

Although the surveys of women participating in the programme revealed that they felt more empowered and self-confident in their professional lives, they did not necessarily become more politically active. Only 10% of the women surveyed said that their involvement in "social functions within the community" increased. Interestingly, their interest in sociopolitical activity even declined as a result of professional involvement (Heeks & Arun, 2010). As regards sustainable development, research indicated that such a model requires almost continuous support and intervention on the part of governments, banks, and local institutions. Although some firms received up to 20% of their revenues from the private sector, most of them relied heavily on public sector contracts. As a result of the development of the IT industry in India, some of them were forced to become call centres or data analysis centres.

On the one hand, these findings show a significant improvement in the quality of life of Kerala's women involved in the project, whereas on the other, they reveal a lack of sufficient training in marketing and customer acquisition. The main problem appears to be the lack of flexibility to go beyond the model imposed from the top. It can be concluded, therefore, that, apart from IT training, the newly recruited employees must be trained in soft skills (as is the case in the procedure proposed by DDD), in economics and marketing, and in the principles of entrepreneurship. Besides skills in specific processes or the production of specific goods, such training may help them become more flexible in adapting their activities to market expectations.

What weaknesses can be identified in ImS as a social version of outsourcing? The first fundamental issue tackled by researchers is the uneven distribution of benefits resulting from the implementation of the process in individual communities. Using India as an example, Anthony D'Costa (2003) observed that the IT industry coexists with heavy industry sectors and, thus, perpetuates differences in growth rates between regions. It is also not clear whether such activity directly leads to developmental transformation.

Numerous authors also point to certain cultural and 'voluntary' constraints. Most of the proposed models assume that local communities will either immediately become strongly involved in a given programme, or that once they have become familiar with its advantages, they will be quickly persuaded as to its effectiveness (Abreu et al,. 2013; Parakala & Udhas, 2012). In fact, this is an oversimplification, since such considerations fail to account for the three basic mechanisms of institutional processes – regulatory, socio-normative, and cultural-cognitive ones (Scott, 2001). As Marquis and Battilana (2009) noted, the cultural-cognitive factor and its impact on the effectiveness of social enterprises often tends to be underestimated. This impact depends on the abstract rules adhered to by the communities concerned to which these programmes may not be adapted. A key role in the success of such programmes is the way the principles and benefits of ImS are presented to local communities (Sandeep & Ravishankar, 2016a). Goffman (1974) introduced the concept of *frame analysis*, which refers to frameworks used by individual communities to interpret the world and the ways of negotiating them, particularly as they apply to social situations. Such a framework can also be called a cultural and social context, or simply an interpretive schema (Snow et al., 1986). In adopting a given framework, we assume the existence of community-specific rules of conduct. As Sandeep and Ravishankar note, the lack of adjustment or negotiation of the framework may pose to be a major obstacle to ImS (2016).

Several effective ways of adapting these frameworks help to facilitate communication and establish the basic rules of interaction. The best known are frame bridging, frame amplification, frame extension, and frame transformation (Snow et al., 1986). Each of these methods assumes at least limited activity in order to effect frame aligning. According to Sandeep and Ravishankar's observations, ImS initiatives still do not make sufficient allowances for the need to adjust the framework to the target beneficiaries. This kind of individualisation of social and value-oriented ImS initiatives is necessary if they are to successfully engage the target community. In particular, narratives expressing a paternalistic and stigmatising approach to the ways of life and value system of a given community should be avoided. A difference in how the buyer treats its product supplier is visible, for example, between offshoring and outsourcing: in offshoring, the supplier tends to be treated as a partner, while in outsourcing – as a lower-status entity (Ravishankar, 2015). As D'Costa argues, referring to the wider cultural context of implementing IT ImS in India, "institutions of cooperation in India, while widespread in simple economic transactions, will be necessarily narrower in scope for the modern industrial setting. Such cooperation is expected to be a product of enterprise paternalism in the wider collective ethos but legitimised with the more immediate rewards of job-satisfaction and economic well-being" (D'Costa, 2003, p. 73).

Moreover, a given cultural and social framework may (and often is) fraught with assumptions that discriminate against certain groups, such as women, caste, or race. As the research by Heeks and Arun (2010) and Lacity and Willcocks (2014) shows, identities based on structural racism present the most common problem in implementing ImS. This is primarily reflected in India's gender and caste restrictions (Ravishankar, 2015) or in the experiences of aboriginal firms that provide their services to non-aboriginal clients (Nicholson et al., 2017, p. 219).

Another problem in implementing such solutions as the main mechanism for combating poverty and inequality is the IT industry's dependence on factors and resources external to poor communities, such as the legal and political environment, access to technology, or the specific IT environment for which people are trained.

IT-based operations in poor areas of the world often face risks associated with governance and political instability. For example, on 5 August 2019, the residents of Jammu and Kashmir were completely cut off from both internet and mobile phone services by the Indian authorities. Naturally, this situation has had much broader consequences than those affecting IT workers.

General statistics compiled on the basis of research on Internet shutdowns shows that this practice was used by the authorities of a number of countries more frequently between 2012 until 2018. The rate slightly decreased in 2019, but Internet and mobile network shutdowns to force communities and politicians of certain problem areas to comply seem to last ever longer.

As was already mentioned, dependence on specific IT solutions and tools can also pose a major problem in mobilising poor communities through ImS. Employees trained to work in a particular operating system, and its specific functions may later find it difficult to adapt to other systems; and, as is well known in the IT industry, such systems tend to have a rather short lifespan and require continuous training-up. In other words, the skills gained in both workshops and internships may be insufficient when trying to find jobs in firms and organisations outside the ImS system. Access to skills and know-how is limited, therefore, as it is imposed by the stronger side of the relationship, i.e. organisations involved in ImS.

Although these are only inconveniences in an otherwise efficient system for helping disadvantaged people, it is worth working towards solutions to enable such employees to achieve a greater flexibility on the labour market.

Conclusion

The concept of impact sourcing stems from the observation that the market for outsourcing services has become global and that the inequality in wealth is increasing worldwide. Under such circumstances, firms and individual organisations can no longer operate exclusively with a view to increasing their profits, as Milton Friedman would have it. With the emergence of the theory of corporate social responsibility and creating shared values, it has become clear that individual outsourcing models should take into account the trust of the societies in which they operate and hence demonstrate their social and environmental responsibility. The requirement to act in accordance with the principles of sustainable development has led to numerous initiatives, the most important of which is impact sourcing. The Digital Divide Data initiative was identified as one of the model examples of implementing the impact sourcing concept. Numerous studies show that given job opportunities, individuals from groups previously excluded or threatened with professional exclusion become more independent, empowered, and self-confident. Nevertheless, this model is burdened with various constraints, which result from the social and cultural framework of the social reality to which it is addressed, such as the underlying discrimination against gender or race; as well as legal and political factors, such as the escalating practice of cutting entire regions off from the Internet and telecommunication services. Moreover, insufficient emphasis is placed on fostering business autonomy and entrepreneurship in programme participants. However, the cited research findings permit moderate optimism about their development potential. Firms and organisations in developed countries should pay particular attention to such solutions in the times of economic uncertainty brought on by the SARS-CoV-2 pandemic, because impact sourcing appears to be a model capable of effectively mobilising the unemployed and retraining former employees for other occupations. The path was already signposted by the President of Estonia Kersti Kaljulaid, who, among other things, decided to subsidise a start-up firm to assist in a temporary transfer of employees from the tourism industry to e-commerce. Taking decisive action to support employees who lose their jobs should now become a priority for all the countries affected by COVID-19 pandemic. In this context, impact sourcing may become one of the methods to be considered in response to changes in the globalised employers' and employees' market, not only during the pandemic but also in the period of market stabilisation once it has subsided.

Note

1 It is precisely this apparent contradiction that Amartya Sen often raised in his work on inequalities and the Human Development Index (HDI).

References

Abreu, C.D., Vilca, C., & Bourdeau, A. (2013). *Recruitment, Training, and Impact Measurement; A Recommended Approach for Impact Sourcing, Accenture. High Performance*. Accenture [accessed from: www.rockefellerfoundation.org/wp-content/uploads/Recruitment-Training-and-Impact-Measurement-A-Recommended-Approach-for-Impact-Sourcing.jpg].

Bowen, H.R. (1953). *Social Responsibilities of the Businessman*. New York: Harper.

Bulloch, G., & Long, J. (2012). *Exploring the Value Proposition for Impact for Impact Sourcing*. Accenture [accessed from: www.rockefellerfoundation.org/wp-content/uploads/Exploring-the-Value-Proposition-for-Impact-for-Impact-Sourcing.pdf].

Carmel, E., Lacity, M., & Doty, A. (2013). *The Impact of Impact Sourcing: Framing a Research Agenda*. The 4th International Conference on the Outsourcing of Information Services, Mannheim, Germany.

Corbett, M.F. (2004). *The Outsourcing Revolution: Why It Makes Sense and How to Do It Right*. New York: Kaplan Publishing.

○Davis, K. (1960). Can business afford to ignore social responsibilities? *California Management Review*, *2*(3), pp. 70–76. https://doi.org/10.4324/9781315259222-10.

D'Costa, A.P. (2003). Institutions and industrial governance in India: Learning to cooperate the Japanese way. *Asian Business & Management*, *2*(1), pp. 63–89. https://doi.org/10.1057/palgrave.abm.9200028.

Freeman, R. (2010). *Strategic Management*. Cambridge, New York, Melbourne, Madrid, Cape Town, and Singapore: Cambridge University Press.

Ganesan, S. (1994). Determinants of long-term orientation in buyer-seller relationships. *Journal of Marketing*, *58*(2), pp. 1–19. https://doi.org/10.2307/1252265.

Goffman, E. (1974). *Frame Analysis: An Essay on the Organization of Experience*. Harvard: Harvard University Press.

Heeks, R., & Arun, S. (2010). Social outsourcing as a development tool: The impact of outsourcing IT services to women's social enterprises in Kerala. *Journal of International Development*, *22*(4), pp. 441–454. https://doi.org/10.1002/jid.1580.

Huang, Y., & Wilkinson, I.F. (2013). The dynamics and evolution of trust in business relationships. *Industrial Marketing Management*, *42*(3), pp. 455–465. https://doi.org/10.1016/j.indmarman.2013.02.016.

Johnson, H.L. (1971). *Business in Contemporary Society: Framework and Issues*. Belmont: Wadsworth Pub. Co.

Lacity, M., & Willcocks, L. (2014). Business process outsourcing and dynamic innovation. *Strategic Outsourcing: An International Journal*, *7*(1), pp. 66–92. https://doi.org/10.1108/SO-11-2013-0023.

Lawson, M., Butt, A.P., Harvey, R., Sarosi, D., Coffey, C., Piaget, K., & Thekkudan, J. (2020). Time to care unpaid and underpaid care work and the global inequality crisis. *Oxfam.org.*, January 20.
Li, P.P. (2012). When trust matters the most: The imperatives for contextualising trust research. *Journal of Trust Research, 2*(2), pp. 101–106. https://doi.org/10.1080/21515581.2012.708494.
Madon, S., & Sharanappa, S. (2013). Social IT outsourcing and development: Theorising the linkage. *Information Systems Journal, 23*(5), pp. 381–399. https://doi.org/10.1111/isj.12013.
Marquis, C., & Battilana, J. (2009). Acting globally but thinking locally? The enduring influence of local communities on organizations. *Research in Organizational Behavior, 29*, pp. 283–302. https://doi.org/10.1016/j.riob.2009.06.001.
Mazur-Bubak, M. (in press). *Nowoczesny paradygmat wojny: Geneza, treść, współczesne znaczenie*. Kraków: Uniwersytet Pedagogiczny im. Komisji Edukacji Narodowej.
McGuire, J.W. (1963). *Business and Society*. New York: McGraw-Hill.
Morgan, R.M., & Hunt, S.D. (1994). The commitment-trust theory of relationship marketing. *Journal of Marketing, 58*(3), pp. 20–38. https://doi.org/10.2307/1252308.
Nicholson, B., Babin, R., & Lacity, M.C. (2017). *Socially Responsible Outsourcing: Global Sourcing with Social Impact*. Basingstoke: Palgrave Macmillan.
Nussbaum, M.C. (2003). *Beyond the Social Contract: Toward Global Justice*. Clare Hall: University of Cambridge [accessed from: https://tannerlectures.utah.edu/_documents/a-to-z/n/nussbaum_2003.pdf].
Parakala, K., & Udhas, P. (2012). *Hub and Spoke Operating Model: A New Business Paradigm for the Indian IT-BPO Industry*. KPMG in India.
Porter, M.E., & Kramer, M.R. (2006). Strategy and society: The link between competitive advantage and corporate social responsibility. *Harvard Business Review*, December.
Porter, M.E., & Kramer, M.R. (2011). Creating shared value. *Harvard Business Review*, January–February.
Ravishankar, M.N. (2015). The realignment of offshoring frame disputes (OFD): An ethnographic "cultural" analysis. *European Journal of Information Systems, 24*(3), pp. 234–246. https://doi.org/10.1057/ejis.2014.5.
Roberts, T., Moser, M., LePan, D., Gaunce, J., & Buzzard, L. (2011). *The Broadview Anthology of Expository Prose* (2nd ed.). New York: Broadview Press.
Ruggie, J. (2011). *Guiding Principles on Business and Human Rights: Implementing the United Nations 'Protect, Respect and Remedy' Framework*. New York and Geneva: United Nations Human Rights Office of the High Commissioner.
Sandeep, M.S., & Ravishankar, M.N. (2016a). Exploring eh 'impact' in impact sourcing ventures: A sociology of space perspective. In B. Nicholson, M.C. Lacity, & R. Babin (Eds.), *Socially Responsible Outsourcing: Global Sourcing with Social Impact*. New York: Palgrave Macmillan, pp. 48–64.
Sandeep, M.S., & Ravishankar, M.N. (2016b). Impact sourcing ventures and local communities: A frame alignment perspective. *Information Systems Journal, 26*(2), pp. 127–155. https://doi.org/10.1111/isj.12057.
Sandeep, M.S., Ravishankar, M.N., & Hislop, D. (2013). *The Establishment of Social IT Sourcing Organizations: An Impression Management Perspective*. ICIS 2013 Proceedings 2013(12).
Scahill, J. (2008). *Blackwater: The Rise of the World's Most Powerful Mercenary Army*. New York: Bold Type Books.
Scott, W.R. (2001). *Institutions and Organizations*. New York: Sage Publications.

Sen, A. (1999). *Commodities and Capabilities*. Oxford: Oxford University Press.

Snow, D.A., Rochford, E.B., Worden, S.K., & Benford, R.D. (1986). Frame alignment processes, micromobilization, and movement participation. *American Sociological Review, 51*(4), pp. 464–481. https://doi.org/10.2307/2095581.

Stott, C., & Reicher, S. (2011). *Mad Mobs and Englishmen?: Myths and Realities of the 2011 Riots*. London: Constable & Robinson.

Thomson-DeVeaux, A. (2020). Which workers are most vulnerable to the economic costs of the coronavirus? *FiveThirtyEight* [accessed from: https://fivethirtyeight.com/features/which-workers-are-most-vulnerable-to-the-economic-costs-of-the-coronavirus/].

Uesseler, R. (2008). *Servants of War: Private Military Corporations and the Profit of Conflict*. Brooklyn: Soft Skull Press.

6 The development of European business services value chains

The perspective of emerging economies

Tomasz Geodecki

Introduction

This chapter is devoted to the development of the business services (BS) sector in the emerging economies of Central and Eastern Europe (CEE). In 2017, this part of the European Union had more than 100 million inhabitants (20% of EU28) in 11 countries (hereafter referred to as CEE11, cf. Table 6.1), which produced 8.3% of EU's GDP. This share dynamically increased from 5.6% in 2004. A special role in this group is played by the four Visegrad countries (V4), i.e. the Czech Republic, Hungary, Poland, and Slovakia. They represent the largest new EU member states with 62% of CEE11's population and contribute over two thirds of the region's GDP. The analysed trends focus on the V4, but the dynamics of the phenomena of interest are compared with changes that have occurred in CEE11 as a whole, whereas the comparative background is provided by the 15 EU member states before the 2004 enlargement (EU15).

Central and Eastern European countries in global value chains

The breakdown of added value creation in European countries

In the V4, a fairly large proportion of GDP is generated by industry (Table 6.1), which, on the one hand, is associated with the traditions of these economies, and on the other, reflects their symbiotic relations with Germany and Austria, the only EU15 member states (except Ireland) where the share of industry did not fall below 25%. As a result, the CEE countries, especially the V4, are characterised by a comparatively smaller share of value added generated by services compared to EU15.

Such a GDP structure has its source in the region's history. After World War II, the entire CEE, except Croatia and Slovenia, came under USSR influence. Industrialisation according to the Soviet model emphasised heavy industry, including metallurgy and traditional engineering sectors. Thus, the 19th-century Western model of industrialisation was copied, and until the 1970s, it permitted those countries to slowly catch up with the West (Bohle & Greskovits, 2012). Industrialisation came hand in hand with universal education. The fairly high level of primary

Table 6.1 GDP structure in European countries in 1995–2017

	1995			*2017*		
	*Agriculture**	*Industry***	*Services*	*Agriculture**	*Industry***	*Services*
European Union – 28 countries	**2.8**	**26.8**	**70.9**	**1.5**	**22.0**	**76.8**
"Old" member states (EU15)	**3.3**	**26.2**	**71.4**	**1.4**	**21.4**	**77.1**
Austria	2.2	28.9	69.0	1.2	25.5	73.3
Belgium	1.3	26.0	72.6	0.6	19.3	80.1
Denmark	2.9	22.1	75.1	1.4	20.5	78.1
Finland	3.8	29.5	66.7	2.3	24.3	73.4
France	2.4	22.3	75.2	1.6	17.2	81.2
Germany	1.0	29.8	69.2	0.8	27.4	71.7
Greece	7.4	19.6	73.0	3.7	15.0	81.3
Ireland	5.6	28.9	65.6	1.2	35.8	63.1
Italy	3.0	26.4	70.7	2.0	21.3	76.8
Luxembourg	0.9	19.2	79.9	0.2	11.2	88.5
Netherlands	3.1	24.1	72.8	1.9	17.7	80.4
Portugal	4.8	24.8	70.4	2.1	19.1	78.8
Spain	3.9	28.3	67.8	2.8	20.2	77.0
Sweden	2.9	26.8	70.3	1.4	22.1	76.4
United Kingdom	1.4	24.8	73.8	0.7	17.6	81.8
Central and Eastern Europe (CEE11)	**7.4**	**31.5**	**61.1**	**3.0**	**28.3**	**68.7**
of which V4 (CZE, HUN, POL, SVK)	**5.1**	**32.1**	**62.7**	**2.7**	**29.4**	**67.9**
Bulgaria	9.2	17.6	73.2	4.1	24.7	71.3
Croatia	5.7	26.8	67.5	2.9	20.8	76.2
Czech Republic	4.0	35.3	60.7	2.1	33.2	64.7
Estonia	4.1	27.4	68.5	2.4	24.0	73.6
Hungary	7.2	25.8	67.0	3.8	25.6	70.6
Latvia	7.7	26.8	65.5	3.5	19.2	77.4
Lithuania	9.9	28.2	62.0	3.5	25.9	70.6
Poland	5.5	33.2	61.2	2.8	28.9	68.3
Romania	18.2	36.4	45.4	4.3	28.9	66.8
Slovakia	2.3	27.7	70.0	2.4	29.0	68.6
Slovenia	4.0	29.6	66.4	1.9	28.4	69.7
Other "new" member states	**3.6**	**23.1**	**73.2**	**1.0**	**11.6**	**86.9**
Cyprus	4.8	20.1	75.2	2.0	11.3	86.7
Malta	2.5	26.0	71.5	0.8	12.0	87.2

*Including forestry and fishery.
**Including construction.

Source: Own calculations based on World Development Indicators, World Bank.

education was accompanied by a quantitatively and qualitatively limited (with certain exceptions) higher education dominated by specialised vocational training (Berend, 1996). From the 1970s onwards, the focus on heavy industry became increasingly anachronistic. The labour and raw material intensity coupled with low quality of manufacturing reduced the competitiveness of what the socialist countries had to offer on international markets. The collapse of global communism found them with obsolete industrial infrastructure and the absence of national capitalists, but with industrial experience and a large disciplined group of trained labour (Bohle & Greskovits, 2012). In this context, transnational corporations became the natural providers of missing capital and managerial expertise (Bruszt & Greskovits, 2009; Gál & Schmidt, 2017). Researchers of trade links emphasise the emergence of a production cluster, which combined the technologically advanced high-wage German economy with low-cost Visegrad economies (IMF, 2013), which Baldwin and Lopez-Gonzalez (2013) call Factory Europe. This is facilitated by geographical and cultural proximity and the complementarity of infrastructure. The last decade has also seen the region's growth in importance as a location for the offshore services industry (Fernandez-Stark & Gereffi, 2010).

Challenges faced by developing countries involved in global value chains: modernisation and emergence or peripherality and dependence?

The distinguishing features of emerging markets include a lower than average per capita income, rapid growth, and a high susceptibility to economic fluctuations. According to the Morgan Stanley Capital International Emerging Market Index, emerging markets include the Czech Republic, Hungary, and Poland. When looking at the issue from a European perspective, they represent economies with a lower average development level, but a faster growth rate. As the other CEE11 countries exhibit similar characteristics, we will also classify them as emerging economies. They rely heavily on foreign direct investment in their development processes through which their markets have been integrated into the global economic cycle. This process has been accelerated by the modern phase of globalisation characterised by the fragmentation of production, i.e. its split into a number of business entities and locations. In order to describe the structural framework of this process, researchers refer to global value chains (GVCs). The main motive for their internationalisation is the prospect of reducing labour costs by offshoring firms (Baldwin, 2012, 2019). However, as Mittelman (1995) argues, the new international division of labour cannot be explained by low labour costs alone. High process efficiency requires reliable suppliers. Hence, countries with stable legal frameworks and a fairly well-educated workforce are chosen as a place for investment. Nevertheless, although participation in a GVC promotes the acquisition of new production and managerial competencies by entities from developing countries, such upgrading is by no means universal. This is because the lead firms in the chains protect their position and the resources that guarantee it. Sometimes investors are not interested in local resources other than low-cost labour. From the perspective of emerging countries, however, the ability to transform from dependent into developmental linkage structures (Dicken, 2015, p. 261) and strengthen the linkages between investors and the local economy is crucial.

Two kinds of challenges for developing countries resulting from their inclusion in GVCs can be identified: those associated with the scale of benefits and prospects for industrial upgrading of local economies and the sustainability of the presence of foreign entities that link local economies to the global economy.

- The first challenge to economic development stems from the fact that while global production sharing has helped developing countries to increase their exports, the value added does not always increase proportionally (Milberg & Winkler, 2013, p. 240). Economies involved in GVCs may participate only in certain stages in the production of a given good or service. This means that semi-finished and finished products processed and exported by individual economies may contain a significant proportion of imported intermediate goods and services from other countries, with a low proportion of domestic value added. This issue is further associated with the fact that the benefits of networking do not necessarily spill over to the local economy. Coe and Yeung (2015), when identifying the category of network embeddedness, refer to the intensity of functional and social links within a given global production network, the permanence of network relations, and their importance for its participants. There is a tension between being embedded in a global network and being embedded in a given territory, as more intense relationships with network participants may entail less intense relationships with local actors. Industrialisation has been promoted in developing countries (cf. Hirschman, 1958) because manufacturing tends to build lasting and intensive links with local industries so that growth in one branch affects production in related ones. The lack of such embeddedness and links between investors and local economies may remove any investment benefits (from the last ones) and lead to creating 'cathedrals in the desert' (Hardy, 1998). In the CEE countries, multinational enterprises (MNEs) in particular have less intense relationships with local suppliers and customers. These efficiency-seeking vertical investments, undertaken due to the differences in labour costs, are characterised by higher exports and employment compared to market-seeking horizontal foreign direct investment (FDI) (Hardy et al., 2011; Gál, 2014; Sass et al., 2018). By its very nature, the former involves the transfer of more labour-intensive stages of value chains to CEE, but as Hardy et al. (2011) note, it creates less skills-intensive jobs. A related problem is whether the offshored activities hosted by developing countries are concentrated in industries susceptible to learning and economies of scale. Capacity growth is considered to be key to development (Amsden, 2001). In their absence, developing countries have to rely on foreign investment in technological development and in the utilisation of managerial skills (Bruszt & Greskovits, 2009). For this reason, CEE is also classified as a peripheral area (Berend, 1996; Bohle & Greskovits, 2012; Grodzicki & Geodecki,

2016; Gál & Schmidt, 2017) with distinct features of dependence (Nölke & Vliegenthart, 2009). As Capik and Drahokoupil (2011) note, the contribution of foreign investors in the business services sector (BSS) to the development of a knowledge-based economy is often limited to creating employment and demand for skilled labour. On the other hand, local vendors lack the capacity to build domestic brands, whereas recipients, including those from developing countries, prefer the services provided by tried and tested global players (Fernandez-Stark & Gereffi, 2010). This has an effect not only on where added value is created but also on the directions of its flow and capital accumulation as profits from foreign investment are partially repatriated (Gál & Schmidt, 2017; Milberg & Winkler, 2013; Kalecki & Sachs, 1966).

- The second challenge is to build lasting relationships between investors and local suppliers of institutions, the community, and to strengthen the positive perception of the benefits of a given location by investors. These elements together make up territorial embeddedness (Micek et al., 2010), which in the CEE countries are considered from the perspective of the threat of relocation (Nölke & Vliegenthart, 2009; Domański & Gwosdz, 2009; Micek et al., 2010). In order to increase the sustainability of the sector in a given location, the key factors are sunk costs in the form of invested capital, the sustainability of the benefits for which investments in this sector were made in this particular location, as well as whether the investor is a local or foreign entrepreneur. Apart from capital, the role of sunk costs may be played by localised capabilities, which are difficult to build at no cost elsewhere. According to Domański and Gwosdz (2009), they are a mediating factor in the territorial embeddedness and prevent the relocation of their activities. Knowledge intensive business activities based on and enabling local competence resources can be an even more valuable local resource because the business services sector is less capital intensive than manufacturing.

The next section describes the scale of engagement in foreign trade and investment in business services covering NACE 2 divisions J58, J62, and J63 (IT business services – IT_BS) and M69, M70, M71, and M73 (professional business services – PROF.BS) (see also Chapter 2).

The sections that follow attempt to answer the research questions about the sustainability of benefits for local economies and investors resulting from the development of business services in the CEE countries:

- First, to what extent are the CEE countries involved in trade in business services in the context of new trends resulting from globalisation? (The growing tendency to outsource intermediate inputs and the increasing role of transnational corporations in coordinating international trade flows.)
- Second, does the growth in value added of the business services sector in the CEE countries correspond with the growth in international trade? To what extent is value-added created in knowledge-intensive services? To what

extent are its suppliers and recipients local and foreign clients? To answer these questions, we employ the GVC approach, which makes it possible to trace value-added flows that accompany international trade (Grodzicki & Geodecki, 2016).

- Third, do the realised and potential benefits to investors determine the sustainability of their firms' interest in investing in the business services sector in the region?

The research was conducted using the world input-output database (WIOD) (Timmer et al., 2015), foreign trade data (UNCTAD), and structural business statistics (Eurostat).

The last point sums up the evaluation of network embeddedness, the sustainability of investment in the business services (BS) sector and proposes directions for further research.

International division of labour in European business services: the role of foreign trade and foreign direct investment

A first glance at the employment and value added in business services reveals that despite a large and growing share in employment, the CEE countries, including the V4, have a comparatively low share in the sector's value added as compared to the entire EU. The left panel of Figure 6.1 shows the share of the largest EU and CEE countries in employment and added value in two BS sectors – IT and PROF. Among the Western countries, the United Kingdom enjoys the highest realised employment potential in BS, and in terms of value added, it takes this advantage even further. Italy is the weakest performer in this respect. The CEE countries compare unfavourably in terms of employment and value added, but in the analysed period, the share of these economies in both categories rapidly increased. Still, if CEE economies have a 19% and 17% share of employment in PROF.BS and IT_BS, respectively, but only 7% and 5% share in value added, it represents about 2.5–3 times less value added per employee than the EU average.

Given the fact that the CEE countries have a total of 100 million inhabitants or account for a fifth of the EU28 population (10 million each in the Czech Republic and Hungary, 38 million in Poland, and 5.5 million in Slovakia), their relative importance of business services in the EU28 is small, whereas that of the Visegrad countries in CEE is disproportionately high (cf. right panels of Figure 6.1.). Especially the Czech Republic and Slovakia compared to the rest of CEE are characterised by an above-average share of value added generated by the business services sector in relation to their populations, whereas Poland's share is below average, especially in IT.

The rapid growth in employment and added value in business services in the CEE countries (see Table 6.2) largely results from the region's growing commitment to international trade in services following the 2004 EU enlargement.

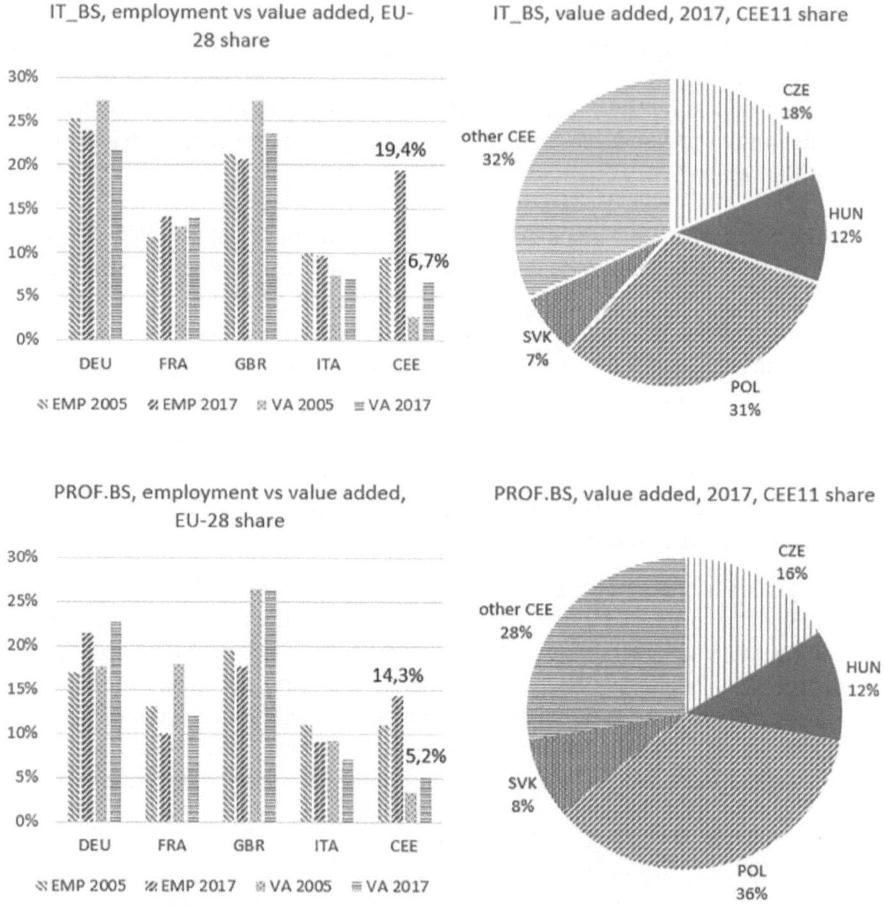

Figure 6.1 Value added and employment in BS in selected EU countries in 2005–2017

Source: Own study based on Eurostat data.

Table 6.2 Exports of IT_BS and PROF.BS sectors (billions of US 2004 dollars and % of EU28)

		EU28		*CEE11*		*V4*	
		IT_BS	*PROF.BS*	*IT_BS*	*PROF.BS*	*IT_BS*	*PROF.BS*
Bn US 2004 dollars	2004	76.1	114.8	3.5	5.5	2.9	3.9
	2014	221.7	216.6	18.0	15.3	11.1	10.3
% of EU28	2004	100%	100%	4.6%	4.8%	3.8%	3.4%
	2014	100%	100%	8.1%	7.0%	5.0%	4.8%

Source: Own study based on WIOD.

Two mutually reinforcing trends can be identified:

- First, the increasing tradability of services, especially those that constitute intermediate inputs in final goods.
- Second, a growing tendency to include CEE suppliers in global value chains coordinated by multinational corporations (MNCs).

A look at the trade statistics proves that business services are increasingly becoming part and parcel of international exchange. This is particularly true for information and communication technology (ICT) services and other business services (OBS), for which the export dynamics in 2009–2017 were significantly higher than the average for services exports (Com.Serv.) (see Figure 6.2).

The input-output statistics, which permit trade flows to be traced back to previous years as well, reveal two other important trends:

- Across the EU, exports of services are clearly growing faster than value added, i.e. in order to produce a unit of value added, business operators in the services sector increasingly rely on international trade. This is true of ICT and professional services (Figure 6.3) to a larger extent than of total services.

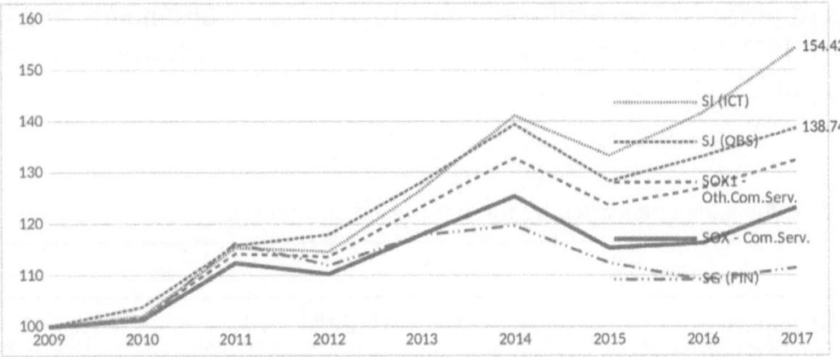

Figure 6.2 Exports of services, EU28 (2009 = 100)

Source: Own study based on UNCTAD trade statistics.

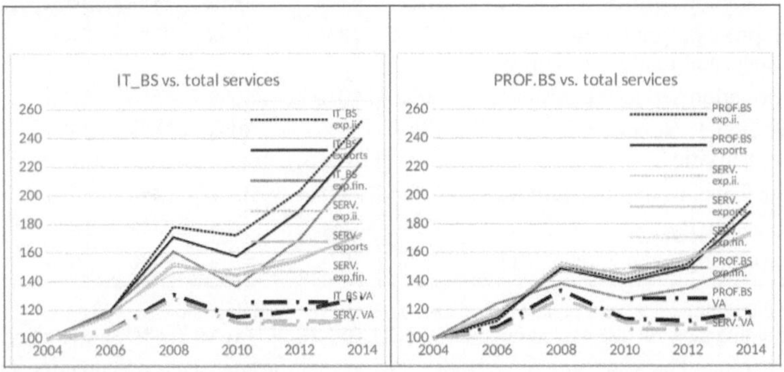

Figure 6.3 Growth in value added and exports in services (2004 = 100; USD 2004 prices)

Source: Own study based on WIOD.

- An increasing share of foreign trade is represented by exports of intermediate inputs (exp.ii), to be processed further in the production of final goods. A higher intensity of trade in intermediate inputs than of final goods (exp. fin.) is evident, especially in IT_BS and PROF.BS. This means that these services in particular are increasingly being provided within globalised value chains as one of many processes leading to the production of final goods.

The growing involvement of the CEE countries in trade in business services has been fostered by a noteworthy increase in activity of MNCs. In 2009–2017, they boosted their share in the generated value added to over 50% in information and communication (J) and over 30% in professional, scientific, and technical activities (M) (Table 6.3).

A comparison with EU28 as a whole justifies the observation that CEE, and especially the V4, is an area significantly dominated by foreign capital.

Figures shown in Table 6.4 confirm the observation that the vast majority of the largest firms in the individual global business services (GBS) divisions in CEE are those with foreign capital. Their greater presence in the group of the largest firms than in the total value added shows that they are the key players on the market. At the same time, the largest share (above two-thirds) can be observed in the three most globalised sectors: computer programming, consultancy, and related activities (J62), legal and accounting activities (M69), and advertising and market research (M73) (cf. Table 6.4; the divisions in question have been shaded).

Table 6.3 Value added generated by foreign-owned entities (%)

Year	*2009*			*2017*		
Groups of countries Activities, NACE 2	EU*	CEE**	V4	EU*	CEE**	V4
C29 Manufacture of motor vehicles, trailers, and semi-trailers	71%	88%	89%	38%	89%	92%
J Information and communication	29%	59%	58%	33%	57%	56%
J58 Publishing activities	23%	41%	46%	31%	40%	38%
J62 Computer programming, consultancy, and related activities	30%	48%	46%	37%	54%	51%
J63 Information service activities	29%	40%	40%	45%	51%	51%
M Professional scientific and technical activities	14%	28%	30%	18%	33%	35%
M69 Legal and accounting activities	2%	21%	23%	4%	31%	34%
M72 Scientific R&D	27%	7%	4%	33%	18%	16%
M73 Advertising and market research	23%	49%	51%	34%	40%	40%

Missing data from 2009 were replaced by data from 2010 for SVK J58 and CZE J63.
Due to missing data: *EU28 excluding: BEL, GRC, HRV, IRL, LUX, MLT; **CEE excluding HRV.

Source: Eurostat: Foreign control of enterprises by economic activity and a selection of controlling countries [fats_g1a_08].

Table 6.4 Top 25 enterprises in each BS sector in CEE countries (2018)

NACE 2 divisions	*Foreign owned entities*
J58 Publishing activities	56%
J62&J63 Computer programming, consultancy, and related activities; information service activities	64%
M69 Legal and accounting activities	80%
M70 Activities of head offices; management consultancy activities	36%
M71 Architectural and engineering activities; technical testing and analysis	44%
M73 Advertising and market research	88%

Source: Own calculations based on data from the Orbis Database, Bureau van Dyke.

The position of the CEE countries in service GVCs

In an era of globalisation, the analysis of exports and imports may be insufficient to identify the benefits that accrue to individual economies involved in international trade owing to the fact that countries may participate only in certain stages in the production of a given good or service. Therefore, over the last decade, researchers have been trying to capture not only the flow of goods and services, but also the flows of added value between individual world economies (see Koopman et al., 2010; Timmer et al., 2013; OECD, 2013).

Value added flows enable us to draw a number of conclusions concerning the embeddedness of operators in business services sectors included in GVCs. When analysing individual positions (links) in a value chain, we shall use the metrics proposed by Grodzicki and Geodecki (2016) to identify where a given branch or a given economy is located in relation to:

- Branches/countries – suppliers of intermediate goods (backward linkages, listed below as FVA [foreign value added], which makes it possible to identify the extent to which a given branch relies on foreign suppliers and subcontractors;
- Branches/countries – producers of final goods in which the value added of the branch/country in question is embodied (forward linkages, listed below as FFG [foreign final goods] indicator); refers to the extent to which the branch relies on foreign producers for its value added.

The FVA values embodied in the final demand of CEE countries were significantly higher in 2004–2014 than those in the Western European countries (EU15) (cf. Table 6.5). This supports the findings of several researchers (e.g. Dicken, 2015; Micek et al., 2010) that linkages between TNCs and local suppliers are denser in developed and larger countries. Using intermediate goods to meet the final

Table 6.5 Position indicators in global value chains: foreign value added (FVA) and foreign final goods (FFG)

Countries	*Years*	*FVA*				*FFG*			
		Total	*Manuf.*	*IT_BS*	*PROF.BS*	*Total*	*Manuf.*	*IT_BS*	*PROF.BS*
EU15	2004	13%	23%	12%	10%	14%	33%	14%	20%
	2014	16%	31%	16%	14%	17%	39%	21%	27%
	Change	3pp.	8pp.	4pp.	4pp.	3pp.	6pp.	7pp.	7pp.
CEE11	2004	20%	31%	19%	17%	19%	40%	20%	25%
	2014	23%	37%	20%	18%	24%	47%	28%	33%
	Change	3pp.	6pp.	1pp.	1pp.	5pp.	7pp.	8pp.	8pp.
V4	2004	19%	32%	18%	16%	20%	42%	21%	25%
	2014	24%	40%	20%	17%	25%	49%	28%	32%
	Change	5pp.	8pp.	2pp.	1pp.	5pp.	7pp.	7pp.	7pp.

Source: Own study based on WIOD.

demand of 1 euro, the V4 countries generated an increase in foreign value added of 19 and 24 cents in 2004 and 2014, respectively. In the same period, in the EU15 countries, globalisation increased the share of foreign value added from 13 to 16 cents per 1 euro.

FFG readouts imply a slightly different situation: the share of foreign entities receiving domestic value added in order to further process it and create final goods increased for the CEE countries significantly for IT and professional business services. Larger discrepancies between imported (FVA) and exported value added within GVCs (FFG) occurred in CEE countries than in EU15. It implies that the CEE countries have become increasingly important providers of business services, which, in turn, generate a considerable proportion of added value.

However, this is accompanied by a decreasing degree of embeddedness of the business services sector, as more and more service recipients are foreign partners as compared to local ones. This process, although not so intense, is also occurring in Western European economies.

To illustrate the benefits of participating in GVCs, we shall use the global value chain income measure (GVCI) (see Timmer, 2013), which includes the added value of a given branch in a given country obtained via the sale of final goods to domestic and foreign recipients (see Grodzicki & Geodecki, 2016). It may provide a reliable basis for comparing the revealed comparative advantage (RCA) subsumed under obtained added value with the advantages in foreign trade. The dotted line in Figure 6.4 represents the RCA in services exports (RCA_Exports). As proposed by Balassa (1965), values above 1 mean that a given country has a larger share of exports of a given product in its export pool than the world average (here EU28).

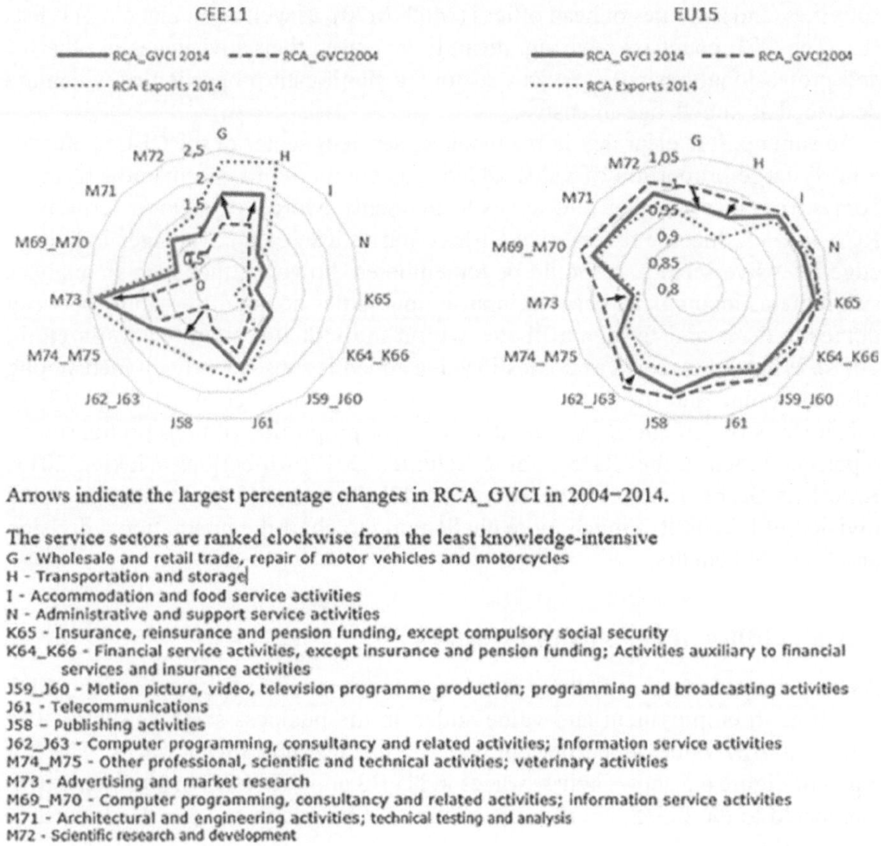

Figure 6.4 Revealed comparative advantages in exports and revenues from participation in global value chains

Source: Own study based on WIOD data.

The comparison of export advantages and the added value obtained shows the capacity of developed countries to carry out activities that bring disproportionate benefits from exports. This is illustrated by the RCA_GVCI line above the exports line (dotted line) for EU15. In CEE11, the GVCI line is below the exports line. Nevertheless, in almost all services, EU15 has seen a decline in the RCA since 2004 (dashed line) accompanied by a rapid increase in RCA_GVCI in CEE11. This suggests that some service tasks have been transferred from EU15 to the new member states. In the business services sector, Western European advantages have dwindled in high offshoring intensity sectors – ICT services (J62&J63) and advertising and market research (M73). EU15 maintained its advantages (RCA_GVCI > 1) in the more advanced divisions of research and development (M72), legal and accounting activities, and activities of head offices (M69_M70), as well as in financial services (K). The CEE countries have significantly increased their advantages in other IT and professional business services sectors, a significant proportion of which are described as knowledge-intensive.

To sum up, it is clear that in the business services sector of the CEE countries, a fairly large proportion of value added – as compared to e.g. manufacturing – comes from local vendors and serves local clients. Moreover, a closer scrutiny of RCA in GVC Income reveals that CEE countries also gain advantages in knowledge-intensive sectors. It should be remembered, however, that such an analysis still remains incomplete, because input-output tables do not differentiate between domestic firms and foreign affiliates within individual sectors (Cadestin et al., 2018). What we perceive as domestic value added is subsequently divided among labour, capital, and the state. Since in CEE a large number of actors in BS are subsidiaries of foreign firms, a relatively larger proportion of their profits can be repatriated than in the EU15 (Gál & Schmidt, 2017; Milberg & Winkler, 2013; Kalecki & Sachs, 1966).[1] In consequence, while it is not difficult to map the global division of labour, it is much more challenging to chart the international division and flows of benefits.

Sustainability of benefits to investors

As was mentioned above, there is a large discrepancy in the share of the CEE countries in employment and value added in the business services sector. The relatively low value added per employee translates into lower wages. The left panel of Figure 6.5 shows hourly wages in IT_BS and PROF.BS in 2004 and 2014. Compared to the EU15, hourly wages in the V4 ranged from 15 to 16 dollars, or

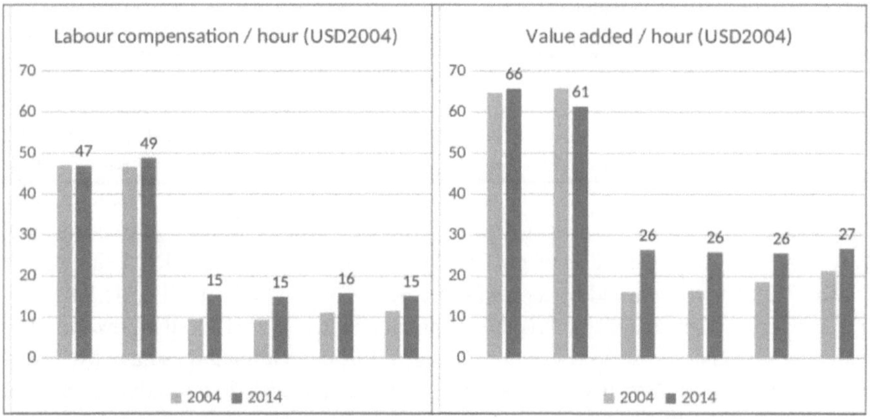

Figure 6.5 Labour compensation and value added in BSS in selected EU countries
Source: Own calculations based on WIOD SEA data.

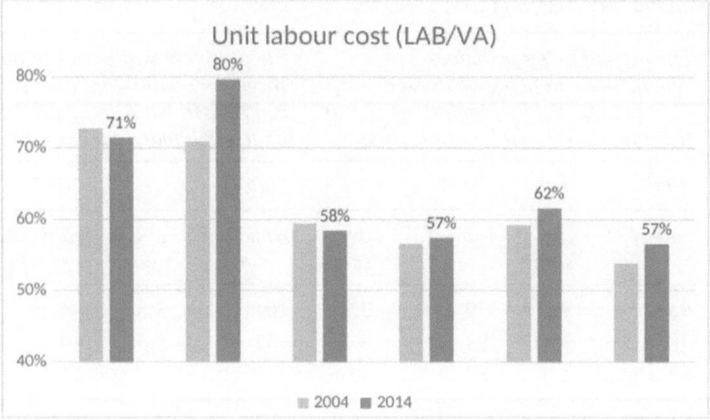

Figure 6.6 Unit labour cost (labour compensation/value added)
Source: Own calculations based on WIOD SEA data.

32% of the EU15 average, whereas productivity ranged from 26 to 27 dollars, or 40–45% of the EU15 average.

Despite a clear increase in wages in the region in 2004–2014, the labour productivity growth rate was fast as well, which made it possible to maintain the unit labour cost (ULC) significantly below the EU15 level, where the ULC in the IT sector exceeded 70% and reached 80% in PROF.BS (see Figure 6.6). The ULC determines the level of cost competitiveness of a given economy and shows that in the CEE BS sector, thanks to the relatively high labour productivity, there is a wage growth potential that still allows investors to achieve higher margins than when investing in business services in developed countries.

Yet another factor that enhances the competitiveness of CEE locations, commented upon by offshoring researchers (see Strange & Magnani, 2018), are lower social and employment standards in the region. In the CEE countries, employers have had much more freedom in this respect than in the EU15, especially in terms of wage flexibility.

Between 2006 and 2017, there was some convergence in this respect – in the post-crisis years, the EU15 slightly relaxed labour protection regulations by allowing more flexible employment forms, whereas in CEE, labour protection increased. This may be considered as compensation of sorts for the greater ability of entrepreneurs to shape wages freely without having to involve the trade unions, which would improve the bargaining position of the world of labour. The employers' capacity to keep a lower labour share (see Table 6.6), and therefore a higher share of profit in value added, are its likely outcomes.

The capacity to create added value is considerably boosted by developing the employees' competencies. Among other things, it resulted from a significant increase in the percentage of university graduates in the 25–34 age band in these countries (cf. Figure 6.7, left panel). Likewise, OECD (PIAAC) studies confirm

Table 6.6 Comparison of hiring and firing practices and flexibility of wage determination in the V4, CEE, and EU15

	Hiring and firing practices The hiring and firing of workers (1 = is impeded by regulations, 7 = is flexibly determined by employers)				*Flexibility of wage determination Wages in country are (1 = set by a centralised bargaining process, 7 = up to each individual company)*			
	2006		*2017*		*2006*		*2017*	
	rank/125	*avg. score*	*rank/137*	*avg. score*	*rank/125*	*avg. score*	*rank/137*	*avg. score*
EU15	95	3.2	79	3.7	101	3.8	94	4.3
CEE11	70	3.8	83	3.5	41	5.5	40	5.4
V4	63	4.0	88	3.6	47	5.5	41	5.3

Unweighted means.

Source: Own calculations based on Global Competitiveness Report 2006–2007 and 2017–2018, World Economic Forum.

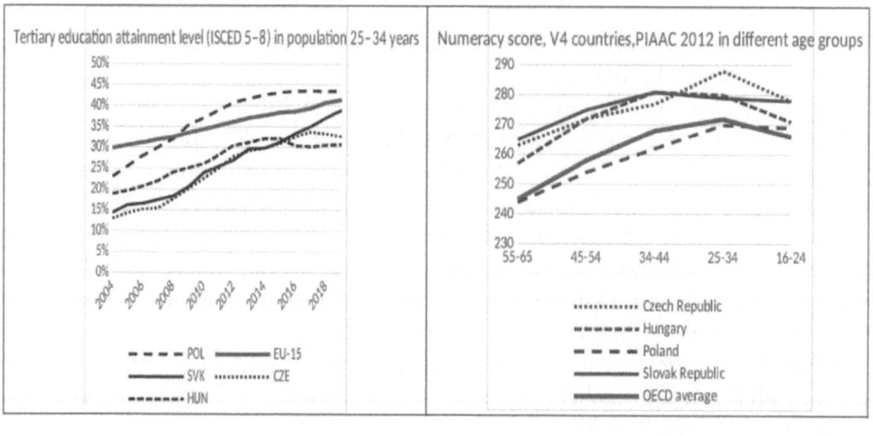

Figure 6.7 Indicators of competences and human capital in the CEE countries compared to EU15 and OECD countries

Source: Own calculations on WIOD SEA, 2014, Eurostat data and OECD data (PIAAC).

the high level of adult competencies and their rapid growth in successive age cohorts (cf. Figure 6.7, right panel).

An important component of the realised and potential benefits for service providers is the talent pool available in the region. The number of students in CEE cities and in the surrounding regions shows the potential for launching labour-intensive processes. Investors do not tend to open their subsidiaries in centres considered to be too small (see chapter on GBS in Krakow and Bratislava). In CEE, Poland ranks first with over 300,000 university students in Warsaw in 2017 while the remaining cities of the region have a much more modest potential. However, in recent years (2013–2018), the number of students in the region significantly decreased (by 20% in CEE and by 22% in the V4), even though it increased by 3% in EU28 in the same period. On the one hand, it results from a significant reduction in fertility rates in the region in the 1990s, and on the other, from the negative migration balance in most of them.

To sum up, the benefits of investing in Central and Eastern Europe, especially in the V4 countries, include an educated labour force capable of implementing complex, high added value processes and relatively low employment costs. These two features contribute to low unit labour costs and thereby to the high attractiveness of the CEE countries, including the V4, as an investment location.

Conclusions and directions for further research

The fluctuations in the global economy, such as the 2009 crisis or the current coronavirus pandemic, time and again raise the issue of tension between globalisation and the embeddedness of business activity. In the times of rising transaction costs and interrupted business relations, firms generally prefer to internalise their processes, which may reduce their propensity to outsource – the main BS growth driver in recent decades. On the other hand, the development of remote working, which is bound to occur along with the expected rapid acceleration in IT development, may stimulate interest in offshoring. As R. Baldwin comments, "The biggest arbitrage or gain for your employers will be to hire people who can do more or less what you can, but for a tenth of the price".[2] The question of embeddedness becomes even more topical: will the factors related to remote communication and labour costs that have contributed to the emergence of the business services sector in Central Europe work in favour of its presence in the region, or will MNEs move to even more competitive locations in the East and South as soon as the technology permits?

The CEE countries demonstrate distinct comparative advantages in terms of revenues from the provision of business services. In the process of creating added value, a fairly large proportion of it – as compared to e.g. manufacturing – comes from local suppliers and serves local clients. However, the share of domestic clients, especially end-users, is clearly lower than that in the EU15, which is due to the region's specialisation in providing business services abroad, often to and by foreign-owned firms. As these entities generate a significant share of value added in the region, doubts may arise as to the extent to which the generated value-added feeds into local economies. This reveals a tension between network and territorial embeddedness: from the perspective of local economies, a greater embeddedness in the global network and the provision of services mostly to international clients means relatively fewer close links with local suppliers and clients.

The CEE countries offer considerable advantages for investors in the form of efficient business processes performed at a lower cost than in nearby Berlin or Vienna and with significantly more flexible labour regulations. However, a tension arises between the various dimensions of embeddedness and investor benefit. Even though lower wages and less social security increase current employers' benefits, in the long run, they may result in a brain drain, i.e. an outflow of population to the richer EU15 countries. This undermines the comparative advantages of the region as gleaned from the student numbers statistics and from the shrinking populations of some countries (e.g. Bulgaria or Lithuania). In 2017–2018, Poland issued the highest number of residence permits for non-EU citizens (1.3 million) of all the EU28 countries in order to help its labour market affected by the net loss of 2 million citizens to emigration after the 2004 EU accession.[3] In the near future, rising employment costs may become a natural obstacle to locating labour-intensive stages of GVCs in the CEE countries, since the region is no longer labour-abundant. A solution to this problem is to implement higher added value processes, also known as industrial upgrading. This is what is meant by overcoming the middle income trap identified by Gill and Kharas (2007) in which countries at a medium development level lose their comparative advantage of a low-cost labour force as they become more affluent. The more expensive the labour, the more their advantages should reflect the uniqueness of the goods and services sold, as the latter make it possible to combine higher wages with maintaining the competitiveness of exports. At present, CEE countries seem to follow this script, as rapidly rising wages are accompanied by even faster growth in labour productivity, which keeps the unit labour cost below the EU15 level. The analysis of added value by sector also showed that an increasing part of it is created in knowledge-intensive business services.

This suggests that the countries of the region have developed specialised capabilities but attempts to evaluate them on a national scale seem to be only moderately successful. In the larger CEE countries, individual urban centres offer very different conditions for the development of business services, as reflected in various rankings of offshoring destinations (e.g. Vashistha et al., 2019). Their league tables include 11 CEE cities, which occupy very different positions even within their national economy (e.g. Krakow and Wroclaw rank 11th and 92nd, respectively). The aggregate analysis of national economies may reflect certain general conditions, such as costs and labour law, or the quality of the educational systems, but the pool of human resources and capabilities resulting from the experience of advanced economic processes are definitely subnational in nature. For this reason, applying economic geography tools to the study of global production networks with their regional actors will significantly enrich the research on global value chains. In this approach, subnational regions are considered to be the key loci of economic development; after all, it is the investor that will ultimately choose Brno over Prague or Warsaw over Budapest.

Notes

1 It is difficult to obtain sector specific data, but the balance of payments suggests that between 2016 and 2018, direct investment income attributable to equity and investment fund shareholders in CEE countries represented on average –5.3 % of GDP, whereas in EU15 it was +1.1% of GDP. Moreover, according to the agreements on avoiding double

taxation, dividend income from foreign subsidiaries is not subject to corporate income tax (CIT) in the host country.

2 Interview for Knowledge@Wharton, 12.03.2019 [accessed on: https://knowledge.wharton.upenn.edu/article/globotics-upheaval/].

3 Eurostat news release, no. 166/2018, 25 October 2018.

References

Amsden, A. (2001). *The Rise of "the Rest": Challenges to the West From Late-Industrializing Economies*. Oxford: Oxford University Press.

Balassa, B. (1965). Trade liberalisation and "revealed" comparative advantage. *The Manchester School, 33*(2), pp. 99–123.

Baldwin, R. (2012). *Global Supply Chains: Why They Emerged, Why They Matter, and Where They are Going*. CEPR Discussion Papers, No. 9103.

Baldwin, R. (2019). *The Globotics Upheaval: Globalization, Robotics, and the Future of Work*. Oxford: Oxford University Press.

Baldwin, R., & Lopez-Gonzalez, J. (2013). *Supply chain Trade: A Portrait of Global Patterns and Several Testable Hypotheses*. Working Paper, No. 18957. National Bureau of Economic Research (NBER).

Berend, I. (1996). *Central and Eastern Europe, 1944–1993: Detour from the Periphery to the Periphery* (Vol. 1). Cambridge: Cambridge University Press.

Bohle, D., & Greskovits, B. (2012). *Capitalist Diversity on Europe's Periphery*. New York: Cornell University Press.

Bruszt, L., & Greskovits, B. (2009). Transnationalization, social integration, and capitalist diversity in the East and the South. *Studies in Comparative International Development, 44*(4), pp. 411–434.

Cadestin, C., De Backer, K., Desnoyers-James, I., Miroudot, S., Ye, M., & Rigo, D. (2018). *Multinational enterprises and global value chains: New Insights on the trade-investment nexus*. OECD Science, Technology and Industry Working Papers, No. 2018/05, OECD Publishing, Paris.

Capik, P., & Drahokoupil, J. (2011). Foreign direct investments in business services: Transforming the Visegrad four region into a knowledge-based economy? *European Planning Studies, 19*(9), pp. 1611–1631.

Coe, N.M., & Yeung, H.W.-C. (2015). *Global Production Networks: Theorizing Economic Development in an Interconnected World*. Oxford: Oxford University Press.

Dicken, P. (2015). *Global Shift: Mapping the Changing Contours of the World Economy*. New York: The Guilford Press.

Domański, B., & Gwosdz, K. (2009). Toward a more embedded production system? Automotive supply networks and localized capabilities in Poland. *Growth and Change, 40*(3), pp. 452–482.

Fernandez-Stark, K., & Gereffi, G. (Eds.). (2010). *The Offshore Services Global Value Chain*. Durham, NC: Center on Globalization, Governance & Competitiveness, Duke University.

Gál, Z. (2014). Relocation of business services into Central and Eastern Europe: Evidence from trade and location statistics. *Romanian Review of Regional Studies, 10*(1), pp. 67–78.

Gál, Z., & Schmidt, A. (2017). Geoeconomics in Central Europe: Implications of FDI. In J. Mark Munoz (Ed.), *Advances in Geoeconomics*. New York: Routledge.

Gill, I.S., & Kharas, H. (2007). *An East Asian Renaissance: Ideas for Economic Growth*. Washington, DC: The World Bank.

Grodzicki, M.J., & Geodecki, T. (2016). New dimensions of core-periphery relations in an economically integrated Europe: The role of global value chains. *Eastern European Economics*, *54*(5), pp. 377–404.

Hardy, J. (1998). Cathedrals in the desert? Transnationals, corporate strategy and locality in Wrocław. *Regional Studies*, *32*(7), pp. 639–652.

Hardy, J., Sass, M., & Fifekova, M. (2011). Impacts of horizontal and vertical foreign investment in business services: The experience of Hungary, Slovakia and the Czech Republic. *European Urban and Regional Studies*, *18*(4), pp. 427–443.

Hirschman, A.O. (1958). *The Strategy of economic Development*. New Haven: Yale University Press.

IMF. (2013). *German-Central European Supply Chain – Cluster Report*. IMF Country Report No. 13/263, August.

Kalecki, M., & Sachs, I. (1966). Forms of foreign aid: An economic analysis. *Social Science Information*, *5*(1), pp. 21–44.

Koopman, R., Powers, W., Wang, Z., & Wei, S.-J. (2010). *Give Credit Where Credit is Due: Tracing Value Added in Global Production Chains*. Working Paper, No. 16426. National Bureau of Economic Research.

Micek, G., Działek, J., & Górecki, J. (2010). *Centra usług w Krakowie i ich relacje z otoczeniem lokalnym*. Kraków: Wydawnictwo Uniwersytetu Jagiellońskiego.

Milberg, W., & Winkler, D. (2013). *Outsourcing Economics: Global Value Chains in Capitalist Development*. Cambridge: Cambridge University Press.

Mittelman, J.H. (1995). Rethinking the international division of labour in the context of globalisation. *Third World Quarterly*, *16*(2), pp. 273–296.

Nölke, A., & Vliegenthart, A. (2009). Enlarging the varieties of capitalism: The emergence of dependent market economies in East Central Europe. *World Politics*, *61*(4), pp. 670–702.

OECD. (2013). *Interconnected Economies: Benefiting from Global Value Chains*. Paris: OECD Publishing.

Sass, M., Gál, Z., & Juhász, B. (2018). The impact of FDI on host countries: The analysis of selected service industries in the Visegrad countries. *Post-Communist Economies*, *30*(1), pp. 1–23.

Strange, R., & Magnani, G. (2018). Outsourcing, offshoring and the global factory. In G. Cook, J. Johns, F. McDonald, J. Beaverstock, & N. Pandit (Eds.), *The Routledge Companion to the Geography of International Business*. London: Routledge, pp. 60–77.

Timmer, M.P., Dietzenbacher, E., Los, B., Stehrer, R., & de Vries, G.J. (2015). An illustrated user guide to the world input–output database: The case of global automotive production. *Review of International Economics*, *23*(3), pp. 575–605. https://doi.org/10.1111/roie.12178.

Timmer, M.P., Los, B., Stehrer, R., & de Vries, G.J. (2013). Fragmentation, incomes and jobs: An analysis of European competitiveness. *Economic Policy*, *28*(76), pp. 613–661.

Vashistha, A., Operti, F., Hallard, K., Jones, R.Y.K., Gallant, W., Tiura, D., Ghosh, D., De Luzuriaga, J., Barrett, M., Wrobel, A., Vashistha, G., & Rajesh, A. (Eds.). (2019). *Tholons Services Globalization Index 2019: Innovation at Scale; Digital Nations & Super Cities*. New York: Tholons.

Part II

Dimensions of embeddedness in the outsourcing, offshoring, and global business services sector

International case studies

7 Bratislava

The development and specific features of outsourcing, offshoring, and the global business services sector

Miroslav Šipikal and Oliver Rafaj

The historical context of GBS development

After the fall of the Iron Curtain, the countries of Central Europe underwent a major economic transformation from centrally planned economies to market ones. These changes have also brought about a significant internationalisation and reintegration into the global economy and, subsequently, into the European Union structures. Especially for the neighbouring countries, such as Germany and Austria, the conditions for investing in this region became very favourable due to its geographical proximity and a good working knowledge of German amongst the local populace. This led to a considerable growth in outsourcing and offshoring from these countries. An average of about 45% of German investment to Eastern Europe represents offshoring from German firms. It decidedly predominates among German investment in the Czech Republic, Bulgaria, and Slovakia (Marin, 2006).

The inflow of global business services (GBS) investment into Slovakia can be divided into two distinct phases. In the early 1990s, horizontal demand-led investments prevailed. Firms primarily sought to take advantage of the new geopolitical situation, new markets, and the advantage of low-cost labour. From the beginning of the 21st century, foreign direct investment (FDI) in the business services sector came to be dominated by vertical investment, when companies began to offshore specific services, such as back office, customer care, or information technology (IT) support. This second stage of investment was much larger in terms of volume and number of firms as compared to the first stage (Hardy et al., 2011).

The second stage was also supported by the launch of investment incentives specifically addressed to strategic services centres in 2005. A strategic services centre (SSC) is defined as a place where the beneficiary provides high value-added services supporting the employment of qualified experts in computer development centres, expert solution centres, centres for the preparation of modified high-tech technologies, and customer support, which mainly deal with such areas as finance, procurement, IT, human resources, and customer care. At least 60% of a SSC staff must have university education (Michalová & Macková, 2015). A total of 10 companies took advantage of these incentives. Another impetus was provided by the adoption of the euro by Slovakia in 2009. This move reduced transaction costs associated with the provision of services to customers from other euro area countries and, at the same time, marked a significant difference from the other Visegrad (V4) countries, which decided to keep their own currencies. However, in both phases, Slovakia lagged behind in terms of both the absolute and relative service sector of FDI inflows and attracted the least amount of high value-added investment among the V4 countries (Sass & Fifekova, 2011; Myszkowska, 2014).

The metropolitan regions of the V4 countries also underwent significant changes. Bratislava gradually shifted away from industrial production towards the service sector. In terms of GDP per capita in PPS, the region reached more than 175% of the EU average as compared with the below-average values at the outset of the transformation (Eurostat). At the same time, these metropolitan cities became gateway cities by attracting a significant number of multinational corporations, which either decided to locate their regional headquarters responsible for business operations in the entire CEE region (Gál, 2015) or established their service centres for their own intracompany services.

As compared to other metropolitan regions of Central and Eastern Europe, Bratislava had a less favourable position in attracting GBS investment, which was due to several factors. Firstly, Bratislava was not the capital after the regime change. Shortly after the Velvet Revolution in 1989, discussions began on the division of Czechoslovakia into the Czech and Slovak Republics. Subsequently, on 1 January 1993, the Slovak Republic was established. Until then, Bratislava had not benefited from the traditional advantages associated with capital inflows. The second disadvantage was the size of the city – Bratislava had fewer than half a million inhabitants, significantly less than the metropolitan regions of Prague, Budapest, or Warsaw.

On the other hand, Bratislava had a number of advantages, typical of the entire Central Europe, compared to global competition for GBS investment, foremost among them being the very low-cost and highly skilled workforce, including foreign language skills (Gál, 2015). Bratislava is located close to Vienna, which has a host of other advantages, one of them being much better access to the world via its international Schwechat airport; and the other, the opportunity to take advantage of Vienna as a place of residence for high-ranking expats or the availability of skilled labour. These advantages were sufficient to create the first offshoring or outsourcing centres in Bratislava. The first ones were established mainly by firms from German-speaking countries or designated to serve the German-speaking market. The Henkel Centre was established in 1991, followed by Siemens and BASF in 1993. Most centres started with only a single activity, but gradually established themselves as important regional hubs of business services. For example, Dell began its operations in Slovakia in January 2003 as a sales and support centre for its German-speaking customers. Subsequently, it was transformed into a European business centre, which gradually evolved into a financial centre for the entire EMEA region (Europe, Middle East, and Africa). In the space of 15 years, it grew into a centre providing a wide range of global services in IT, finance, marketing, sales, and technical and business operations support. In fact, it represents a typical example of GBS development in Slovakia.

Characteristics of the sector

At present, more than 40 international companies operate in the field of business services outsourcing and offshoring. The first companies arrived in the early 1990s, when Henkel Slovakia, Siemens, Johnson Controls, and SIA Central Europe established their centres in Bratislava. In the second half of the 1990s, they began to invest in other regions of Slovakia. For example, Danfoss Power Solutions was founded in 1995 in the Trenčín Region; in 1996, the Uniqa Group Service Centre was established in the Nitra Region; in 1997, Embraco was founded in the Košice Region; and in 1998, ON Semiconductor Slovakia was established in the Trnava Region. At the time, a number of these firms were not primarily oriented towards business services, but offshored services operated alongside industrial production.

In the early 2000s, 14 major international players in the GBS sector operated in Slovakia. Thanks to the above-mentioned favourable business conditions and Bratislava's attractive location, the second wave of investment arrived in the area. In subsequent years, other international companies, such as Accenture, IBM, and Dell established their subsidiaries in the region. By 2013, the number of companies increased by 15. Soitron, Lenovo, PricewaterhouseCoopers, and Deutsche Telekom Services in Bratislava, and T-System and Lafarge Holcim European Business Services in Košice were among the most important ones. In recent years, they were joined by such well-known brands as Siemens Healthcare, Swiss Re Management, Lenovo Global Technology, and ING Business Shared Services in Bratislava, and Ledvance in the Nitra Region. GBS firms in Slovakia are strongly concentrated in Bratislava and represent over 65% of total employment. Moreover, firms operating in Slovakia's capital are larger and generate higher added value than those in the rest of the country: more than 70% of total revenues of the sector and more than 75% of total value added are created centrally. Table 7.1

Table 7.1 Slovakia's top 10 GBS firms

Name	*Location*	*Year established*	*No. of employees*
IBM International Services Centre s.r.o.	Bratislava	2003	4941
T-Systems Slovakia s.r.o.	Košice	2006	3853
AT&T Global Network Service	Bratislava	1999	3800
Dell s.r.o.	Bratislava	2002	2328
DXC Technology	Bratislava	2000	1996
JOHNSON CONTROLS INTERNATIONAL spol. s r.o.	Bratislava	1993	1613
HENKEL SLOVENSKO, spol. s r.o.	Bratislava	1991	1510
Accenture Technology Solutions	Bratislava	2003	1055
Siemens s.r.o.	Bratislava	1993	1006
Adient Slovakia	Bratislava	2016	880

Source: Compiled by authors based on data from *Trend* (17/2019).

shows the basic data for 10 largest GBS firms in Slovakia, which confirms the dominance of Bratislava. Only one firm from this list operates in Košice, Slovakia's second largest city.

Although the sector constitutes a more important part of the economy in the Bratislava region than in the entire Slovakia, its share is smaller in comparison with other metropolitan regions in the V4 countries. This is also due to the impact of foreign investment in manufacturing in the region. The final accounts of companies (FinStat, 2016) show that the GBS sector accounts for 7% of the total value added generated by all firms in Slovakia. More than 5% of total value added is generated by GBS firms located in Bratislava. In terms of total sales, this sector accounts for 2.5% of total sales generated by firms in Slovakia, while GBS firms in Bratislava account for 1.75% of total sales.

Figure 7.1 shows the growth in total sales in the GBS sector[1] in millions of euros. From 2009 to 2015, the total sales in the sector posted a slight growth. Conversely, in 2016, firms located in Bratislava reported lower sales than in the previous year. From the point of view of sales in other regions of Slovakia, the figures show that total sales increased during the whole period under review. Part of the growth, however, was due to the arrival of new firms. The sharp growth at the beginning of the new millennium thus significantly slowed down.

The data on the development of the sector's added value (Figure 7.2) show that it grew throughout the period under review both in Bratislava and in other regions of Slovakia. The economic importance of Bratislava in this respect also results from its increasing share in the total value added generated by the GBS sector. While in 2009 approximately 60% of its total added value was generated in the capital, in 2016 the city's share exceeded 75%. More importantly, added value grew more robustly than sales, which suggests an ongoing streamlining process taking place in existing firms and their good competitive position.

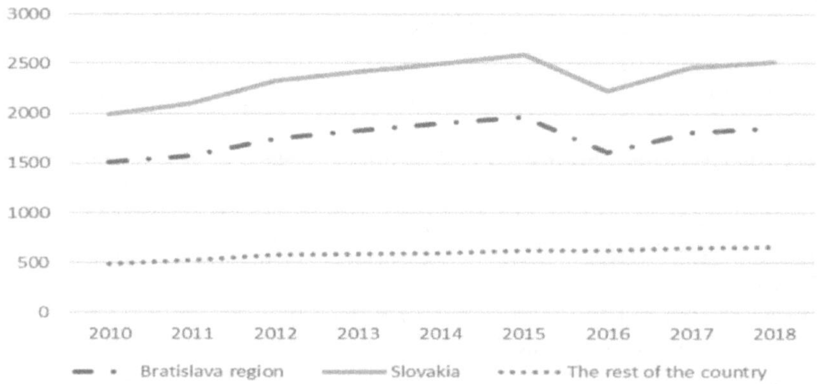

Figure 7.1 Total sales of GBS firms in Slovakia (in millions of euros)

Source: Own study based on data from FinStat.

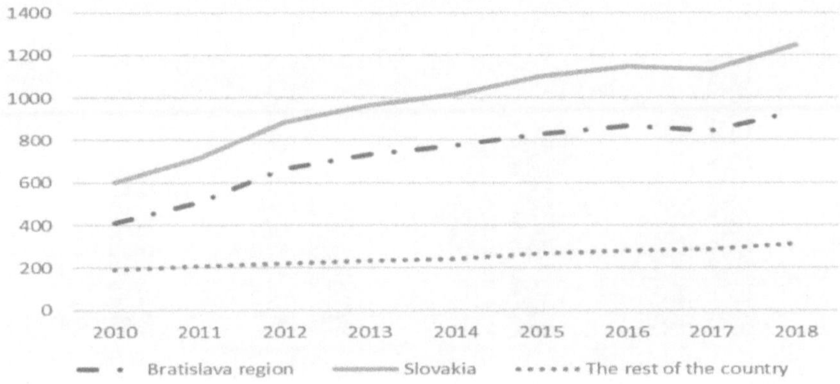

Figure 7.2 Growth in value added in Slovak GBS (in millions of euros)

Source: Own study based on data from FinStat.

The added value generated by the sector increased at an even faster pace than did employment. However, employment growth in the sector is considerably slowing down. In total, more than 30,000 employees worked for GBS firms, 7,000 more than five years ago. At the same time, the growth of employment is mostly due to the arrival of new enterprises. This may also be partly due to the emerging labour shortage, which certainly affects the plans of firms to expand service provision.

In terms of the composition of the sector, recent years have seen a gradual change in its makeup. In 2009, companies providing IT services (36%) predominated, followed by customer services (25%), and various support services in specific industries (21%), whereas the rest comprised financial services and accounting firms (18%). Fewer than 10 years later, the structure of the market changed. IT services firms (30%) were the largest, followed by financial services and accounting (25%), and customer services (25%). The remaining 20% includes firms providing services to specific industries. This comparison is presented in Figure 7.3. The growth in the share of financial and accounting services was mainly due to the arrival of new firms, such as LafargeHolcim European Business Services in Košice, Ledvance in Nitra, or ING Business Shared Services and Covestro (Slovakia) Services in Bratislava. This change was mainly due to the reduced availability of skilled labour, which was first noted in IT-related professions. The impact of this factor on the development of the sector will be discussed later in this chapter.

In terms of geographical coverage, all Slovak GBS firms provide services to other European countries. Moreover, 59% of them also serve North America, 45% Africa, 41% Middle East, 32% South America, and 32% Asia and the Pacific (MH SR, 2016).

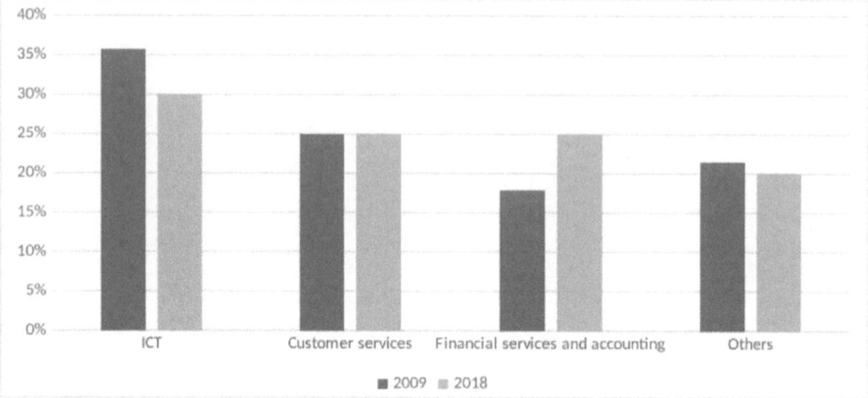

Figure 7.3 GBS industry composition as share of firms in specific sub-industries (in %)
Source: Own study based on data from *Trend* and FinStat.

Prospects and challenges

Despite the constant expansion, the representatives of the global business centres themselves agree that the growth heyday for this sector in Bratislava is long gone (Nejedlý, 2019b). What is most likely to happen in the near future is slower growth. According to a survey conducted by the Corporate Service Centres Forum (an organisation representing employers in the area), most of its members anticipate a modest annual growth rate of 5–10% in the future, but only a third revealed that they consider departing from Slovakia as one of the possible scenarios (Nejedlý, 2019a). Several key factors needed to support development in this sector on a regional scale at best remain stagnant. As a result, the position of Bratislava as an outsourcing or offshoring target is gradually deteriorating. For example, Bratislava ranked 49th in the Tholons Services Globalization Index (Tholons, 2019) in 2007, but slipped to 79th place in 2018, with all its major competitors in CEE doing significantly better (Prague, Budapest, and Warsaw were ranked in the top 25). Likewise, Slovakia's attractiveness for business services appears to be decreasing. According to the Global Services Location Index compiled by Kearney (Kearney, 2019), Slovakia ranked 35th, the lowest of its direct competitors, such as the V4, the Baltic countries, or Bulgaria and Romania. Compared to 2007, when it ranked 12th, this represents a significant drop. Slovakia scored lowest on the labour force indicator.

Apart from the long-term factors, such as the considerably smaller size of Bratislava compared to other metropolitan cities in CEE and thus the smaller pool of suitably qualified labour, three key factors currently affect the sector in Slovakia, namely the deployment of 4.0 technologies, labour market development, and the quality of the business environment and government support activities.

4.0 technologies

The introduction of 4.0 technologies, particularly digitalization, and the use of artificial intelligence in service delivery processes has been an important factor in the last decade with the potential to affect the entire business model as well as the distribution of GBS. This development can also be perceived in Slovakia. The process did not start in recent years; for example, in 2005, the IBM International Service Centre automated and digitalized its invoice accounting, which had previously been done manually. At present, multiple automated processes are handled by the centre, including the conversion of old Lotus Notes databases to cloud-based web applications, finance dashboards, IT network security risk assessment portals, or earning release reports for their services units. So far, over 28,000 hours of work have been automated on an annual basis (Liptáková, 2020).

Currently, on average, a third of the processes in these companies are automated. Basic areas include accounting automation, chatbots, or analysis programs used to predict supply chain disturbances (Nejedlý, 2019a). Process automation removes the monotony of repetitive transactional activities, speeds up data processing, and increases the quality of outputs. It enables companies to reassign the labour thus freed up to activities with higher added value (Liptáková, 2020). The BSCF survey (Liptáková, 2020) confirms the strengthening automation trend in Slovakia's business service centers (BSCs). As many as 30% of the surveyed centres plan to automate more than 20% of their key processes or functions in the next two to three years; 27% of BSCs plan to automate 10–20% of such processes.

4.0 technologies primarily benefit more advanced economies with a highly skilled workforce. Conversely, low-cost countries are losing jobs due to increased automation in the sector. New jobs that require higher skills are being created in certain, usually more developed, countries in order to manage the demands resulting from automation (Kearney, 2019). These developments thus make the appropriately skilled workforce even more critical to the success of GBS.

Workforce

A key factor for the functioning of GBS is the availability of skilled labour. In the early phases of GBS inflow to Bratislava, it represented the most significant competitive advantage (Hardy et al., 2011; Gál, 2015). The labour force was well qualified, fluent in foreign languages, and inexpensive in comparison with Western Europe. This fully satisfied the needs of the GBS firms at a time when a good command of at least one foreign language (English in particular) was a prerequisite for all jobs, except perhaps some back-office activities (Hardy et al., 2011). These criteria were met mainly by young university-educated people; hence the mean age of workers was very low. Those people were enthusiastic and willing to work very hard, as they mostly had no family commitments. GBS firms were able to offer very competitive wages; no wonder that they were often able to recruit the best candidates available in the region. The recruitment procedure was extremely selective with assessments and interviews taking up several days. Fewer than 10% of applicants were successful and turnover was extremely low (Hardy et al., 2011).

Once Slovakia's economic performance improved, this particular advantage gradually began to wane. The availability of labour itself became the primary problem. According to the statistics held by the Slovak Centre for Labour, Social Affairs and Family (www.upsvar.sk), while at the beginning of the second wave of GBS inflow in 2000, unemployment in the Bratislava Region was over 6%, in January 2010, it dropped to 4.4% and in January 2020, it fell further to only 2.84%. An even more significant difference can be seen throughout Slovakia, from where Bratislava drew a considerable part of its workforce thanks to the availability of convenient commuting services. In 2000, the average unemployment rate in provincial Slovakia was 18.6%; in 2010 it fell to 12.66%, whereas in 2020, it was only 5.8%.

The demographics and developments in higher education also contributed to the situation. The worsening demographic trend characterised by a lower absolute number of people entering the labour market each year, combined with the fact that a significant proportion of young people went to study abroad, led to a sharp drop in the number of university graduates. According to official data compiled by the Slovak Centre for Scientific and Technical Information (www.ctvisr.sk), in the first phase of new GBS investment in 2003, there were 17,686 graduates, more than half of whom lived in the Bratislava region. Moreover, there was a prospect of steady growth in the number of university graduates due to a gradual increase in university education across the population. In 2010, there were 41,843 graduates. The last decade, however, has seen an inverse trend: in 2019, the number of graduates declined to 29,250, of whom just over a third live in the Bratislava region. The increased market competition for the required skills forced firms to increase wages, invest more in the education and training of employees, and offer more benefits (Hardy et al., 2011). Naturally, as consequence, the number of university graduates employed dropped, which was accompanied by an increase in the number of qualified candidates with secondary education. The proportion of employees with university degrees in GBS centres decreased from 82% in 2014 to 71% in 2018 (Nejedlý, 2019a). Deteriorating trends can also be noticed in language skills. A survey of graduates (Horný & Ďurina, 2014) revealed that the greatest discrepancy between what employers expect and the level of proficiency acquired at school occurs in language skills. This trend is also confirmed by a CEO of the largest GBS in Slovakia (Nejedlý, 2019b), although he does not consider it to be a major problem for the functioning of his company.

The shortage of labour and the positive economic developments were also reflected in the increased wages in the region. Specifically, since 2016, Slovakia has experienced a significant annual percentage increase in employee costs compared to Western European countries (Morvay et al., 2019). These costs were not fully offset by labour productivity growth, which contributed to the slight loss of Slovakia's competitive edge.

This is partly due to the stronger pro-trade-union policy in Slovakia in recent years. Trade unions also began to be founded in Slovakia's GBS firms, which was not conducive to their competitive position.

> If you have a shortage of people in the market, high turnover, additional costs caused by unpredictable changes in laws, and unions arise in your company, you logically do not say at the headquarters that you want a new project that can bring hundreds of new jobs.
>
> (Kvašňák, 2018)

Moreover, trade unions put an extra administrative burden on host firms, since as soon as a trade union begins to operate, the latter must completely review and possibly re-set internal processes for employees.

Due to this development, Bratislava ceased to be attractive to new GBS firms and no large new centres have been established in recent years. Instead, smaller centres began to emerge in provincial cities across the Slovak Republic, where the shortage of available labour is not so acute and the wage demands are lower. Having said that, the existing centres are still very efficient within their company structures thanks to the use of 4.0 technologies, no new competition is arriving in the region, and so far, GBS firms are not planning to leave Bratislava. This is also due to the fact that the average age of the labour force is very low compared to similar centres abroad, which is due to the recruitment of a large number of fresh university graduates with language skills when these firms first arrived in Slovakia.

The business environment

The last area that significantly affects the operation of GBS centres is the very quality of their business environment. In this respect, certain negative developments have occurred in Slovakia in recent years. In 2018, the Business Environment Index, which is compiled annually by the Slovak Entrepreneurs' Alliance, fell to its lowest reading since it was launched in 2001. It shows two clearly distinct development phases. The first one is marked by a gradual increase from 2001 to 2007, which approximately corresponds with the second wave of GBS inflow to Slovakia. After 2007, the index declined every year from 124 to 40 points (aliancia.pas.sk). The index is based on entrepreneurs' opinions concerning the key aspects of doing business, which include corruption, law enforcement, the condition of the judiciary, infrastructure, legislation, and taxes. A similar ranking of global competitiveness by the World Economic Forum put Slovakia in 42nd place, with the lowest scores in such areas as the quality of institutions, innovation capacity, and labour market – all very important aspects for GBS. In the V4, Slovakia came third behind the Czech Republic and Poland (WEF, 2019). From the perspective of GBS firms, negative developments include the high tax burden on labour and legislative changes resulting in increased staff-related costs for employers (e.g. the obligation to provide employees with leisure vouchers to be spent in Slovakia).

The above-mentioned problems were recognised by the Ministry of the Economy of the Slovak Republic, which prepared a strategy to foster the development of strategic service centres, subsequently approved by the Slovak Government (MH SR, 2016). The document identifies as the main issues the diminishing availability of labour with appropriate soft and hard skills, including the ability to communicate in several foreign languages; the discrepancies between school curricula and practice; high staff turnover and the resulting difficulty in retaining valuable manpower owing to increasing regional and global competition. The strategy proposes 21 measures to improve the attractiveness of Slovakia to GBS firms. In our opinion, however, most of these measures are likely to have a negligible impact on improving the functioning of the sector, even though a significant proportion of conceptual work was directed to finding workable solutions (such as the plan to establish a comprehensive database of existing centres, or to attract skilled labour from outside the country both by encouraging Slovaks working abroad to return home and by opening doors to foreign workers). Apart from the above-mentioned factors, the capacity to provide external help to GBS centres is also limited by the limited spillover effects from the latter. Research shows little evidence of transfer of managerial knowledge and technology from foreign-owned to domestic firms. In other words, learning and knowledge acquisition appear to have been taking place within a closed circuit, with virtually no leakages (Hardy et al., 2011). Still, most proposed measures are only just being phased in. Hence, their impact on Slovakia's capacity to attract GBS investment or promote the development of the sector cannot yet be reliably assessed.

Note

1 The GBS sector cannot be accurately identified by its selected NACE code, which subsumes only firms in a specific sector. Therefore, no official statistics are available. For this reason, the data in the analysis is a compilation of individual data on companies in this sector, which were identified by a specialized magazine *Trend* and the Business Service Centre Forum, an organisation whose membership includes companies in this sector operating in Slovakia. Thus, the data may underrepresent the actual development of the sector, as some smaller firms may not have been captured.

References

FinStat. (2016). *Database of Slovak Companies – FinStat 2016* [accessed from: www.finstat.sk].

Gál, Z. (2015). Development of international financial centres in Central and Eastern Europe during transition period and crisis. The case of Budapest. *Studia regionalne i lokalne*, *16*(60), pp. 53–80.

Hardy, J., Sass, M., & Fifekova, M.P. (2011). Impacts of horizontal and vertical foreign investment in business services: The experience of Hungary, Slovakia and the Czech Republic. *European Urban and Regional Studies*, *18*(4), pp. 427–443.

Horný, P., & Ďurina, J. (2014). *Prenositeľné kompetencie absolventov slovenských vysokých škôl*. Centrum vedeckotechnických informácií SR [accessed from: https://vysokoskolacidopraxe.cvtisr.sk/files/horny_durina_prenositelnekompetencie-absolventov-slovenskych-vs.pdf].

Kearney, A.T. (2019). *Global Services Location Index* [accessed from: www.kearney.com/digital-transformation/gsli/2019-full-report].

Kvašnák, L. (2018). IBM aj AT&T musia na Slovensku riešiť ďalší problém. *Odborárov Trend*, 50/2018.

Liptáková, J. (2020). Automation increases effectiveness of business service centres. *Slovak Spectator* [accessed from: https://spectator.sme.sk/c/22313599/automation-increases-effectiveness-of-business-service-centres.html].

Marin, D. (2006). A new international division of labor in Europe: Outsourcing and offshoring to Eastern Europe. *Journal of the European Economic Association*, *4*(2–3), pp. 612–622.

MH SR. (2016). *Koncepcia podpory podnikových služieb na Slovensku* [accessed from: www.mhsr.sk/uploads/files/cSmjK0ZS.pdf].

Michalová, V., & Macková, D. (2015). Offshoring a tvorba pracovných miest v sektore služieb, *Studia commercialia Bratislavensia*, *8*(32), pp. 592–608.

Morvay, K., Lábaj, M., Jeck, T., Hudcovský, M., Frank, K., & Dujava, D. (2019). *Economic Development of Slovakia in 2018 and Outlook up to 2020*. SAV, Bratislava.

Myszkowska, M. (2014). The scale and characteristics of services offshoring in the Visegrad countries. *Entrepreneurial Business and Economics Review*, *2*(3), pp. 33–46.

Nejedlý, T. (2019a). Po expanzii šetrenie a konsolidácia. Bizniscentrá na Slovensku vstupujú do novej éry. *Trend*, 17/2019.

Nejedlý, T. (2019b). Slovenko bola skvelá voľba, no vrchol už máme zrejme za sebou. *Trend*, 17/2019.

Sass, M., & Fifekova, M. (2011). Offshoring and outsourcing business services to Central and Eastern Europe: Some empirical and conceptual considerations. *European Planning Studies*, *19*(9), pp. 1593–1609.

Tholons. (2019). *Tholons Services Globalization Index* [accessed from: www.tholons.com/digitalnationsupercities/].

WEF. (2019). *The Global Competitiveness Report 2019*. Geneva, Switzerland [accessed from: www3.weforum.org/docs/WEF_TheGlobalCompetitivenessReport2019.pdf].

8 Budapest

The development and specific features of outsourcing, offshoring, and the global business services sector

Zoltán Gál and Robert Marciniak

Introduction: global business service hubs in CEE

A key feature of the second global shift is the relocation of a range of service functions from the USA and Europe to low-cost developing countries. The second global shift is part of a worldwide structural shift towards service-based foreign direct investment (FDI) and also as a new direction of managerial and localization strategy of corporations (Blinder, 2006; Bryson, 2007; Hardy, 2006). Supporting this, "fragmentation" and "trade in task" theorems developed by Jones and Kierzkowski (1990) and Grossman and Rossi-Hansberg (2008) examine the new role of services in international trade. Advances in this process have made it easier for companies to disaggregate their value chains around the globe, all the while maintaining management control over them, or to disperse service production among numerous supplier firms even in distant locations.

The rapid surge in globalisation, opening up of formerly isolated regions such as Eastern Europe, Russia, and China to global trade, has substantially boosted task trade and service-related cross-border investment. Many Eastern European countries invigorated by the EU enlargement became important locations for offshoring services. The relocation of service offshoring-related activities, such as outputs, value-added, employment, foreign direct investments, and exports in services has grown rapidly, particularly after 2000 in the new EU member states (NMS) in Central and Eastern Europe (CEE) (Czech Republic, Hungary, Poland, and Slovakia, though 'latecomers,' such as Romania and Bulgaria, have also begun to attract this kind of investment) (Gál & Sass, 2009).

The relocation of services also reflects the types and impacts of foreign direct investment (FDI) on business services within the Global Production Network (Gereffi & Fernandez-Stark, 2010). A bulk of research examines offshoring as a part of a worldwide structural shift towards service-based FDI (Gereffi et al., 2005; Bryson, 2007; Grote & Täube, 2006; Bevan & Estrin, 2004). Due to the problems with collecting data on business service investment, in recent studies, statistics are supplemented with qualitative research (Hardy, 2006; Fifekova & Hardy, 2010; Hardy et al., 2011, Capik & Drahokoupil, 2011).

In 2003, CEE with its $1 billion share in the global offshoring market (which is worth an estimated $40 billion) lagged far behind the more prominent locations (McKinsey, 2004). The share of Visegrad countries (V4) in the global business services FDI was less than 1% in 2008. Nevertheless, the share of CEE is rapidly growing. In 2003, only 5% of services-related global FDI projects were realised there, while in 2006, 22% of related FDI projects were undertaken in individual regions in these countries. However, the number of current projects in Western Europe exceeded the number of CEE-based projects – 1,600 and 220, respectively in 2009 (Sass, 2008; Gál & Sass, 2009).[1]

The position of Budapest/Hungary as a BPO hub

The second global shift and its associated boom started in 2000, when services-related FDI reached almost 60% of total FDI in the region by 2013. Since 2000, the share of services sector FDI in total FDI flows reached 70% in the Czech Republic, 55% in Hungary, 60% in Poland, and 40% in Slovakia. Overall, the tertiary sector received more than 60% of the foreign capital inflows into the V4 region (Sass et al., 2018).

Due to the scarcity of statistical data, we conducted an approximate comparative analysis based on foreign trade data, which serves as a kind of proxy, to examine the scale and sectoral characteristics of services offshoring (Gál, 2014). Based on this, we determined the weight and sectoral specialisations of individual countries, such as Hungary and specifically, Budapest. Gál (2014) measured the size of trade in offshorable services. Information and communication technology (ICT) services and other business services (OBS) can be regarded as potentially offshorable activities. Exports in services in NMS-6 have been expanding from a very low base of 63 billion euros by 2007 and 82 billion in 2012, which represents an almost fourfold increase on 1996. The share of NMS-6[2] in global service exports is still modest (2.4% in 2012). In absolute terms, Poland, the Czech Republic, and Hungary are the leaders in this field. The total value of offshorable services in the NMS-6 totalled 27.2 billion euros in 2012, and within this aggregate, business services overwhelmingly predominated (78% on average). In absolute terms, Poland is the largest trader (ca.10 billion euros) followed by Hungary (ca. 6 billion euros). The Czech Republic is similar in size to Hungary (Figure 8.1).

In terms of sectoral composition of service exports, in 2007, the dominance of other business services in Hungary (28% of total service exports) is outstanding compared to 17–19% in other V4 countries. ICT services predominated in the Czech Republic, whereas financial services have a larger share in Poland (Sass et al., 2018).

Sass et al. (2018) examined FDI stocks of the four subsectors in offshorable services, namely business services, financial services, telecommunications, and computer-related services. Their combined share exceeds 25% in the V4 countries in 2013. In Poland, it is more than 30%, whereas in Hungary it exceeds 47%.

Business and IT services contribute greatly to the overall value of services exports. The shares of these two services industries in total services exports grew

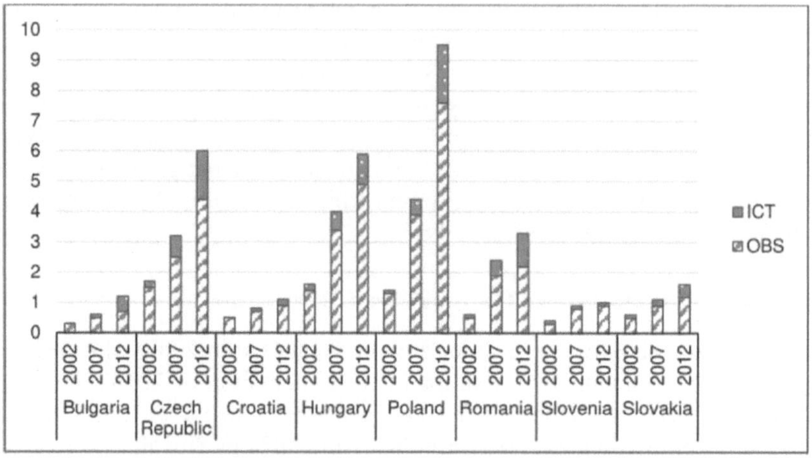

Figure 8.1 Exports of offshorable services and its sectoral composition in 2002 and 2012 (in billions of euros)

Source: Authors' calculations based on Eurostat BoP data and Gál (2014).

Notes: ICT = Information and Communication Technology Services; OBS= Other Business Services.

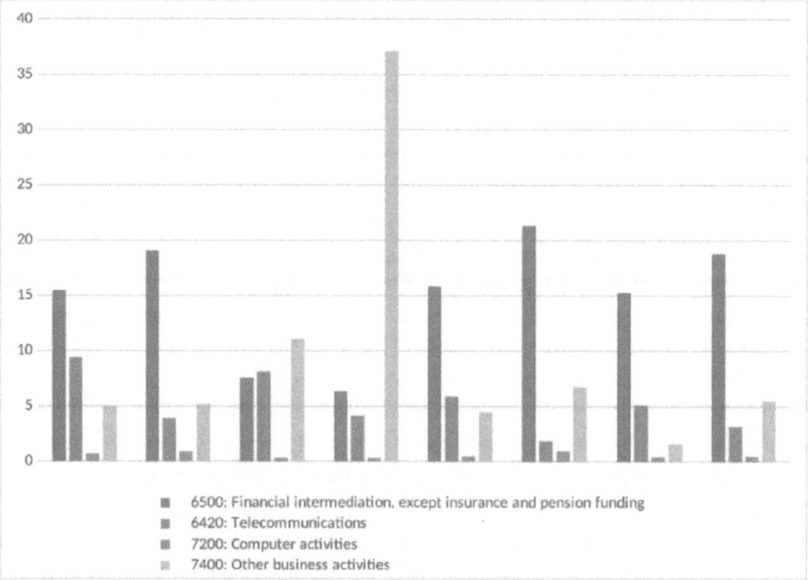

Figure 8.2 Share of the analysed services industries in total inward foreign direct investment (IFDI) stocks (%)

Source: Data compiled by the authors based on http://stats.oecd.org/Index.aspx?DatasetCode=FDI_POSITION_INDUSTRY (International Standard Industrial Classification of All Economic Activities (ISIC)).

between 2005 and 2013, whereas the shares of the other two services industries declined. The combined share of the four industries was the highest in Hungary (37%). Business services are by far the most export-oriented, with above 40% export/output ratios. Hungary stands out from the V4 with its export to output ratio at almost 90%. Computer and IT services follow, with at least 15% export to output ratio (Sass et al., 2018). Therefore, out of the four industries studied, other business services have the strongest export-generating effect in Hungary, followed by telecommunications services.

The development of Budapest as a GBS hub

The first business process outsourcing centre (HP, Accenture) in CEE opened in Budapest in 1991–92, but the real boom in the industry began with IBM opening its office in Budapest in 1997 and accelerated after the turn of the millennium. The first shared services centre (SSC) was opened in Warsaw in the same year. As a location, Budapest can be considered as the pioneer of the GBS sector in the region. During the first stage of service offshoring, captives[3] in the form of SSC were the main service providers, but later independent global vendors also opened new offshore outsourcing centres in Budapest to serve their European clients (Gál & Sass, 2009). The first upswing in SSC's founding boom lasted until the 2008 crisis (the SSC sector was concentrated in Budapest). In 2006 and 2007, 8–8 new centres were opened every year in the Hungarian capital.

Like Bratislava, Budapest boasted one of the highest geographical concentrations of GBS within its borders, which led to a number of adverse consequences such as higher costs, greater attrition, and relative labour shortages. In the mid-2000s, Hungary took part in the process of services outsourcing and offshoring (O&O) mainly as a host country; however, contrary to what is suggested by the media, Hungary's (and other NMS countries') share is smaller in the services outsourcing process, even if transactions within Europe are factored in. The majority of services (offshore) tend to be outsourced to developed countries, even as India (and to some extent China) are the new rising locations. In Europe, Ireland is traditionally the most important host country, with Great-Britain, Portugal, and Spain as important targets, but the largest projects tend to be outsourced to India, even from Europe (Sass, 2008; Gál & Sass, 2009).

A boom in services-sector FDI started in Hungary around 2001–2002, and since then its role has steadily increased, including its contribution to overall Hungarian economic performance. Hungary hosts 45–50 such projects, the figures being similar in Poland and the Czech Republic. After Hungary's accession to the European Union, the number of projects in GBS started to grow rapidly. In 2005, around 20,000 people worked for various service centres in Hungary; around 75% of total workforce was employed in Budapest, including the captive service centres.

Budapest proved to be especially attractive for this type of investment; in fact, it was among the first target cities in CEE. The main reasons were that this particular type of FDI needed a fairly advanced infrastructure, especially IT, and a skilled workforce. For European firms (overseas firms serving their European clients),

Table 8.1 SSCs in Hungary in 2008

Company	*Country*	*Location*	*Number of jobscreated (planned)*
ExxonMobil	USA	Budapest	1200
IBM ISSC	USA	Budapest	1300
Diageo	Great Britain	Budapest	600
Getronics	The Netherlands	Budapest	510
Jabil	USA	Szombathely	719
SAP	Germany	Budapest	600
Tata	India	Budapest	450
Convergys	USA	Budapest	282
EDS	USA	Budapest, Szeged	1150
InBev	Belgium	Budapest	380
Budapest Bank	USA	Békéscsaba	530
Morgan Stanley	Great Britain	Budapest	450
Citigroup	USA	Budapest	302
Vodafone	Great Britain	Budapest	746
T-Systems	Germany	Budapest, Debrecen	1750
British Telecom	Great Britain	Budapest, Debrecen	700
CEMEX	Mexikó	Budapest	330
Alcoa (Orkla)	USA (Norway)	Székesfehérvár	100
AVIS	USA/Great Britain	Budapest	300
SEI/Verety	USA	Debrecen	70
Sykes	USA	Budapest, Miskolc	700
Transcom	Sweden (Luxembourg)	Budapest	200?
Genpact	USA	Budapest	600
ING (2007closed)	The Netherlands	Budapest	?
HP	USA	Budapest	?
GM/Daewoo	USA, South Korea	Budaörs	?
Renault-Nissan	France/Japan	Győr	80
BAT	Great Britain/USA	Pécs	?
GE Lighting	USA	Budapest	30+
Lufthansa Systems	Germany	Budapest	100
Marsh	USA?	Budapest	50
National Instruments	USA	Debrecen	240
Microsoft (GTSC)	USA	Budapest	50
GEM	Great Britain (NI)	Debrecen	250
Celanese	USA	Budapest	150
Porsche	Germany	Budaörs	110

Source: Compiled by the authors based on Sass (2008).

cultural and language links also matter. Hungary's advantages over the other V4 countries included high FDI growth, the lowest average salary, which translated into the lowest labour costs for investors, and the best transport infrastructure (Grudowski & Muchlado, 2015). Budapest's growing importance as a business services centre is attested to by the fact that India's largest vendor firm, TATA, has set up its business process outsourcing (BPO) headquarters there, making it its only expansion centre located in CEE.

As regards the impact of the 2008 crisis, despite the initial decline in financial services, the vertical-type business services managed to maintain their strong export orientation, despite a slowdown in their export dynamics due to demand-side factors (Sass et al., 2018). SSCs were the only sector of the Hungarian economy that continued to perform strongly after the crisis. The industry created thousands of new jobs in Hungary since the first centres were established in the late 1990s. When PricewaterhouseCoopers (PwC) released its previous survey in 2013, the 80 SSCs operating in Hungary employed 35,000 people. According to the Hungarian Investment Promotion Agency (HIPA), the number of centres exceeded 100. Moreover, they employed 38,000 people in 2016 and 46,000 in 2018 (HIPA, 2018). In the last 10 years, the infrastructure of the country has significantly improved, and the real estate market has matured as new developments meet the specific requirements of tenants. Although fewer new services centres opened in the last few years, those already operating are continuously expanding in terms of occupied office space and the number of employees.

Characteristics of the Budapest GBS sector

For many years, the business services sector (BSS) has been one of the fastest growing segments of the Hungarian economy. After the early period, when most business process outsourcing (BPO) providers settled down in Hungary, the number of shared services centres (SSC) sharply increased and today the latter represent the majority of the market (Drótos et al., 2019; Marciniak, 2015). The umbrella term – business services centre (BSC) – includes BPOs, SSCs, and other service units, such as Centres of Excellence (CoE).

As regards the size of the BSS, Hungary topped the region's investment league tables for some time and then gradually slipped due to the competition on the part of larger markets and their potential labour pools. Now Hungary ranks third in CEE after Poland and the Czech Republic. For many years, Hungary has enjoyed a stable position in the top 30 of global service location selection rankings (Sethi et al., 2019; Vashistha et al., 2019). As a result, one of the most advanced service markets has developed in Hungary. Some of the BSCs operating there were merged or acquired, but very few have left the country. As a result, today 50% of the domestic market consists of over 11 year-old entities (Drótos et al., 2019). This represents a mature service market with the necessary expertise, human labour, supplier base, and office space to deliver the right level of service.

Certain locations, including Budapest (and also Cracow, Warsaw, and Prague) appeared to be close to capacity in terms of the kinds of jobs that were being relocated to or established in these markets. As a result, high staff attrition rates have been driving up the cost base.

Budapest is the most saturated amidst the V4 countries in terms of capital, which is partly due to its high concentration within the country. Despite this, Hungary's capital experienced the third largest new office space capacity growth between 2010 and 2013, following Warsaw and Cracow.

When we consider the size of the O&O sector in each city, relative to the operational cost of doing business and the size of its talent pool, it is clear that the expansion of the industry within the region is not cost-driven. Budapest's costs base was the highest in the region after Warsaw. In terms of the ease of doing business, as well as regulatory and institutional stability, the capitals of the region are much closer to the OECD average than their competitors in other emerging regions. However, in terms of this indicator, Warsaw and Bratislava also overtook Budapest by a few places in 2013.

The BSS is a continuously growing and fairly crisis-resilient sector of the Hungarian economy. According to our market analysis conducted in the late 2019, ca. 150 BSCs were in operation in Hungary. These centres are primarily affiliates of international corporations and employ approximately 67,000 mostly multilingual graduates. Fourteen of the Hungarian service centres employed more than 1,000 staff in 2019; 25% of them employed over 500, and another 15% about 400 staff. Over the last decade, the sector has created an average of 3,000 jobs annually (Juhász, 2019). It made the business services sector not only one of the fastest-growing segments of the Hungarian economy in the last decade, but also one of the most important labour markets for graduates (Drótos et al., 2019).

The constant growth of BSS is important for the Hungarian economy due to several economic multiplier effects. Although the integration and embeddedness of BSS in the CEE countries' economy are generally not as high as in the automotive industry, BSCs offer above-average wages in those countries. The greatest impact on the host economy occurs through taxes on labour (personal income tax) and the effects of spending by well-paid employees on a variety of services (food, drinks, transportation, accommodation, health, culture, and sports). The high number of BSCs positively affects the commercial real estate market as well (Kislovska & Tamošiūnienė, 2016).

According to the HOA-HIPA survey in 2019, 75% of BSCs expected further growth and a further 14% planned to open new service units in Hungary in the next 2–3 years (Drótos et al., 2019). As was the case in the past, the first sites are typically established in Budapest to be followed by other locations outside the capital.

Hungarian centres follow international trends with a slight lag mainly because they typically operate as subsidiaries of large international companies. That is where the transformation of centres into multifunctional, multi-location, and multi-sourcing units takes place. For the past 20 years, former single-function centres have extended their service portfolio and become multifunctional, while initially almost exclusively low-value-added activities have been increasingly complemented and superseded by more complex, knowledge-based higher value-added work (Marciniak, 2016; Drótos et al., 2019). Based on Deloitte's research, the proportion of multifunctional centres exceeded 60% already in 2015 (Juhász, 2019).

Today, half of the centres still provide purely lower value-added transactional services, but 80% of executives across the entire market plan to deploy more advanced services (Drótos et al., 2019). Companies gradually expand their operations by adding new, high value-added activities. The workforce comprises mainly fresh graduates, mostly speakers of foreign languages. The sector has created hundreds of new jobs. Companies establish BSCs in Hungary to serve their subsidiaries or to provide outsourced services to other companies. Most Hungary-based regional BSCs offer finance, accounting, IT, customer service, HR, and other back-office activities. Besides conducting simple transactions, these centres carry out more complex activities with higher added value. In many cases, one half of the market has moved up the international value chain as a Centre of Excellence (CoE) (Marciniak, 2012).

As far as the impact on the host economy is concerned, it is not easy to find spill-over effects for services, since the latter tend to use little local supply. The main advantage of FDI in services is that young employees work in an international environment for a fairly good salary, take advantage of training opportunities, and pursue a career in the company. For many graduates, for whom finding a job is not that easy, these projects offer more or less suitable job opportunities. The principle that FDI attracts FDI is true even for these kinds of projects. Considerable impacts

Table 8.2 Activities carried out by Hungary-based BSCs

Back office	*Customer contact*	*Common corporate functions*	*Knowledge services and decision analysis*	*Research and development*
►►►*Increasingly complex transactions*►►►				
Transaction processing Document management Data entry Data processing	Call centres Telemarketing	HR Accounting Administrative services Financial services IT call centres Other IT services Quality management Cost planning Service delivery (after sales) Supply chain management	Program and project management Financial program management Integration engineering Analytical accounting services Business performance analysis Cost analysis	(Original) software development Mathematical modelling

Source: Compiled by the authors based on Gál and Sass (2009) and McKinsey Global Institute.

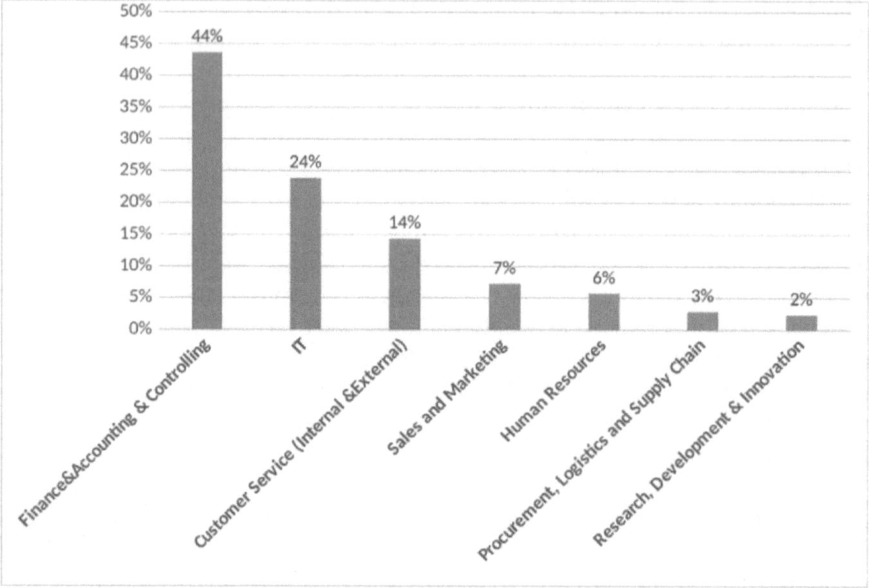

Figure 8.3 Services provided by Hungarian BSCs
Source: Compiled by the authors using the data from the HOA-HIPA survey (Drótos et al., 2019).

on other related branches are also visible, especially on real estate, telecommunication, infrastructure, etc., including those intended to improve the quality of the primary services.

In Hungary, BSCs utilise a high degree of standardisation and digitalisation by applying end-to-end (E2E) process control. The GBS model responsible for service processes has not only a regional appeal but is also integrated with global value chains. In 2019, 59% of the BSCs provided their services globally (Drótos et al., 2019).

Most service centres in Hungary have a US background, but there are also a fair number of British and German companies. Slightly more than half of the players are captive centres, i.e. they only provide services within their company group. Nearly one-third of the centres provide services internally and externally as well (hybrid centres). The proportion of these centres has steadily grown in recent years as the service centres' model of operation has matured. The share of the BPO centres, which initially predominated in the Hungarian market, is now only 17% (Drótos et al., 2019).

BSCs in Hungary deliver services primarily in the areas of finance and accounting and IT, but customer service, sales, marketing, HR, procurement and supply chain, and research and development and innovation (R&D&I) are also growing in importance. These service functions are typical in the whole CEE region, but their shares differ by country.

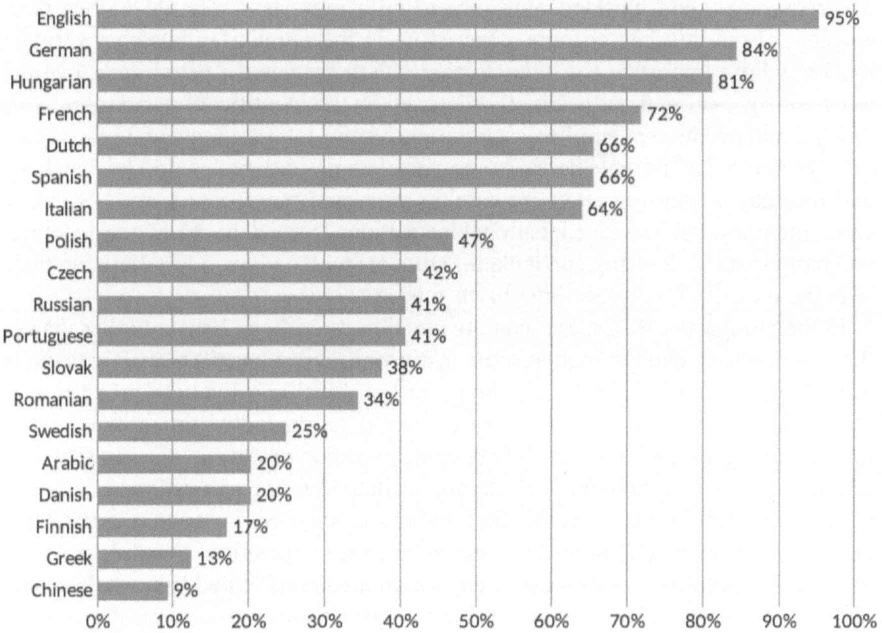

Figure 8.4 Languages supported by Hungarian BSCs

Source: Compiled by the authors based on the data from the HOA-HIPA survey (Drótos et al., 2019).

As one of the most important nearshore locations in the CEE region, Hungarian BSCs excel at providing multi-language services. On average, more than eight languages are spoken at an individual centre, and 41% of the responding units support at least 10 languages (Drótos et al., 2019). The largest number of languages used in a service unit exceeds 30. The most popular foreign languages in the Hungarian BSCs are English, German, French, Dutch, Spanish, and Italian, but the rarer and more 'exotic' languages (such as Chinese or Arabic) are steadily gaining share (Juhász, 2018).

In Hungarian services centres, 75% of the employees are highly qualified university graduates with an excellent command of several foreign languages. The average age of the workforce employed in those centres was close to 32 years in 2019, but in some smaller and more recently established units, it is as low as 23. These values are likely to increase as the segment matures and the complexity of the service portfolio increases (Drótos et al., 2019).

Recruitment is becoming more difficult owing to the international reach of the service centres and the requirement to speak at least two foreign languages. Moreover, the number of graduates in the Hungarian labour market has been decreasing for several years due to such factors as demographics, educational policy, and emigration. During the economic boom, the difficulties were compounded by fierce competition for qualified manpower as well.

For these reasons, screening for the right competencies during recruitment and retaining talent have become increasingly important. The development of employer branding has become a key issue in the Hungarian business services market, whose importance is likely to continue to grow in the near future. In order to ease the pressure, firms originally focussed on the identification and training up of loyal and productive employees, but now, on-the-job training and flexible work arrangements (e.g. flexible hours, home-based work, part-time work, teleworking, and four-day working weeks) are gaining more and more popularity. BSCs also enter into partnership with educational institutions in the delivery of guest lectures and participate in devising curricula for students with a view to familiarising them with the industry (Nagy-Stellini, 2018; Juhász, 2018).

In the Hungarian BSCs, the average attrition rate of ca. 20% is higher than in the other sectors, even though in some institutions it can be still higher, even up to 40% (Nagy-Stellini, 2018). The primary reason for this is the high proportion of transactional work done in BSCs. For the newly graduated in junior positions, an initially interesting job may quickly become monotonous and routine. In search of promotion and development, they do not hesitate to move to a different company or sector. Another problem is that for a long time, the BSCs used to recruit people mainly based on their command of foreign language to positions that did not necessarily correspond with their education, which also contributed to the subsequent high attrition rate. This phenomenon puts unrelenting pressure on the centres, which were hoping for a stable future growth. This shortage of labour leads to wage inflation in the context of already high wages, which is not conducive to the sector's international competitiveness or growth. The sector as a whole relies on high-intensity activities, with their staff costs ranging from 40–60% of the total

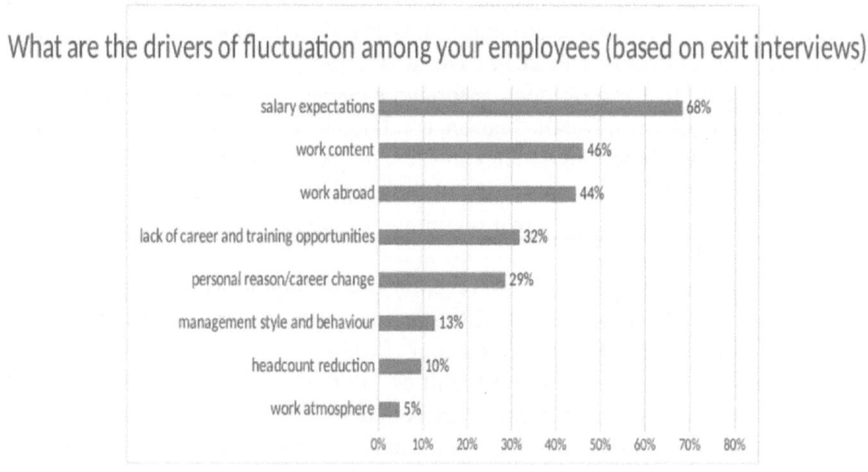

Figure 8.5 Reasons for the high voluntary attrition rate in Hungarian BSCs

Source: Compiled by the authors based on the data from the HOA-HIPA survey (Drótos et al., 2019).

operating costs (in some cases, the figures are still higher), which means that the human labour intensity in the sector is very high. For this reason, there is a noticeable and steadily accelerating trend to increase the proportion of foreign workers among the BSC staff, which now averages at 16%. Today, in some centres with about 2,000 employees, more than half of the workforce is Asian.

Belated decentralisation of the SSC sector in Hungary

In Hungary, 75% of the service centres and 80% of the employees are located in Budapest. The rest is mainly spread among larger regional centres like Debrecen, Székesfehérvár, Szeged, Pécs, and Miskolc. Unlike Poland, most investment is concentrated in the capital, which is due to the fact that the Hungarian government agency failed to redirect new investment to medium-sized cities in the early 2000s. While BPO was selected by the Polish and Czech investment promotion agencies as a priority, the Hungarian agency came under serious criticism on account of its marketing activity. As is the case in other areas in Hungary, Budapest dominates both the BPO and information technology outsourcing (ITO) sectors. Hungary lacks secondary cities of similar size to the Polish and Czech ones; moreover, there is no suitable office space available in its medium sized cities. In the early 2000s, firms did consider more provincial locations, but invariably returned to Budapest due to the lack of facilities to choose from. Alternative options to the costly Budapest tended to come across the border, such as Bucharest, Cluj-Napoca, or even Kyiv rather than Miskolc, Pécs, or Debrecen. Capital cities are the main hosts to BSCs, both vertical and horizontal ones, though there are a few vertical captive centres located close to the production sites, such as the US Alcoa, which established its financial operations centre in Székesfehérvár, or National Instruments' SSC in Debrecen. Budapest tends to be appreciated for higher-value work, while lower-level processing occurs in secondary locations that offer much lower costs and much lower attrition rates. It is understandable that demand-led horizontal investment tends to locate in the capital, where the demand for its services is highest. For supply-driven vertical investment, the main attracting factor in the capital is the large supply of appropriately qualified workers (Hardy et al., 2011; Gál, 2014). Vertical investment is more inclined to locate in smaller cities, especially if firms cannot recruit the required number of qualified staff in big cities.

Recently, 20–25% of SSCs located their operations outside the capital, mostly in larger cities with strong universities, such as Győr, Debrecen, Pécs, or Miskolc, which also possess outstanding logistics networks. Provincial university cities which can supply suitable graduates with language skills are prime candidates for this type of investment. After the crisis, local municipalities started to realize the importance of the SSC sector and are now actively looking for new investment as well as offering support to potential investors in their site selection process. The significance of locations outside Budapest will likely continue to grow in the next few years as the capital's labour market becomes more saturated and more favourable state incentive schemes are created. Overall, vertical business service investment has a more positive impact than the horizontal one, especially when

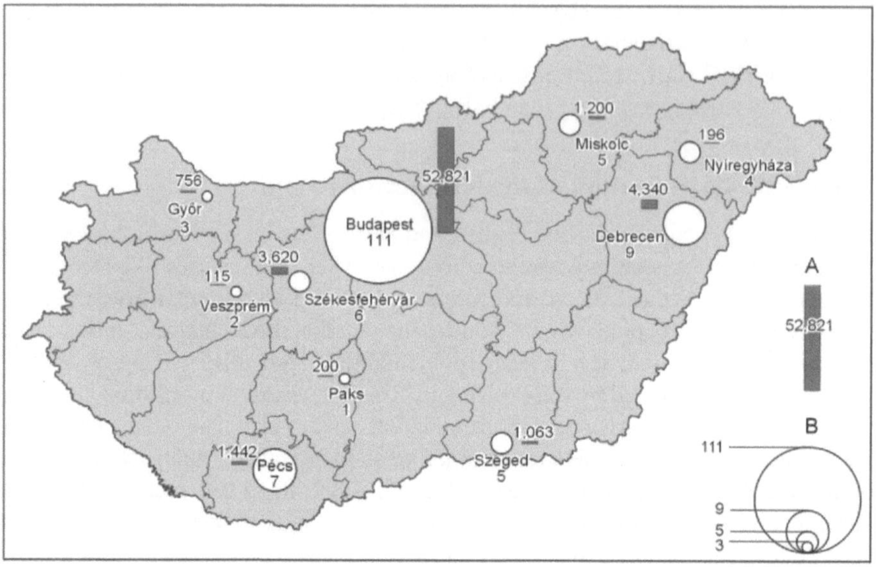

Figure 8.6 Geographical breakdown of BSCs in Hungary, 2019

Legend: A = No. of Employees
B = No. of BSC units

Source: Edited by the authors.

companies are forced to spread out to provincial cities as the capital runs out of suitable workers.

Prospects and challenges

The further growth potential of Hungarian BSCs should be analysed in several areas. The new wave of digitalisation and automation is likely to radically alter the present-day operation of service centres. The implementation of digital technologies will replace a substantial amount of human transactional work with software solutions (Marciniak & Berend, 2017; Marciniak, 2019). The manpower freed up from lower value-added tasks may help firms to develop new, more complex, and knowledge-based service operations. It may translate into a clear step up in the global value chains provided that service centres take advantage of the situation.

The principal regional cities in Hungary have a labour potential that could provide a reserve for BSCs' further growth. Admittedly, they may not be the first choice for service units, but they are likely to suffice as secondary satellite sites.

The huge wage inflation in the Hungarian economy may adversely affect the popularity of the local BSS, but the depreciation of its currency against the euro and the dollar helps to keep them competitive.

As the global value chains (GVCs) are becoming shorter globally, investors tend to relocate their service centres closer to the clients, with a preference for nearshore locations, such as Hungary. In this FDI contest, the Hungarian government needs to continually devise new investment promotion schemes.

The shortage of educated manpower in the last years has had a strong negative effect on the entire Hungarian labour market, but the BSCs find themselves in an even more difficult position since they need to recruit graduates fluent in foreign languages. The COVID-19 pandemic will certainly slow down the global economy, leading to layoffs in a number of sectors. Although it will negatively affect some of the BSCs as well, but in general, owing to the crisis-proof characteristic of the BSS, BSCs may use this as an opportunity to absorb this labour supply.

Crises and emergency situations like this also tend to highlight the importance of cybersecurity and uninterrupted provision of business services given the fact that BSCs are implementing more and more digital tools and solutions, with process control becoming more complex on account of multi-sourcing models.

Unlike high value-added financial and business services hosted by international financial centres (IFC), shared services centres are less embedded in their national and regional hinterlands. These supply- and efficiency-driven vertical investments across national boundaries are prospecting for low-cost global locations within global production systems. Another difference is that shared services centres involve low- and medium-value tasks and, as such, they do not have a strong institutional base. Moreover, their centres do not exercise control and command functions as is the case in the core financial institutions. Due to their low level of territorial embeddedness, the impact on their host location are limited. Factors of economic embeddedness linked to employment relations (tax payments, improvement of service culture) and real estate management (most important tenant in the high level office market) are determinative, and the sector's ratio in export and gross value added (GVA) output, as one driver of the digital economy in Hungary, are growing continuously. Project specific, R&D-related embeddedness factors (like service innovation and technology developments) are low, whereas institutional embeddedness focuses mostly on recruitment (e.g. cooperation with educational institutes) and participation in chambers and industry associations. Consequently, SSC locations in CEE are unlikely to naturally evolve towards IFCs due to the absence of the prerequisite geographical concentration of indigenous financial firms of international importance and the exercise of command and control functions by their headquarters (Gál, 2015).

Notes

1 Investors come from various countries: 41% of total business centres have been established by US companies, 45% by Western European, 3% by Indian ones, and 11% by others. The areas range from IT services (33%) to supply chain management (3%). Forty percent of these business services centres provide their services globally, 52% to selected regions, whereas only 8% to a single country (ABSL, 2015).

2 NMS-6 (6 new member states): Bulgaria, Croatia, Czech Republic, Hungary, Poland, and Romania.

3 Captive centres: wholly owned subsidiaries that provide services in the form of back-office activities to the parent company from an offshore location.

References

ABSL [Association of Business Service Leaders]. (2015). *Business Services in Central & Eastern Europe*. ABSL Report [accessed from: https://www.absl.cz/docs/CEE_report_final.pdf].

Bevan, A., & Estrin, S. (2004). The determinants of foreign direct investment into European transition economies. *Journal of Comparative Economics*, *32*(4), pp. 775–787.

Blinder, A. (2006). Offshoring: The next industrial revolution? *Foreign Affairs*, *85*(2), pp. 113–128.

Bryson, J. (2007). The second global shift: The offshoring or global sourcing of corporate services and the rise of distanciated emotional labour. *Geographiska Annaler, Series B. Human Geography*, *89B*(Supplement 1), pp. 31–43.

Capik, P., & Drahokoupil, J. (2011). Foreign direct investments in business services: Transforming the Visegrad four region into a knowledge-based economy? *European Planning Studies*, *19*(9), pp. 1611–1631.

Drótos, G., Marciniak, R., & Ránki-Kovács, R. (2019). *Business Services Hungary 2019: Report on the Hungarian Business Services Industry*. Budapest: Hungarian Investment Promotion Agency, Hungarian Service and Outsourcing Association.

Fifekova, M., & Hardy, J. (2010). *Business Service Foreign Direct Investment in Central and Eastern Europe: Trends, Motives and Impacts*. Brno: The Economy and Society Trust [accessed from: www.czechinvest.org/data/files/fdi-project-report-1981-en.pdf].

Gál, Z. (2014). Relocation of business services into Central and Eastern Europe: Evidence from trade and location statistics. *Romanian Review of Regional Studies*, *10*(1), pp. 67–78.

Gál, Z. (2015). Development of international financial centres in Central and Eastern Europe during transition period and crisis: The case of Budapest. *Regional and Local Studies/Studia Regionalne i Lokalne*, *2*(60), pp. 53–80.

Gál, Z., & Sass, M. (2009). Emerging new locations of business services: Offshoring in Central and Eastern Europe. *Regions Magazine*, *274*(1), pp. 18–22.

Gereffi, G., Humphrey, J, & Sturgeon, T. (2005). The governance of global value chains. *Review of International Political Economy*, *12*(1), pp. 78–104. https://doi.org/10.1080/09692290500049805.

Gereffi, G., & Fernandez-Stark, K. (Eds.). (2010). *The Offshore Services Global Value Chain*. Durham, NC: Center on Globalization, Governance & Competitiveness, Duke University.

Grossman, G., & Rossi-Hansberg, E. (2008). Trading tasks: A simple theory of offshoring. *American Economic Review*, *98*, pp. 1978–1997.

Grote, M., & Täube, F. (2006). Offshoring the financial services industry: Implications for the evolution of Indian IT clusters. *Environment and Planning*, 38, pp. 1287–1305.

Grudowski, P., & Muchlado, M. (2015). Offshoring and outsourcing in Visegrad countries: Advantages and disadvantages. *Research on Enterprise in Modern Economy – Theory and Practice*, *1*(1), pp. 5–18.

Hardy, J. (2006). Bending workplace institutions in transforming economies: Foreign investment in Poland. *Review of International Political Economy*, *13*(1), pp. 129–151.

Hardy, J., Sass, M., & Fifekova, M. (2011). Impacts of horizontal and vertical foreign investment in business services: The experience of Hungary, Slovakia and the Czech Republic. *European Urban and Regional Studies*, *18*(4), pp. 427–443.

Hungarian Investment Promotion Agency (HIPA). (2018). *Business Services Hungary 2018 Survey* [accessed from: https://hipa.hu/images/dokumentumok/hipa-hoa-business-services-hungary-2018-survey.pdf].

Jones, R.W., & Kierzkowski, H. (1900). The role of services in production and international trade: A theoretical framework. In R.W. Jones and A. Krueger (Eds.), *The Political Economy of International Trade*. Oxford: Basil Blackwell, pp. 31–48.

Juhász, K. (2018). A hazai ssc szektor humán erőforrás kérdései [Human resource issues in the domestic ssc sector]. *TAYLOR – Gazdálkodás- és szervezéstudományi folyóirat*, *X*(31), pp. 25–33.

Juhász, K. (2019). Merre tovább? – HR kérdések a hazai SSC szektorban [Where to next? – HR issues in the domestic SSC sector]. *TAYLOR – Gazdálkodás- és szervezéstudományi folyóirat*, *XI*(35), pp. 15–25.

Kislovska, K., & Tamošiūnienė, R. (2016). Economic multiplier effect of shared service centres. *Ekonomika a Management*, *2016*(4), pp. 1–10.

Marciniak, R. (2012). Center of Excellence as a next step for shared service center. *Journal of International Scientific Publication: Economy and Business*, *6*(3), pp. 230–238.

Marciniak, R. (2015). *Osztott szolgáltatások – egy innovatív szervezeti forma értékelése [Shared Services – Analysis of an Innovative Organizational Form]*. Miskolc: University of Miskolc.

Marciniak, R. (2016). Relocation of service function as a strategic tool of corporate operation. In D.B. László (Ed.), *Management Challenges in the 21st Century. Volume II: Further Challenges*. Saarbrücken: Lambert Academic Publishing, pp. 35–46.

Marciniak, R. (2019). *Digital Business Services Centre: As the Future State of Maturity*. Bor, Serbia: University of Belgrade.

Marciniak, R., & Berend, D. (2017). Disclosing RPA trend in the business services. In *Management Challenges in the 21th Century. Volume III*. Saarbrücken: LAP LAMBERT Academic Publishing, pp. 119–132.

McKinsey Global Institute. (2004). *Offshoring: Is It a Win-Win Game?* San Francisco, CA: McKinsey Global Institute [accessed from: www.mckinsey.com/knowledge/mgi/offshore].

Nagy-Stellini, T. (2018). *HAYS Salary Guide 2018*. Budapest: HAYS Hungary.

Sass, M. (2008). A szolgáltatások relokációja – európai folyamatok [Relocation of services – European processes]. *Európai Tükör*, *XIII*(évf. 7.-8. szám), pp. 85–100.

Sass, M., Gál, Z., & Juhász, B. (2018). The impact of FDI on host countries: The analysis of selected service industries in the Visegrad countries. *Post-Communist Economies*, *1*, pp. 1–23.

Sethi, A., Suman, V., & Gott, J. (2019). *Digital Resonance: The New Factor Impacting Location Attractiveness. The A.T. Kearney Global Services Location Index*. New York: A.T. Kearney.

Vashistha, A. et al. (2019). *Tholons Service Globalization Index 2019 – Innovation at Scale – Digital Nations & Super Cities*. New York: Tholons.

9 The development and specific features of outsourcing, offshoring, and knowledge intensive business services in the Czech Republic

The case of Prague and Brno

Stanislav Klazar, František Ochrana, Michal Plaček, and Gabriela Vaceková

Introduction

This chapter is structured as follows: first, we provide an overview of the development of industry in the Czech lands and the emergence of broadly defined business services (BS) and knowledge intensive business services (hereinafter referred to as KIBS) in the Czech Republic to briefly analyse the historical context of their evolution. Next, we focus on Prague and Brno to explore the selected characteristics of the sector (such as employment, structure, and relations with its external environment). Finally, we examine the challenges and prospects of outsourcing and offshoring KIBS in the Czech Republic.

Historical evolutionary overview of the development of industry in the Czech lands and the emergence of BS and KIBS in the Czech Republic

Before the establishment of Czechoslovakia, the territory of the current Czech and Slovak Republics had been a part of the Austro-Hungarian Monarchy, the second largest European state after Russia. Its economy developed outside the then mainstream colonial economies. From a global point of view, Austro-Hungary was a semi-peripheral state with its economic interests oriented towards Germany, the Balkans, and Eastern countries. Compared to the Western European countries, the Monarchy's industry was less developed and the accumulation of venture capital was slower (Urban, 2003).[1]

The Habsburg Monarchy was economically and ethnically heterogeneous (Mathias & Pollard, 1989). The Czech lands (i.e. the territory of the present-day Czech Republic) together with Lower Austria (the territory of the present-day federal state of Nieder Oesterreich) belonged among the industrial-agrarian centres of the Monarchy (Průcha, 1974). In the 1890s, the Czech lands produced about two-thirds of the total industrial output in Austria (Urban, 1991).[2] After the dissolution of the Austro-Hungarian Monarchy, one-fifth of its area, one-quarter of its population, and two-thirds of all the industry passed to Czechoslovakia. Within Czechoslovakia, industrial production concentrated in what is now the Czech Republic.[3]

The historical evolutionary trajectory of industrial production in the Czech lands was extremely adversely affected by the communist regime (1948–1989), which ushered in an era of centrally managed economy with an emphasis on heavy and defence industries.[4] At that time, the Czechoslovak economy developed extensively and, unlike the developed Western countries, did not detect or respond to the latest technological trends; as a result, it lost its former status of an industrially developed country.

The low labour productivity and the inability to flexibly respond to demand revealed the systemic failure of the centrally managed economy. The system started to fall apart in the 1980s. Its decline was completed with the political revolution in 1989. Czechoslovakia, previously separated from the Western world by the Iron Curtain, opened to the rest of the world. These events marked the restoration of capitalism and transformation to a market economy (1990–1992). Nationalised property was privatised in three stages: restitution, small privatisation, and large privatisation. As part of restitution, the nationalised property was returned to its original owners. Small privatisation involved retail and services facilities being auctioned off to private entities. Thus, the ‘class of sole traders’ was born, and the services sector began to take shape. Large privatisation applied to medium-sized and large businesses.[5] The goal was to bring the first private owners to formerly state-owned businesses. However, the legislative provisions for large privatisation proved to be inadequate, which opened the pathway to fraud and corruption.

A large majority of the former large state enterprises did not survive. Some of the originally Czech (Czechoslovak) automotive firms (located in Prague and Kopřivnice) and engineering plants (Brno) closed down. Others – mostly those that were taken over by foreign owners – now successfully compete on the international market (e.g. the car factory in Mladá Boleslav). From the point of view of the current trends in business services (BS) and KIBS, it can be hypothesised that this process of ‘trimming’ the previously heterogeneous industrial production ultimately proved to be favourable for the Czech Republic. This observation corresponds with the empirically documented development of countries that experienced a major political upheaval or economic crisis (e.g. Germany and Japan after the World War II), which subsequently enabled them to dictate new trends in industrial development (Olson, 1982).

Characteristics of the sector (employment, structure, and relations with the external environment)

Changes in the shares of individual sectors (by NACE classification) in total employment from 1993–2018 are illustrated in Figure 9.1.

Figure 9.1 shows a gradually declining share of manufacturing industry, which, however, remains predominant in the Czech Republic, and the growth of sectors generally considered to be related to BS and KIBS, namely information technology (IT), communication, professional services, scientific, engineering, administrative, and support activities. This trend confirms the global conclusions of the study on KIBS (Wirtz et al., 2015).

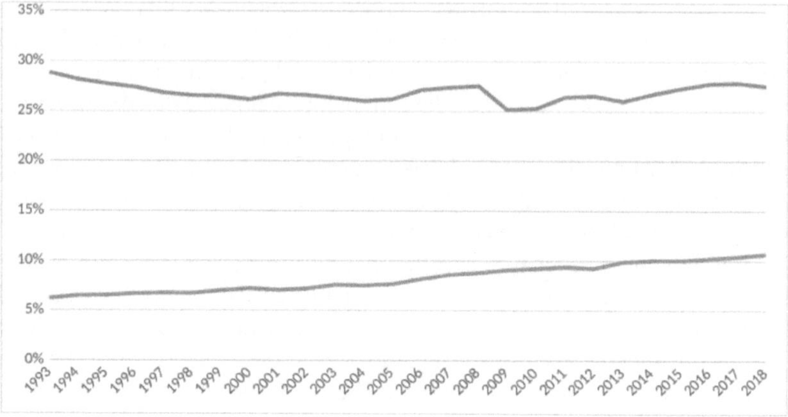

Figure 9.1 Change in employment shares in selected sectors

Source: Czech Statistical Office 2020.

*note: upper line – manufacturing industry; lower line – ICT.

These changes are also evidenced by the data on the value added generated by various sectors, with (G)BS historically ranked highest. According to Eurostat, BS include the following (Table 9.1):

Table 9.1 Gross value added of KIBS in the Czech Republic (year-on-year volume indices in %)

ID NACE Rev2	*Description*	*Mean (short run) 2013–2018*	*Mean (medium run) 2008–2018*	*Order (short run)*	*Order (medium run)*
TOTAL	Whole economy	102.85	101.72	x	x
N78	Employment activities	118.26	104.95	1	12
J631	Data processing, hosting and related activities, web portals	110.26	107.78	5	3
J582	Software publishing	109.13	105.32	7	10
J62	Computer programming, consultancy, and related activities	106.78	105.85	8	7
M69	Legal and accounting activities	103.85	101.06	28	43
M702	Management consultancy activities	103.71	105.13	31	11
M71	Architectural and engineering activities, technical testing and analysis	101.6	100.3	50	48
M731	Advertising and market research	99.6	99.57	65	56

Source: Czech Statistical Office – Database of National Accounts – gross value added. Online http://apl.czso.cz/pll/rocenka/rocenka.vysledek?mylang=EN&hl_text0=TB0001B1Gd

The highest value-added growth (calculated as the geometric mean for 2013–2018) was achieved in the '78 Employment activities' sector, followed by the '63 Information service activities' sector (ranked 5th), '58 Publishing activities', and '62 Information technology service activities' (ranked 7th and 8th, respectively, out of 89 monitored items). Slightly above average results were achieved in '69 Legal and accounting activities' (28th) and '70 Activities of head offices; management consultancy activities' (31st). '73 Advertising and market research' ranked distinctly below average (65th).

Wirtz et al. (2015) point to the problem with statistical data collated on the basis of NACE. For this reason, we have decided to supplement them with the data on Knowledge Intensive Services (KISA). Typical examples of KISA include research and development (R&D), management consulting, information and communications services, human resource management and employment services, legal services (including those related to intellectual property rights), accounting, financing, and marketing-related service activities. Figure 9.2 shows the development of the employment share in the KISA sector and in high-technology manufacturing, where the latest technologies are used to create state-of-the-art products.

This juxtaposition demonstrates that the KIBS sector plays a much more significant role in employment than is conveyed by the conventional NACE classification. Interestingly, a comparison with the high-technology manufacturing sector, which, according to the assumptions adopted by the proponents of the historical evolutionist approach should build on the Czech Republic's industrial tradition, reveals an opposite trend.

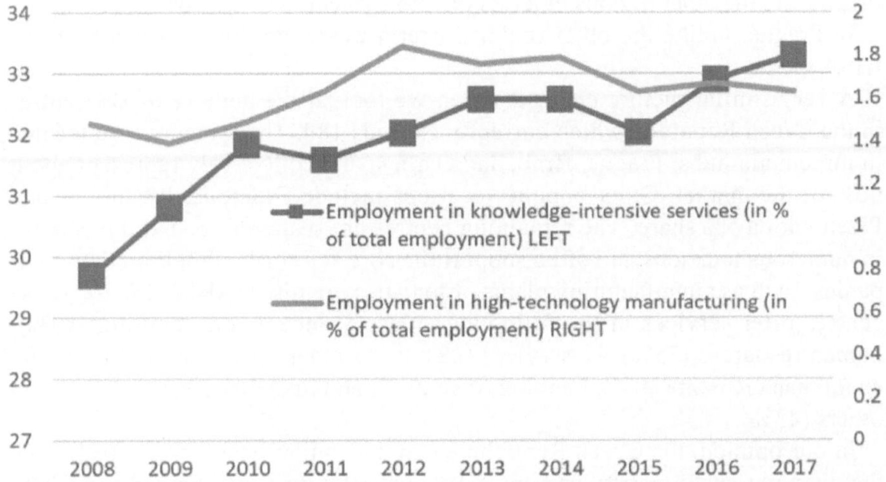

Figure 9.2 Changes in employment shares in KISA and high-technology manufacturing

Source: Authors own study based on data from Regional Innovation: Knowledge and high technology industries (https://stats.oecd.org/).

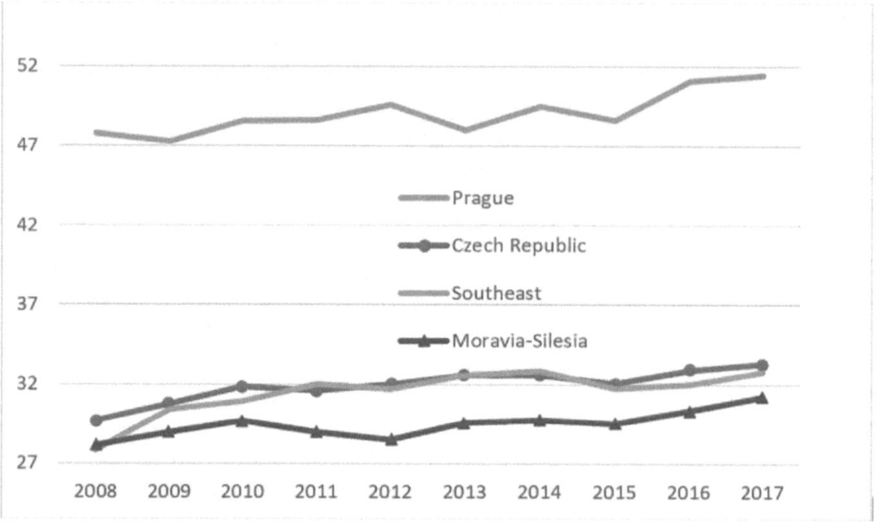

Figure 9.3 Differences between Prague and the other regions of the Czech Republic in employment in the KISA sector

Source: Authors own study based on data from Regional Innovation: Knowledge and high technology industries (https://stats.oecd.org/).

From the geographical point of view, it logically follows that KISA activities should be concentrated in Prague. Figure 9.3 shows the differences between Prague and the other regions in terms of employment in the sector.

In Prague, unlike the other regions, nearly every other person works in the KISA sector.

A very similar picture emerges when we look at the number of BS centres in the Czech Republic, which currently exceeds 180. These centres are located in three main hubs: Prague, Brno, and Ostrava and collectively represent about 90% of the market. Other popular locations include Olomouc, Pardubice, and Plzen with a 5% share. The remaining centres are scattered around the country in numerous locations and often support the core activities of their mother companies, such as manufacturing plants or logistics premises (ABSL, 2016). These centres offer services in the following areas: finance and accounting (89%); human resources (75%); IT services (62%); customer operation (53%); supply chain management (38%); banking, insurance, and financial services (6%); and others (43%).

In our opinion, the Czech Republic entered a similar development path once the 'painful transformation' had opened the gates for investment in BS and KIBS. Prague and Brno are cases in point, since economic activity in them has currently shifted towards the services sectors (Vollrath, 2020).

According to ABSL, the following criteria are important for investors in business centres: the quality of public transport in the city, its image, transport accessibility, availability of modern office space, and cooperation with local authorities (ABSL, 2019b). In terms of these criteria, Prague and Brno rank as the top two cities in the Czech Republic, followed by Ostrava by a large margin (ABSL, 2019a).

Numerous factors contribute to individual decisions of international organisations and firms to invest in Prague and Brno, but the crucial ones are always economic. They include, in particular, good access by road and by air, comparatively low rents, low administration costs and energy prices, as well as lower staff costs per employee in Prague and Brno compared to London or New York. Cultural and historical arguments cannot be discounted either: Prague is the fifteenth largest city in the EU, whereas Brno's history dates back to the Middle Ages. Moreover, Brno is located close to Vienna, a major European metropolis. Thus, Prague and Brno offer very attractive environments for employees of international firms. Last but not least, Prague ranked 13th among 113 cities in terms of the quality of life (PICSA Index, 2019). The index comprises the following components: GDP, access to housing, medical care, access to education, and social and economic justice. Prague scored particularly high on safety and the number of physicians. According to D&L Partners, Prague has one of the densest networks of consulting rooms globally. A comparison of world cities shows that the richest ones are not necessarily the most comfortable to live in. For example, out of the ten richest cities in the world, London ranked 33rd, whereas New York 38th. The already mentioned Vienna traditionally ranks highest in the list, which, in turn, makes the neighbouring Brno more attractive for the employees of international firms headquartered there.

Table 9.2 Prague and Brno fact sheet

Prague	*Brno*
• main location for business services with over 100 centres and 40.000+ employees • meets all the requirements of international firms: excellent public transport system, modern office space, well-developed internal infrastructure, and large expatriate community • political, educational, cultural, and economic centre of the country • renowned among expatriates as one of the most attractive places to live in Europe	• second largest city in the Czech Republic • highly attractive city with excellent infrastructure, cultural life, and lower costs of living compared to Prague • the sector plays a crucial role in the city, over 30 major centres, 20% annual growth, and over 15,000 employees • several world-class universities, large talent pool in ICT, economics, and business • IT hub of the Czech Republic

Source: CzechInvest (2017).

Table 9.3 compares Prague and Brno in terms of the key factors important for taking investment decisions:

Table 9.3 Prague and Brno in figures

Factor/City	*Prague*	*Brno*
Unemployment rate	2.9	4.8
Number of university students 2016/2017	124,674	67,244
Business administration students	30,641	11,700
ICT students	10,334	8,615
Law students	4,700	2,667
Language skills	English 68%, German 41%, Russian 40%, French 9%, Spanish 6%	English 54%, German 48%, Russian 40%, French 5%, Spanish 2%
Labour cost – management (euro)	68,000–87,000 (finance accounting) 68,000–87,000 (HR) 68,000–87,000 (procurement) 81,000–99,000 (IT)	37,000–83,000 (finance, accounting) 37,000–70,000 (HR) 37,000–83,500 (procurement) 32,400–55,400 (IT)
Labour cost – operative (1–3 years' experience) (euro)	18,700–30,000 (finance, accounting) 18,700–30,000 (HR) 18,700–30,000 (procurement) 18,700–30,000 (IT),	14,000–21,000 (finance, accounting) 14,000–18,500 (HR) 14,000–21,000 (procurement) 15,000–19,200 (IT)
Units of office stock	3.2 million m^2	0.5 million m^2
Rental price (euro/m^2/month)	Prague city centre 18.5–19.5 Prague inner city 15–16.5 Prague outer city 13–14.5	11–13
Key advantages	Main location for business services with over 100 centres and over 40,000 employees; meets all the requirements of international companies; political educational, cultural, and economic centre of the country; one of the most attractive places to live in Europe	Second largest city in the Czech Republic; excellent infrastructure, cultural life; lower costs compared to Prague; several world class universities; large talent pool in ICT, economics, and business; hub of the Czech Republic

Source: CzechInvest (2019), Deloitte (2019).

Another important perspective on both destinations was offered by the managers of firms headquartered in Prague and Brno, respectively. We conducted a content analysis of interviews carried out by Deloitte with 11 managers of those firms (five from Prague and six from Brno) who were asked the following simple questions depending on where they were based: why Prague or why Brno (Delloitte, 2019)?

- In Prague, most respondents agreed that the city functioned as a proxy for their business in Western countries. The managers also emphasised the advantages of the location and the possibility to attract qualified labour from various continents. The cost and availability of suitable candidates as well as the region's stability were also of great importance.
- In Brno, respondents emphasised the availability of qualified labour. Managers mentioned the local 'pool of talents' and 'top-notch universities'. The latter reflects the fact that Brno's universities are particularly renowned for their focus on IT. Other reasons included the convenient geographic location and problem-free relocation for foreign staff.

From our point of view, the main difference between Prague and Brno should be perceived in terms of their maturity. Prague can be described as a mature Western centre on account of its advanced infrastructure, language skills of the populace, and the quality of education offered at its universities. Brno can be seen as a still growing challenger that benefits particularly from its low-cost qualified labour supply as well as the innovative environment of its universities.

The case studies of Prague and Brno demonstrate the role of the KIBS sector, outsourcing, and offshoring in the economy of the Czech Republic. These phenomena emerged only when the centrally managed system with its predominant industrialism ceased to exist. The Czech economy was transformed from

Figure 9.4 Selected investors in the Czech Republic

Source: CzechInvest (2017).

an autarkic economy to an open one. Where the centralistic state intervened in the past, the economic regulator role predominates now. The first decade after the fall of the communist regime saw a rapid growth of BS, which reflected the shift from local production to the provision of outsourced services. This shift, as a phenomenon accompanying the increasing specialisation and integration of global economy, constitutes one of the "drivers of economic growth" (Wirtz et al., 2015, p. 565).

The analysis of BS and KIBS sectors in Prague and Brno shows them to be typical examples of post-transformation cities of a former centrally managed economy. As such, they can be used to demonstrate two basic evolutionary modes in the development of BS, namely outsourcing and offshoring.[6] From the point of view of KIBS, outsourced services include IT. Hence, outsourcing in KIBS is a purely economic decision taken, on the one hand, to reduce costs (cf. Ricardo's law of comparative advantage) and on the other, to help a firm to concentrate on its core activities in order to increase its competitiveness and enhance the quality of services.

The first instances of outsourcing in IT occurred soon after the transformation and were mostly driven by economic interest. Firms started to subcontract the development and maintenance of their own IT systems. Foreign companies used the services of Czech computer firms to design, build, and administer their information systems. Brno became an important centre of such services. The analysis of the BS in the Czech Republic shows that KIBS are characterised by a high propensity to offshore and globalise and, consequently, a high level of outsourcing. The studied cases of KIBS confirmed the following characteristics of the sector identified by Wirtz et al. (2015):

- Typical objectives: cost savings, efficiencies, compliance, service focus, agility, scalability, and innovation;
- Scope: many processes and many providers; combination of shared services and outsourcing/offshoring; not just transactional activities; includes also critical business processes;
- Agility: high, because coordinated centrally;
- Governance: centralised and coordinated;
- Culture: transformational change; service-focused culture is fundamental; work as a single team regardless of shared services or outsourcing.

Outsourcing can be used as an example to demonstrate the phenomenon of path dependence (Peters, 1999). The phenomenon emerged in market economies in the 1970s and was implemented in practice by international corporations (e.g. Kodak, Xerox, and GM) on a larger scale in the following decade. Firms removed their support activities from internal corporate processes and subcontracted them to external providers. In Czechoslovakia, outsourcing appeared with a delay due to historical circumstances, specifically, with the breakdown of the centrally planned economy and its replacement with a market economy.

Challenges and prospects

KIBS can be defined as "multifunction, multi-region, multisource, and multi-business all at the same time which have a common leadership and governance structure that is closely tied to the firm's organisational objectives" (Wirtz et al., 2015, p. 573). The core drivers of future change are as follows (ABSL, 2019b):

- The range of services in the future will be expanded and more multidimensional owing to the adoption of a multi-channel and holistic approach;
- The role of people in business services centres (BSCs) will be more unique as the most conducive to satisfaction and loyalty, whereas the synergy between humans and machines will dramatically increase the capacity of operations;
- Business services will continue to be digitalised and the new technologies will drive the changes using the personalisation affecting the experience and expectations of the emerging generations;
- The importance of data security will increase and will impact the sector's standards.

A report by the World Economic Forum states that 65% of children entering primary school today will end up working in completely new job types that do not yet exist. Five years from now, over one-third of skills (35%) considered important in today's workplace will have changed. Currently, about one-tenth of the total workforce performs jobs that are likely to grow in percentage terms, whereas around one-fifth are in occupations that will likely shrink. All this means that approximately seven in ten people are currently doing jobs whose future is, at best, uncertain. The key findings about skills suggest that job redesign coupled with workforce retraining may promote growth in KIBS (ABSL, 2019b). It can be expected that KIBS will continue to grow as a result of overall economic growth as well as an increased proportion of new activities being delivered using the shared services model. The prospects for expansion are now to be found in big data, data mining, analytics, and research & development, i.e. in the areas previously restricted to a handful of specialised groups operating within individual firms (ABSL, 2019b). The focus of BS is no longer just to reduce costs or improve service value. Its role is changing from being a service provider to a business partner on an equal footing with other functions and departments in an organisation or service consumer. Leading firms are undergoing organisational transformations, which involve a number of business functions being shifted to KIBS (ABSL, 2019b).

Traditional skill sets needed in KIBS are to an ever-greater extent affected by the availability of new technologies that will replace certain parts and aspects of human work, thereby leading to a far-reaching workforce transformation. BS will develop and expand utilising their big data processing capacity (including customer data, transactional data, employee data, and analytics). Digital trends will primarily affect the following areas (ABSL, 2019b):

1 Shared services will have to quickly upscale their range in order to move up the value curve and invest in digitalisation, including data security. The transitional aspect of work will be handed over to the digital workforce.
2 To be able to move the range of services to the next level, employees will need to acquire a different set of competencies. Employees will have more value-added jobs and they will have to be upscaled in order to handle more strategic and analytical work. To succeed, organisations must focus on training and developing these new skills. Allowing the employees to focus on value-added tasks will also require different management skills in motivating a highly skilled workforce. The focus will also shift on the quality of the work done.

The Czech Republic has become an important location for business shared services and the sector is now one of the fastest growing industries. Its role in the domestic labour market is considerable, as it currently employs over 75,000 people, with the figure projected to reach 100,000 by 2020. Firms with an established presence are expanding throughout the Czech Republic as the portfolio of their activities is becoming more complex and advanced. The country offers several attractive locations for business shared services apart from Prague and Brno (CzechInvest, 2017).

The main factors that make the Czech Republic an excellent location for KIBS include (CzechInvest, 2017):

- Location in the centre of Europe;
- Well-developed internal infrastructure;
- Talented, skilled, and competitively priced workforce;
- Availability of office space;
- Telecommunication and data networks;
- Cosmopolitan society, large expat community;
- Government support.

Based on the report by CzechInvest (2017), understanding the impact of robotics and cognitive technologies on education, skills, workplace, labour market, recruitment, and retention will be crucial to ensuring that the Czech Republic is able to manage the risks and opportunities associated with workforce changes for further economic growth. Businesses will have to focus on and articulate the competencies needed now and in the mid-term future. Governments, businesses, and society need to work together to support a dynamic workforce capable of constantly reskilling and upskilling. This means revisiting education, career models, and approaches to lifelong learning and work, regardless of geography, and innovating public-private partnerships. Policies that underpin the basic fundamentals of the workforce, such as regulation of the gig economy, need revising in a way that provides for inclusive growth and facilitates innovation and long-term unemployment solutions.

Considering the anticipated impact of technological changes on the business service sector (BSS) (ABSL, 2019b), the Czech Republic should take the following steps to remain competitive in the KIBS world:

1 Computer science, technology-related, and innovation-focused education must become a priority at all the levels of schooling starting at elementary schools.
2 Closer cooperation between the academic and corporate sectors should be promoted to align curricula to the latest demands of the job market, including compulsory internships during the last two years of study.
3 Government should support innovation, technology start-ups, and new technologies in general via technology incubators and economic, administration, and tax support.
4 The Czech Republic should be promoted as an innovative country that can offer a platform for R&D and innovations and as an attractive destination for global experts in modern technologies. The latter should be attracted by streamlining the immigration procedures for selected professions and professionals.

Conclusion

In this chapter, we discussed the current situation and development trends that affect KIBS in the Czech Republic based on the examples of Prague, its capital city, and Brno, its second largest city. We provided a brief historical overview of the development of industry in the Czech lands and the emergence of the phenomenon of BS and KIBS in the country, analysed the selected characteristics of the sector, and looked at the challenges and prospects for outsourcing and offshoring KIBS in the Czech Republic. KIBS is also an interesting domain for policymakers since the latest developments have been driven by market forces based on private initiative. Nevertheless, a free development of an industry does not automatically lead to the best possible welfare outcomes. Targeted, stimulating action may in some cases seize welfare opportunities that otherwise would have remained underdeveloped. The Czech government aims to support increasing specialisation and integration of KIBS in order to foster economic growth by organising debates about the sources of value added in KIBS. The increased popularity of outsourcing has led to a new wave of KIBS that further stimulates foreign trade of the Czech Republic. By comparison, offshoring services are a relatively new phenomenon in the country. We may expect an expansion of outsourcing and offshoring to a range of KIBS. Furthermore, future economic growth shall be driven by the competitiveness in services that have become an important catalyst for continuous development, bringing new socio-economic and political challenges.

Acknowledgement

This research was funded by the Czech Grant Agency GAČR Project No. GA19–06020S

The text was prepared also as one of the outputs of a research project of the Faculty of Finance and Accounting at the University of Economics "Economic and institutional aspects of public finance" registered by the Internal Grant Agency of University of Economics, Prague under the registration number F1/7/2019.

Notes

1 The Czech Republic has been an EU member state since 2004. Together with Slovakia, Poland, and Hungary, it belongs to the Visegrad Four (V4). The historical predecessor of the Czech Republic was the Czechoslovak Republic established after the collapse of the Austro-Hungarian Monarchy in 1918. Czechoslovakia existed until the end of 1992 when it was divided into two separate states – the Czech Republic and the Slovak Republic.

2 At the turn of the 20th century, the automotive industry and motorcycle manufacturing developed in Mladá Boleslav and Kopřivnice. The first aviation experiments were carried out in the territory of the present-day Czech Republic. New technologies (electric, gasoline, diesel engines, steam turbines, and high-grade steel production) were gaining ground as new industrial sectors (the arms industry, chemical industry, and electrotechnical industry) developed. A prominent role in this respect was played by the German population of the Czech lands. Germans were invited to the Kingdom of Bohemia in the Middle Ages, during the reign of the Přemyslid dynasty. They became the founders of towns, master craftsmen, and subsequently contributed to the emergence of industry. Germans were displaced (in 1945–1946) on the strength of a decision made by the victorious powers after the end of the World War II (1945). Formally, it was ordered by the Decrees of the President of the Czechoslovak Republic Edvard Beneš. The territory of Bohemia became ethnically uniform. The Hungarian ethnic minority remained in Slovakia. As regards the Jewish population, only a small number of the Jews who survived returned after the war. Some of them later emigrated to Israel and the USA.

3 The other territories of Czechoslovakia (Slovakia and Transcarpathia) were agrarian regions (Půlpán, 1993). The dynamic development of industry was hampered by the scarcity of raw materials, which had to be imported (cotton, flax, silk, and iron ore). It is worth mentioning that in 1924, Czechoslovakia ranked 10th among the richest countries of the world (Hickmann & Fischer, 1927). The global economic crisis had an extremely negative impact on the Czechoslovak economy. The industrial production index dropped by 40%. Nevertheless, in 1934 Czechoslovakia again ranked 10th among the industrially most developed countries of the world (Janda, 1934). After the Munich Agreement (signed by Great Britain, France, Italy, and Germany) in 1938, Czechoslovakia was forced to cede to Germany the borderlands (the so-called Sudetenland), where the German population predominated. As a result, the key industrial sites were taken over by Germany. After Slovakia withdrew from the Czechoslovak state in 1939, the Protectorate of Bohemia and Moravia headed by the acting Reich Protector was declared on the remaining territory of Bohemia and Moravia. The country's administration and economy were subordinated to the German Third Reich. After Nazi Germany was defeated, the property of Germans (except for German anti-fascists) and collaborators was nationalised, and Germans were expelled from the territory of Czechoslovakia. The cosmopolitan character and multi-ethnic spirit of the former Czechoslovakia was lost. This also applied to Prague and Brno, which had sizeable German-speaking populations.

4 The orientation of the economic development was determined by the subsequent congresses of the Czechoslovak Communist Party (Komunistická strana Československa,

KSČ). Plans were drafted for five years. Altogether, from 1949–1989, there were eight such plans. The first plan (1949–1953) focused on the development of heavy industry, collectivisation of agriculture, and industrialisation of Slovakia. The subsequent five-year plans were strongly oriented towards heavy industry (with an emphasis on the arms industry), steel production, chemical industry, and agriculture. Czechoslovakia was part of the Eastern Block, with the Council for Mutual Economic Assistance acting as its economic organisation.

5 The so-called voucher privatisation. Every citizen could buy a book of vouchers for CZK 1,000 and exchange the vouchers for company shares or invest them in a privatisation fund. Currently, the large privatisation is customarily called 'grand theft in broad daylight'.

6 As Part I of this book shows, outsourcing is the opposite of insourcing. A firm may choose to perform its manufacturing activities on its own, deploying its own capacity (in-house) or subcontract some of the non-core activities to another company, which specializes in respective activities. The reasons for such a decision are economic in nature. Offshoring involves the relocation of a business process from one country to another – typically an operational process, such as manufacturing, or supporting processes, such as accounting (Zuckerman, 2008).

References

ABSL. (2016) *Business Service Sector in the Czech Republic* [accessed from: www.absl.cz/report2016/].

ABSL. (2019a). *Brno. City Profile: A Guide to Business Services Sector* [accessed from: www.absl.cz/docs/Brno_City_Profile_FINAL.pdf].

ABSL. (2019b). *Business Service Sector in the Czech Republic* [accessed from: www.absl.cz/report2019/].

CzechInvest. (2017). *Annual Report 2017* [accessed from: www.czechinvest.org/cz/O-CzechInvestu/Ke-stazeni/Vyrocni-zpravy-cs].

CzechInvest. (2019). *Annual Report 2019* [accessed from: www.czechinvest.org/cz/O-CzechInvestu/Ke-stazeni/Vyrocni-zpravy-cs].

David, P.A. (2007). Path dependence: A foundational concept for historical social science. *Cliometrica, 1*(2), pp. 91–114.

Delloitte. (2019). *Prague – City Profile. A Guide to Business Services Sector* [accessed from: www2.deloitte.com/content/dam/Deloitte/cz/Documents/strategyoperations/ABSL_Prague_City_Profile_EN.pdf].

Hickmann, A.L., & Fischer, A. (1927). *Prof. Hickmann's Geographisch-statistischer Universal-Atlas*. Freytag & Berndt.

Janda, B. (1934). *Encyklopedie výkonnosti*. Praha: Bohumil Janda Sfinx.

Mathias, P., & Pollard, S. (1989). *The Cambridge Economic History of Europe: The Industrial Economies: The Development of Economic and Social Policies*. Cambridge: Cambridge University Press.

Olson, M. (1982). *The Rise and Decline of Nations: Economic Growth, Stagflation, and Social Rigidities*. London: Yale University Press.

Peters, B.G. (1999). *Institutional Theory in Political Science*. London and New York: Continuum.

PICSA Index. (2019). *Creating an Inclusive Prosperity Cities Index Background and Methodology* [accessed from: www.picsaindex.com/the-picsa-index/].

Průcha, V. (1974). *Hospodářské dějiny Československa v 19. a 20. Storočí*. Bratislava: Pravda.

Půlpán, K. (1993). *Nástin českých a československých hospodářských dějin do roku 1990*. Praha: Praha Univerzita Karlova.

Urban, O. (1991). *České a slovenské dějiny do roku 1918*. Praha: Svoboda.

Urban, O. (2003). *Kapitalismus a česká společnost. K otázkám formování české společnosti v 19. století*. Praha: NLN.

Vollrath, D. (2020). *Fully Grown: Why a Stagnant Economy is a Sign of Success*. Chicago: The University of Chicago Press.

Wirtz, J., Tuzovic, S., & Ehret, M. (2015). Global business services. *Journal of Service Management*, *26*(4), pp. 565–587.

Zuckerman, M.A. (2008). The offshoring of American government. *Cornell Law Review*, *94*(1) [accessed from: http://scholarship.law.cornell.edu/clr/vol94/iss1/10].

10 Krakow vs. other Polish destinations of outsourcing, offshoring, and the global business services sector

Janusz Górecki

Characteristics of the sector in terms of employment, structure, and relations with the external environment

For years, the key determinants of attractiveness of particular geographical areas for investment in business services centres have invariably included the availability and quality of labour, costs of doing business, good access by road and by air, availability of appropriate infrastructure (including modern office space), the image of a given area (including the previous investment experience of other firms and the quality of investor service) and its internationalisation, the availability of investment incentives, the quality of life, etc. As a result of a combination of these factors, more than one-half of the number of jobs in the analysed sector in Poland was created in the three largest business services centres: Krakow, Warsaw, and Wroclaw (ABSL, 2019, p. 15). Most remaining investment and employment concentrates in regional centres such as Tricity, Upper Silesia and Zagłębie Metropolitan Area, Lodz, and Poznan. In recent years, the Polish business services map has also seen the emergence of Bydgoszcz, Lublin, Szczecin, and Rzeszow.

In the first quarter of 2019, there were 1.4 thousand export-oriented business services centres in Poland, with a total employment of 307,000 (ABSL, 2019, p. 7). Most of the employment generated by foreign investment comes from countries such as the USA (27%), the Nordic countries (10%), the United Kingdom (9%), France (9%), and Germany (7%) (ABSL, 2019, p. 31). The dynamics of employment growth in service centres in Poland has been decreasing since 2016. The compound annual growth rate (CAGR) for 2016–2019 was 12.8%. The main factors that affect this indicator include challenges on the labour supply and cost side (ABSL, 2019, p. 9). The CAGR of employment in the seven main business services centres has been between 11% and 16% in the last years (2016–2019) (ABSL, 2019, p. 18). The lowest values were observed in Krakow and Wroclaw, i.e. the most developed (next to Warsaw) business services markets in Poland. It is worth mentioning that due to Warsaw's lower saturation with business services centres (i.e. fewer employees in the sector), the growth rate in the capital (14%) is higher than in Krakow or Wroclaw.

Shared services centres (SSC/GBS) are responsible for the largest proportion of employment in this sector in Poland (33%). Information technology (IT) centres (with 32%) come second in the employment structure. Business process outsourcing (BPO) centres employ 18% of total labour in the sector, whereas research and development (R&D) centres utilise a further 13%. The remaining share of employment (4%) is generated by hybrid entities (ABSL, 2019, p. 12). The target countries for business services have remained unchanged for years and include Germany, the UK, and the US (ABSL, 2019, p. 35). Among several dozen languages in which the services are provided by Poland-based centres, the most popular ones, apart from English, are German, Polish, French, Italian, and Spanish (ABSL, 2019, p. 40).

In the employment structure broken down by process categories, IT services come out at the top with a 29% share. Financial and accounting services (F&A) generate 22% of jobs, followed by customer contact services (14%) and banking, financial services and insurance (BFSI) with 13%. The four above-mentioned process categories account for more than three-quarters of jobs in the sector in Poland (ABSL, 2019, p. 33).

Business services centres operate in nearly 50 Polish cities, with 19 centres employing at least one thousand people (ABSL, 2019, p. 15). A large number of locations with the right combination of factors for investors is a characteristic feature of Poland as compared to other CEE countries. Figure 10.1 shows the largest service centres in Poland complete with employee headcount data.

It is worth noting that apart from metropolitan areas, service centres are also established in medium-sized cities (50,000–250,000 inhabitants). However, the development of the sector in these centres faces a number of barriers (such as insufficient supply of adequate human capital).

According to researchers on the potential of medium-sized cities in Poland for BPO, SSC, IT, and R&D investment,

> among the enterprises representing the modern business services sector, IT firms are likely to most strongly affect the development of the analysed sector in medium-sized cities. Due to the specificity of the business, it is easier for IT firms to establish small branches in medium-sized cities and take advantage of business development opportunities based on local human resources.
>
> (Ministerstwo Inwestycji i Rozwoju, 2019, p. 169)

Another kind of investment, although much less popular, involves medium-sized satellite branches of large outsourcing and shared services centres already operating in metropolitan cities. These new branch offices usually offer less knowledge-intensive services, which reflects the locally available human resources. It is worth noting that

> the prime candidates for such functions are conveniently located and easily accessible centres (cities), where larger companies have their headquarters.

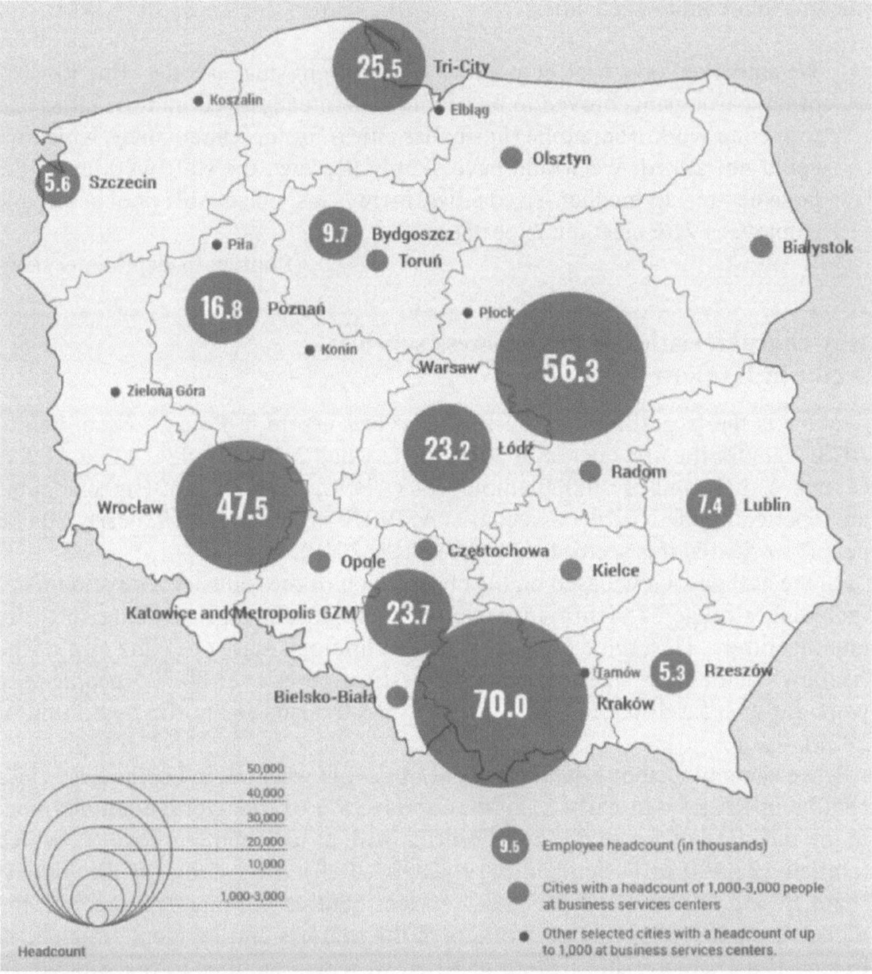

Figure 10.1 Headcount at BPO, SSC/GBS, IT, and R&D centres in selected business services locations in Poland

Source: ABSL (2019).

> However, such cities must provide a certain minimum internal potential (i.e. number of eligible candidates); otherwise they will only constitute a recruitment area for firms operating in the metropolis.
>
> (Ministerstwo Inwestycji i Rozwoju, 2019, p. 169)

The limited opportunities offered by medium-sized cities to prospective business services centres are perhaps best summed up by the words of a manager in a global outsourcing firm operating in Poland, which decided to explore the labour markets in medium-sized cities:

> We embarked on a project to attract people from smaller cities. But 60–70% of the participants proved to be people who already lived in those cities and wanted to work from home (in smaller cities) for the same money, which we could not afford. We would have simply depleted the staff working in the large centres. In medium-sized cities, there is just no suitable pool of eligible employees who meet our expectations.
>
> (Source: In-depth interview)

Key characteristics of the business services sector in Krakow

Krakow is the largest modern business services centre in Poland. According to ABSL data for the first quarter of 2019, the city had 217 BPO, SSC, IT, and R&D centres with a total of 70,000 employees (ABSL, 2019, p. 50). Higher figures are reported by the Krakow association ASPIRE: in January 2019, nearly 80,000 people worked in this sector locally (ASPIRE, 2019).

In the author's view based on his observation of the industry's development, including a range of IT firms working for foreign clients (including software manufacturers, IT service providers, and technology start-ups), the size of the Krakow business services sector can be estimated at over 80,000 people who work for at least 300 BPO, SSC, IT, and R&D firms (as at the beginning of 2020).

If we accept the above data, the share of people working in business services centres in Krakow in early 2020 was about 36% of the average employment in the business sector in the city (in firms with at least ten employees), which totalled 222,300 in December 2019 (GUS, 2020). This is by far the highest share among all the major business services centres in Poland. Moreover, the highest proportion of foreign workers in the sector's employment structure in Poland is a characteristic feature of Krakow, which testifies to the strength of its external relations.

As is the case in Warsaw, Wroclaw, and Tricity, the largest share in the employment structure of Krakow's business services centres by origin of the parent company belongs to American firms (32%). Krakow also stands out among the main centres in Poland in terms of the lowest (apart from Katowice) share of jobs generated by firms from the Nordic countries (6%). The share of jobs in Polish centres is also the lowest (11%), which means the largest investment internationalisation ratio among the surveyed cities. Conversely, the city ranks first in terms of the share of British companies in employment in the sector (16%), and second (to Wroclaw) in terms of the share of jobs provided by Swiss companies (9%) (ABSL, 2019, p. 32).

Interesting conclusions can be drawn from the analysis of the employment structure of the main business services centres in Poland by type of centre (i.e. by its

Table 10.1 Investments in business services in Krakow by category

BPO	*SSC*	*IT*	*R&D*
Accenture	ABB	Ailleron	ABB
Alexander Mann Solutions	Amway	Air Liquide	Akamai
Aon	Cathay Pacific	Atos	Aptiv
Apply Capnor	Electrolux	Autodesk	Assa Abloy
Capgemini	FedEx	CD PROJEKT RED	BWI Group
Capita	Heineken	Codewise	Dassault Systems
Cognizant	Herbalife	Comarch	DreamLab
Euroclear	HSBC	EPAM	EC Engineering
Genpact	International Paper	Ericsson	GlobalLogic
Hays	Jacobs	Grand Parade	IBM Software Lab
IBM BTO	Kimberly–Clark	GrapeUp	Motorola Solutions
Itekna	Kingfisher	HCL Technologies	Nokia
Majorel	Lufthansa	Luxoft	Ocado Technology
PeopleScout	PMI	Miquido	Pegasystems
Red Flag Group	Revolut	NOVOMATIC Technologies	Qualtrics
Teleperformance	Rolls–Royce	OEConnection	Samsung
TTEC	Shell	Sabre	Schibsted Tech
WilsonHCG	State Street	Sii	Valeo
Wipro	Uber	Stefanini	Varroc Lighting Systems
Xceedance	UBS	Yggdrasil Gaming	Zendesk

Source: Own study.

predominant activity profile). It turns out that Krakow has the highest proportion of employment in shared services centres (45%) and the lowest in IT centres (19%). The percentage of jobs in BPO centres comes close to the national average (18%), while employment in R&D centres (17%) is higher only in Wroclaw (ABSL, 2019, p. 14).

The largest employers in the sector studied in Krakow are British-Dutch Shell, representing the petrochemical industry (since 2006) and the French Capgemini. Apart from Credit Suisse, Nokia, and IBM in Wroclaw and Atos in Bydgoszcz, they also run the largest business services centres in Poland. The BFSI sector, represented by State Street, HSBC, UBS, BBH, and Euroclear, among others, enjoys a very strong position in Krakow's employment structure. Besides Capgemini, the most important investors representing the professional services sector are American IBM BTO and British Aon. The largest investors in the IT sector include the Polish firm Comarch and the American companies Sabre and Cisco.

Numerous technologically advanced software houses, i.e. firms that develop software for external clients, usually foreign ones, have also found their niche on Krakow's map of business services. As was noted by the authors of the report on the perspectives of Poland's IT industry (SoDA, 2019, p. 24),

> An extremely important distinguishing factor in the industry is the territorially unlimited nature of the software-writing firms. Despite the fact that as much as 64% of the surveyed entities provide services to Polish customers, exactly the same proportion declares revenues from the American market. The figure is only a little smaller in the German or British markets.

It is worth adding at this point that Krakow is one of the most important development centres of Poland's video game industry. The city's strong position is confirmed by the fact that it regularly hosts the Digital Dragons conference, one of the largest events in the video game industry in Europe.

Other important contributors to the technological development of the city's economy are start-ups, often considered as indirect effects of the robust present of the analysed sector in Krakow (particularly in the area of IT). An interesting example is Talent Alpha, founded in 2018, which translated the long-standing experience of its founders in the Polish IT labour market into an innovative technological solution in the form of a platform intended to match IT service providers (e.g. software houses) with large global customers in order to enable the latter to fill the staffing gaps in the implementation of their technological projects.

The youngest business services centres in Krakow, established in 2019, include the IT centre of the British EQ Tek (part of the Equinity group), the American software supplier Q88 LLC, the British technology company WorldRemit, the American GainCapital, the German GFT Technologies, shared services centre of American PepsiCo, the German logistics company Havi, the British Vesuvius, the research and development centre of Varroc Lighting Systems, and the centre established by Universal-Investment. These new investments are characterised by considerable diversification and planned employment scale, which usually does not exceed 200 in a single service centre, although in the case of PepsiCo, it is over 500.

The range of services offered by Krakow's centres

Subsequent years of business process services have seen an increased range of activities in most centres located in Krakow. The attendant inflow of new competencies to a number of units contributed to their increasing importance in the international operating structures of parent companies. Table 10.2 lists selected centres that perform a variety of key business service functions for their global parent companies.

Table 10.2 Activity profiles of selected business services centres in Krakow

Name	*Type of centre*	*Year activities in Krakow began*	*Parent company headquarters location*	*Employment range in Krakow*	*Activity profile*
ABB Global Business Services	GBS	2017	Switzerland	1,500–2,000	Finance, Human Resources (HR), Information Systems (IS), Supply Chain Management (SCM)
Capgemini, Business Services, Capgemini Cloud Infrastructure Services	BPO/IT	2003	France	4,000+	Business Services: F&A, banking operations, HR, customer service, marketing supply chain management. Cloud Infrastructure Services: technical support and remote management of client's IT infrastructure
HSBC Service Delivery	GBS	2008	UK	ca. 3,000	Operations, Technology, Finance, Risk, Transformations
Motorola Solutions	R&D	1998	USA	1,000–1,500	Software Development of Public Security Systems TETRA/APCO–25 and Public Safety LTE
Sabre Global Development Centre	IT	2000	USA	1,500–2,000	Technology Services: data solutions, mobile, online commerce, platform services, software
Shell Business Operations	GBS	2006	Netherlands	4,000+	Finance Operations, Customer Service, HR Services, Order to Delivery, Contracting & Procurement
State Street Bank	GBS	2007	USA	3,000–3,500	Fund Accounting, Financial Reporting, Key Investor Information Document (KIID), Security Valuation Services, Derivatives, Hedge Funds, Collateral Services, Conversion, Anti-Money Laundering, Support Functions

Source: Own study based on the websites of individual firms.

The historical context of GBS development

The modern business services sector in Poland began to develop in the 1990s and involved the first foreign investments in IT service centres, business process outsourcing (BPO), and research and development centres (R&D). Somewhat later, in the first half of the 2000s, shared services centres (SSC) also arrived at the scene. In the initial stage, investment concentrated in a handful of the largest metropolitan centres, which have remained the industry's leaders until today.

Krakow was one of the first cities to attract the attention of investors planning to establish their business services centres in Poland. This was mainly due to its strong internationalisation compared to other large cities, and the size of its academic community. In the initial stage of development of the studied sector, the city primarily attracted IT services and R&D centres, such as:

- Comarch, founded in 1993, still ranks among the largest Polish IT companies;
- Ericpol – a branch of a Polish IT company established in Krakow in 1996 (in 2016, it became part of the Swedish corporation Ericsson);
- ABB – research and development centre of the Swiss-Swedish multinational corporation, launched in 1997;
- Motorola Solutions – software development centre established in 1998.

The early stages of outsourcing to Krakow were also marked by the arrival of such firms as PricewaterhouseCoopers (now PwC), whose outsourcing department was taken over and expanded by Capgemini (since 2003), or the IBM BTO service centre in operation since 2002. The entry of globally recognized outsourcing brands into Krakow, the development of software centres, such as Motorola and ABB, and the inflow of shared services centres (SSCs) of international corporations in 2003–2005 (Lufthansa, International Paper, PMI, Electrolux) triggered further development of the industry in the city (imitation effect).

The Krakow Technology Park (KPT) – a specialised business environment institution operating since 1997, which manages Krakow's Special Economic Zone (SEZ) and the Technology Park – certainly contributed to strengthening the position of the business services sector in its first years in Krakow. The park's offer in the form of, among other things, investment incentives has had a positive impact on interest in doing business in Krakow. The first permits to operate in the SEZ were issued in 1999 (the recipients included Comarch and Motorola). In 2000, the permission to operate in the SEZ was granted to ABB's R&D centre. In 2004–2005, the zone was also opened to BPO and SSC centres.

An important development impulse for the sector was the positive response of investors to Poland's accession to the European Union in 2004, associated with greater legal and economic stability. However, the development of the sector on a global scale (affected, among others, by technological factors) and the attendant drive to find suitable cost- and quality-enhancing human capital locations that would meet the firms' demand for business services played a decisive role in the robust growth in the number of new service centres in the second half of the 2000s.

The pace at which the sector developed led to the founding of industry associations in 2009, which brought together firms with business services centres located in Poland: the local, Krakow-based ASPIRE, and the nationwide ABSL. It is worth emphasising that ASPIRE is the first organisation in Krakow that represents foreign investors based on industry rather than their country of origin (Micek et al., 2011). The ABSL is currently the largest employer organisation in Central and Eastern Europe in the business services sector.

In 2009, only a dozen or so thousand people worked in Krakow's business services centres (although it was the largest figure in Poland), hence the latter were not as important to the city's economy as they are now. Today, business services provide a distinctive example of one of the several modern sectors of Krakow's economy. Outsourcing centres (BPO) and shared services (SSC) can be considered as classic examples of a development path based almost exclusively on external impulses. In contrast, IT services owe their development to both external impulses and academic entrepreneurship (Micek et al., 2017, p. 39).

A noticeable increase in the impact of academic potential on the city's economy manifests itself, among others, in the development of the business services sector in Krakow both in quantitative (employment, number of centres) and qualitative terms (moving up the value chain). Therefore, the development of the studied sector is path-dependent in a broad sense of the term (see Gwosdz, 2004; Micek et al., 2017, p. 40). Currently, business services, apart from higher education and tourism, is the most important sector of Krakow's economy. For over a decade, the largest employer in the city has been the Jagiellonian University rather than the Arcelor-Mittal steelworks (currently ranked fourth in terms of employment). Shell and Capgemini make up for the remaining two in the top three.

A fact worth mentioning is that some firms, drawing on their positive investment experience in Krakow, not only decide to expand their existing facilities, but also open up new local centres with different activity profiles. Examples include the Motorola Solutions financial and accounting services centre (established in 2007), the IBM R&D centre (IBM Software Laboratory), which started operating in the late 2005, and the Aptiv financial services centre in operation since 2017.

The established position of Krakow on the global business services map results, among others, from its growing recognition among investors. The city owes its positive image to the fact that it invariably comes out on top of a variety of investment rankings compiled with the participation of global consulting firms, to mention only the Tholons Services Globalization CITY INDEX report. The global brand of Krakow as an advanced and mature business services centre encourages firms to analyse their position on the labour market and ask themselves whether and how they can attract staff (brand strength, offer for employees, etc.). However, due to the high likelihood of being able to recruit appropriate staff, the risks for a company entering Krakow for the first time is much lower than settling for a location that does not have a proven pool of experienced candidates (or the positive experience of previous investors).

Two decades of office market development in Krakow

The development history of the modern office space market in Krakow is closely linked with the inflow of investment in business services centres. The first modern offices were built in the second half of the 1990s. In the early stages of Krakow's office market, the demand of investors for appropriate quality office space considerably exceeded supply. As a result, the office space vacancy rate remained very low. Some investors, faced by the lack of suitable office space in Krakow, decided to temporarily operate from the premises of their client firms (in the case of outsourcing companies) or to use those offered by other institutions. A good example is the Motorola Solutions – Krakow Software Design Center, which initially operated from a building owned by the Jagiellonian University (Micek et al., 2010, p. 49).

By the end of the first decade of the 21st century, over 70 business services centres were established in Krakow. Subsequent investment translated into a growing demand for office space. The largest office buildings constructed at the time were Buma Square (2006), Philip Morris International (2003), Rondo Business Park (2007), Vinci (2010), Cracovia Business Centre/K1 (1998), and Euromarket (2000), each with an area of at least 16,000 m^2.

Krakow has no business district as such. Currently, modern office space tends to be scattered around the city and its agglomeration (e.g. Eximius Park). It is worth noting that the last few years have seen increased demand for flexible workspace from Krakow's service centres. The provision of co-working space in modern office buildings enables firms to optimise the space they occupy, for example, in case of increased employment for the purposes of launching a new service project. This kind of lease is thus not only the domain of start-ups or micro-enterprises. It is estimated that in the first half of 2019, there were 3,900 workstations in flexible offices in Krakow (CBRE, 2019).

Krakow is second only to Warsaw in terms of total office space. In the last 11 years (from the first quarter of 2009 to the fourth quarter of 2019), the office space stock in the city (including its agglomeration) increased by about one million m^2 (from less than 400,000 m^2 to just over 1.4 million m^2) (Marketbeat, 2009; JLL, 2020). In 2019, office space rental prices remained lower than in 2009 (currently approx. 13.5–15.5 euros per m^2), even though its quality has significantly increased. It is worth noting that most office space lease transactions in Krakow in 2018, as in previous years, involved firms representing the business services sector (ABSL, 2019, p. 61).

Challenges and prospects

The analysed sector is subject to a variety of local and international impacts, which have affected its structure and development directions both in Krakow and in other business services centres across Poland. Table 10.3 lists selected key trends that currently shape the sector and the challenges faced by firms operating in the area of business services in Poland, all of which (unless their impact is limited by other geographical factors) also apply to the situation of the sector in Krakow.

Table 10.3 Selected trends and challenges in the business services sector in Poland

TRENDS	• Continued strong demand for German- and French-speaking employees. • Continued high interest of German and Scandinavian firms in nearshoring. • Stable number of new investors opening business services centres at about 40 per year and stable investment in expansion of existing activities in Poland at the maximum of 10 per year (mainly in the IT area). • Increased share of foreign labour in the employment structure of the sector (16–17% estimated average for Poland; 20% for Krakow) and Poles who have gained relevant work experience abroad. • Warsaw's increased share in the employment structure of the business services sector in Poland and stable shares of the main regional centres. • Slowly increasing use of IPA (Intelligent Process Automation) solutions in service centres, mainly in order to reduce their operating costs. • Increasing proportion of advanced, comprehensive, knowledge-intensive tasks in the structure of services provided by BPO, SSC/GBS, IT, and R&D centres and the associated emergence of new positions so far non-existent in the Polish labour market. • Decreased average planned employment in the newly created service centres, which marks the inflow of smaller specialist investment (usually several dozen people) in a single business area. • New shared services centres in Poland reflect investment by smaller foreign firms (as different from global operators), whose previous operating structures did not comprise such units (SSCs).
CHALLENGES	• Ongoing intense competition among the business services centres for staff with the right skills. • Scarcity of high-quality human capital in a large number of Poland's medium-sized cities, which poses a serious obstacle to the expansion of business services centres and makes it difficult to recruit appropriate staff even in metropolises. • Persistent mismatch between the educational offer of universities and the needs of the services sector. Developing innovative solutions in the area of shaping the talent pool. • Developing soft competencies among employees (as part of internal staff development programmes) and delivering eligible candidates for business services centres (as part of the offer of universities and business environment institutions). • Intensification of cooperation (an ecosystem of connections) among business services centres and universities, secondary schools, and organisational units in local governments responsible for implementing pro-investment policy measures. • Urban policy focus on the quality of life, which can be a decisive factor in attracting international talent/firms. A case in point is Krakow's fight against air pollution. • Implementing appropriate local transport policies to respond to the demand from the sector (especially in cities where service centres have the strongest impact on the labour market, e.g. in Krakow and Wroclaw). • Instability of legal solutions at the national level (including regulations unfavourable to the business services sector).

Source: Own study.

The business services sector in Poland is entering the process maturity stage, which is likely to gather momentum in the coming years. It will be accompanied by further development of competencies needed by the sector, particularly due to the increasing demand for highly knowledge-intensive services. While the main categories of processes handled by the centres will remain the same, their characteristics will change. The progressive standardisation of processes will involve applying intelligent automation on a much larger scale, but the coming years are unlikely to see a breakthrough in this area in Poland (in terms of the proportion of processes handled using IPA). The dynamics of employment growth in the service centres, typical of the previous several years, has significantly slowed down. It can be estimated that in the short-term, the number of jobs in the sector will increase at the rate of 5–10% per year (depending on the centre) to reach at least 350,000 in Poland's export-oriented service centres in 2021. A combination of the following factors will have a considerable impact on the situation in the sector:

- The widening demographic gap (insufficiently compensated for by importing qualified staff from abroad);
- Saturation of local labour markets from the perspective of the sector's needs;
- Rising operating costs;
- Changes in the legal environment;
- Global trends in the industry (e.g. increasing intelligent automation of business processes).

Already a decade ago, it was remarked that Krakow's modern business services market was becoming saturated (Micek et al., 2010). The following years, however, proved that concerns about the lack of space or opportunity for new investment were premature. The share of employment in services in the sector's total employment in the city (firms with at least ten employees) may reach as much as 40% within the next two years. This means that the headcount in BPO, SSC, IT, and R&D centres, likely to exceed 90,000, will enable Krakow to maintain its leading position in terms of employment volume among the business services centres both in Poland and in Central and Eastern Europe. Next to Warsaw and Wroclaw, Krakow promises to inspire innovative business solutions in the area of the studied sector.

References

ABSL. (2019). *Business Services Sector in Poland 2019*. Warsaw: ABSL.

ASPIRE. (2019). *ASPIRE Headcount Tracker 2019*. Krakow: ASPIRE.

CBRE. (2019). *Rynek biur elastycznych w Polsce 2019*. Warszawa: CBRE.

GUS. (2020). [accessed from: https://krakow.stat.gov.pl, 05 February 2020].

Gwosdz, K. (2004). Koncepcja zależności od ścieżki (path dependence) w geografii społeczno-ekonomicznej. *Przegląd Geograficzny*, *76*(4), pp. 307–326.

JLL. (2020). *Rynek biurowy w Polsce. Luty 2020 r*. Warszawa: JLL.

Marketbeat (2009). *Raport o rynku nieruchomości w Polsce, Wiosna 2009*. Warszawa: Cushman & Wakefield.

Micek, G., Działek, J., & Górecki, J. (2010). *Centra usług w Krakowie i ich relacje z otoczeniem lokalnym*. Kraków: Wydawnictwo Uniwersytetu Jagiellońskiego.

Micek, G., Działek, J., & Górecki, J. (2011). The discourse and realities of offshore business services to Krakow. *European Planning Studies*, *19*(9), pp. 1651–1668.

Micek, G., Gwosdz, K., Kwiatkowski, T., & Panecka-Niepsuj, M. (2017). Nowe branże gospodarki w Krakowie: Czynniki i mechanizmy rozwoju. *Studia Ekonomiczne. Zeszyty Naukowe Uniwersytetu Ekonomicznego w Katowicach*, *320*, pp. 18–45.

Ministerstwo Inwestycji i Rozwoju. (2019). *Potencjał miast średnich w Polsce dla lokalizacji inwestycji BPO/SSC/IT/R&D*. Warszawa: Ministerstwo Inwestycji i Rozwoju.

SoDA. (2019). *Czy Polska ma szansę stać się hubem IT Europy*. Warszawa: Fundacja Citi Handlowy im. L. Kronenberga.

11 The degree of embeddedness of the business process outsourcing sector in the Visegrad Group in the context of its current development trends and case study findings

Marcin Zawicki

Introduction

The Visegrad Group (V4) is an important region on the world map of the business services market.[1] Relatively low labour costs, large labour resources, high substantive, linguistic, technological, cultural, and communication skills of the staff, favourable relationships between the quality and cost of living, good transport accessibility of cities and quality of public transport, access to modern office space, political as well as economic stability, and a friendly attitude of public authorities and local communities towards investors are important factors for locating business services centres in the Czech Republic, Hungary, Poland, and Slovakia. The business process outsourcing sector includes service activities provided by business process outsourcing (BPO) centres, shared services centres (SSC; for internal clients), global business services (GBS), information technology outsourcing (ITO/IT) centres, research and development (R&D) centres, and hybrid service centres (GBS, IT/ITO, R&D, and hybrid centres can provide services for both internal and external customers). In the literature, the business services sector is often analysed from the point of view of the evolution of these services and changes in their organisational forms; the impact of offshoring and outsourcing on the economic efficiency of firms; targets and criteria for locating service centres; the impact of the development of the business services sector on the economies of countries that import and export these services; and the role of the business services sector in creating global value chains. The aim of this chapter is to outline the prospects for the embeddedness of the business services sector in the V4 countries in the context of key development trends in this sector and its characteristics in individual V4 countries and selected cities, which are presented in Chapters 7–10 of this part of the book.

The size and structure of the business process outsourcing sector in the V4 countries

The Tholons Services Globalization City Index is a recognised barometer of the attractiveness of cities for business services. It has been compiled since 2006 based on data collected and validated from an extensive network of industry stakeholders, including enterprise buyers, service providers, governments, trade bodies, and associations (Tholons, 2019). In 2019, the top 100 super cities include seven cities from the V4 countries. The highest, 11th place in the ranking, was occupied by Krakow (6th in 2018), 21st by Warsaw (22nd in 2018), 22nd by Budapest (23rd in 2018), 19th by Prague (16th in 2018), 40th by Brno (27th in 2018), 80th by Bratislava (70th in 2018), and 92nd by Wroclaw (52nd in 2018). For many years now, Asia has been the global centre of business services. In the top ten of the 2019 Tholons City Index, there are as many as seven cities from this continent, including Bangalore and Manila, which hold the top positions, as well as single cities in South America (Sao Paulo), North America (Toronto), and Europe (Dublin) (Tholons, 2019).

The business process outsourcing sector in the V4 countries has been developing since the first half of the 1990s. Its origins date back to the neoliberal economic reforms implemented in this part of the world after the fall of communism, which aimed to liberalise their economies, privatise state-owned enterprises, and open up to foreign direct investment. A significant proportion of investment was in manufacturing and trade, which triggered a demand for tailored business services. In the host countries, foreign investors created dedicated units that served the business processes, often in the vicinity of their production plants. In subsequent years, many of them were transformed into SSCs. BPO service centres were also established to provide services to external clients.

The current potential of the business process outsourcing sector in the V4 countries is evidenced by statistics, according to which in 2019, the sector employed over 520,000 people (as compared to nearly 350,000 in 2016), and the number of service centres established exceeded 1.9 thousand (over 1.3 thousand in 2016) (cf. Table 11.1). In 2016–2019, the mean annual employment growth rate in this sector was 14.7%.

Table 11.1 Number of business process outsourcing centres (BPO, SSC/GBS, IT, R&D) and employment in these centres in the V4 countries and selected cities

	Number of business services centres		*Number of employees in business services centres*	
	2016[1]	*2019*	*2016*[1]	*2019*
Czech Republic	200	310[6] (2020)	65,000	112,000[6]
Prague	100+	157[6]	40,000	56,000[6]
Brno	30+	53[6]	15,000	24,600[6]
Hungary	100+	150[2]	45,000	67,000[2]
Budapest	90	98[3]	40,000	48,000[3]
Poland	936	1,400[4]	212,000	307,000[4]
Krakow	138	300[5] (2020)	50,300	80,000[5] (2020)
Slovakia	100+	65+[7]	25,000	37,000[7]
Bratislava	40+	40+[7]	18,000	24,000[8]

Source: Own study based on: [1] (ABSL, 2016); [2] (Gál & Marciniak, 2020); [3] (Drótos et al., 2019); [4] (ABSL, 2019b); [5] (Górecki, 2020); [6] (ABSL, 2020); [7] (Sario, 2019); and [8] (finstat.sk).

The dynamic development of business process outsourcing centres in the V4 countries would not have occurred if it had not been for the tangible economic benefits they bring to investors. The largest business services market in the region is Poland with over 300,000 employees in 1,400 business process outsourcing centres, which constituted 59% of total employment in the sector in the V4 countries (2019). The second largest one is the Czech Republic with 112,000 employees in 310 service centres (21% of employment in the sector), followed by Hungary with 67,000 employees in 150 service centres (13%). In Slovakia, over 65 service centres were established, which, in 2019, employed about 37,000 people (7%). Apart from citizens of the V4 countries, business process outsourcing centres employ an ever-growing proportion of foreign workers. In the Czech Republic, their share has already reached 43% of the sector's workforce, whereas in Hungary it totals 16%, in Poland 15%, and in Slovakia 9%.

In the Czech Republic, the centres are located in three main hubs: Prague (56,000 employees), Brno (24,000), and Ostrava (12,000). These three cities cover about 90% of the market. Other popular locations include Olomouc, Pardubice, and Plzen with 5% of the share (Klazar et al., 2020). In Hungary, 66% of the business process outsourcing centres and 70% of the employees are located in Budapest (48,000 employees), while the rest is scattered across larger regional centres like Debrecen, Szekesfehervar, Szeged, Pécs, and Miskolc (Gál & Marciniak, 2020). More than one half of the jobs in this sector in Poland were created in the three largest business process outsourcing centres, including Krakow – the largest business process outsourcing centre in the V4 countries (80,000 employees), followed by Warsaw (56,000), and Wroclaw (47,700). The remaining centres have been located in regional centres: Tricity, Upper Silesia, and the Zagłębie Metropolitan Area, Lodz, Poznan, Bydgoszcz, Lublin, Szczecin, and Rzeszow (ABSL, 2019b; Górecki, 2020). In Slovakia, about 70% of the business process outsourcing centres are located in Bratislava. Most of the others are located in Kosice, Trnava, Zilina, Nitra, and Presov (Sario, 2019).

According to ABSL data, in the Czech Republic, the largest proportion of employees works in IT centres (40% of the total workforce) and SSCs (37%). The remaining part of employment is made up of employees of R&D centres (13%) and BPO outsourcing centres (10%) (ABSL, 2020). The structure of the business process outsourcing sector in Hungary is dominated by SSCs, which account for 51% of all entities in this sector. Thirty-three percent of them are hybrid centres, whereas 17% are BPOs (Drótos et al., 2019). SSC/GBS are responsible for the largest part of employment in the sector in Poland (33%) followed by IT centres (32%). BPO outsourcing centres employ 18% of the sector's workforce, whereas R&D centres another 13%. The remaining part of employment (4%) is generated by hybrid operators (ABSL, 2019b, p. 12).

The general picture of the structure of the business process outsourcing sector in the V4 countries would not be complete without the areas of services that they provide. Centres in the Czech Republic offer services in such areas as finance and accounting (89%); HR (75%); IT services (62%); customer operations (53%); supply chain management (38%); banking, insurance, and financial services (6%); and other (43%) (Klazar et al. 2020). BSCs located in Hungary provide services in the areas of finance, accounting, and controlling (44%); IT (24%); internal and external customer services (14%); sales and marketing (7%); HR (6%); procurement, logistics, and supply chain (3%); and research, development, and innovation (2%) (Gál & Marciniak, 2020). In Poland, most people are employed by centres providing IT services (29%) and financial and accounting services (22%), followed by customer contact services (14%) and banking, financial, and investment services (13%). The above four categories of business processes account for over 75% of jobs in the services sector in Poland (ABSL, 2019b, item 33). The structure of services provided in Slovakia's business process outsourcing sector is dominated by financial and accounting services (29%) and IT services (22%). Sales and marketing services (13%) and customer services (11%) (Sario, 2019) make up the rest.

Embeddedness in the business process outsourcing sector in the V4 countries in the context of challenges

Karl Polanyi argued that the functioning of an economy could not be understood disassociated from the social world in which it was embedded. Therefore, certain organisations, but also the economy as a whole, need to be understood as parts of larger, historically derived, institutional, or social structures. And hence, since individuals are always primarily social beings, rather than economic ones, embeddedness is a necessary and basic condition of the economy (Polanyi, 1944). Sharon Zukin and Paul DiMaggio (1990) introduced a distinction between cognitive, cultural, structural, and political embeddedness. Cognitive embeddedness denotes "the ways in which the structured regularities of mental processes limit the exercise of economic reasoning" (1990, p. 15). They define cultural embeddedness as "the role of shared collective understandings in shaping economic strategies and goals" (1990, p. 17). Structural captures "the contextualization of economic exchange in patterns of on-going interpersonal relations" (1990, p. 18), whereas political embeddedness determines "the manner in which economic institutions and decisions are shaped by a struggle for power that involves economic actors and nonmarket institutions" (1990, p. 20).

In Martin Hess's view (2004), embeddedness basically signifies the social relationships between both economic and non-economic actors (individuals and groups of individuals), and economic action is grounded in 'societal' structures. Accordingly, he identified three kinds of embeddedness: societal, network, and territorial. Societal embeddedness comprises the cultural, political, institutional, and regulatory framework the actor is located in. The term *network embeddedness* refers to the structure of relationships among a set of individuals or organisations, whereas *territorial embeddedness* explains the extent to which an 'actor' is anchored in particular territories or places (Hess, 2004).

Hess's system is often used in research on the embeddedness of businesses and economic sectors. It informs, among others, the work of Neil Coe and Henry Wai-Chung Yeung (2015), co-founders of the theory of global production networks. They interpret societal embeddedness as "the importance for economic action of the cultural, institutional, and historical origins of the economic actor" (2015, p. 17). In the context of the business process outsourcing sector, this can be understood as the sociocultural patterns of work, management, working conditions, employee benefits, customer relations, relations with public authorities, etc. that a firm has acquired in the past and brings to a new location together with its investment. According to Coe and Yeung, network embeddedness is "the degree of functional and social connectivity within a global production network, the stability of its agents' relations, and the importance of the network for its participants" (2015 p. 17). It seems that, in the business process outsourcing sector, this kind of embeddedness may apply not only to the production network, but also to any other type of network which, by virtue of being part of it, brings specific benefits to firms (such as information networks, experience exchange networks, policy networks, etc.). Territorial embeddedness, as Coe and Yeung point out, "captures how firms and related organisations are anchored in different places" (2015, p. 18). This most readily discussed kind of embeddedness refers to the issue of firms' dependence on local resources, labour markets, implemented public policies (Coe & Yeung, 2015), as well as the number and intensity of their links with local suppliers, clients, public authorities, and institutions, as well as the local community (Micek et al., 2010).

The trajectory of development of the business process outsourcing sector to date shows that it was originally determined by two kinds of strategic business choices – the choice of directions for the development of services in response to the needs of clients and stakeholders, and the choice of service centres' locations which were optimal for the implemented business models. However, further embeddedness of the business process outsourcing sector in the V4 countries will not be determined by past business profits but by the sector's perception of future benefits from the centres' operations in specific locations. These benefits may include expected savings or gains and, more importantly, the prospects for service development in accordance with global industry forecasts.

The key anticipated development directions of the business process outsourcing sector worldwide include: 1. information technology development; 2. business process automation; 3. the emergence of global business services; and 4. competition for talent.

Until early 2020, the fourth industrial revolution (Schwab, 2016), which fundamentally restructured human participation in economic processes, could still be considered the main megatrend that sets out and integrates various business services development directions. However, the mega-changes that occur within its framework not only redefine technology as such, but above all society as a whole (Csath, 2018). This leads to the conclusion that the transformation of the business process outsourcing sector not only has economic, technological, and organisational effects but also social and civilisational ones. From 2020 onwards, it has become clear that the unexpected but very important megatrend in the transformation of the business process outsourcing sector will be the various consequences of the COVID-19 epidemic. Although they are still difficult to appreciate and estimate, the industry forecasts cannot ignore them.

Information technology development

Information technologies develop in all economic sectors and kinds of enterprises. Every firm with a global reach knows perfectly well that if it wants to remain competitive, it must become a technology firm. This will lead to the separation of IT processes, increased demand for services provided by IT centres, as well as for specialists in this field (Roszkowska, 2019). Business services will be subject to further digitalisation as new technologies drive the changes using the personalisation affecting the experience and expectation of the emerging generations. The use of big data, data mining, analytics, research and development, and the importance of data security, which already affect many service provision standards, will increase (ABSL, 2019a).

Foreign direct investments made in recent years suggest a growing demand of firms for advanced technological processes, the main area of activity subject to internationalisation being software and the IT services sector. Business services come third, whereas financial services sixth (Roszkowska, 2019). Information technologies also constitute an inseparable element of business process optimisation. Their development is stimulated by changing relations between services centres and their customers. More and more attention is being paid to the end result, i.e. to measurable economic effects achieved by the client, not only to the quality of the customer service process. For example, client orientation no longer consists solely in timely invoice processing, but in looking for various ways to optimise processes, such as improving a firm's liquidity by optimising payment terms. Demanding clients also expect a greater emphasis on analytics to support business decisions more effectively and on further process automation, the highest level of which is robotics (Piwowarczyk, 2017).

Satisfying the large and growing demand for IT experts already poses a major challenge for global firms. The now fashionable professional development path via start-ups, which is pushing away the readiness to climb the corporate career ladder, makes it more difficult for corporations to recruit IT specialists. Global firms, if they want to remain competitive, must constantly tap external resources. To this end, they scout young technology firms and create venture capital funds (Roszkowska, 2019).

The territorial embeddedness of the business process outsourcing sector in the V4 countries is therefore becoming increasingly conditional on access to IT specialists, especially IT/ICT graduates. Of the five cities in the region, the largest number of IT students is to be found in Budapest (12,300), Prague (10,300 thousand), and Brno (8,600). There are 6,600 and 6,000 of such students in Krakow and Bratislava, respectively (and 13,800 in Warsaw, which was not covered by the study). Local technology start-up markets will also increasingly determine the territorial embeddedness of the business process outsourcing sector. Firms with this profile are already attracting substantial capital and human resources investments of global corporations.

Business process automation

As a result of the development of technological synergy between humans and machines, the capacity of operations will dramatically increase. Traditional skills needed to perform work in business services are under an ever-increasing pressure of the availability of new technologies that will replace certain parts and aspects of human work. It will lead to a transformation of the workforce (ABSL, 2019a) and will likely result in slower growth and perhaps also decreased employment in the sector (Piwowarczyk, 2017). Across the economy as a whole, occupational groups whose tasks can be most readily automated are facing the greatest risk of losing their jobs. This is particularly true of people working in predictable environments (production workers, drivers, transport equipment operators, general mechanics) and office workers. In the business process outsourcing sector, the decrease in employment will first of all affect the finance and accounting, HR, and administrative services departments (McKinsey, 2017, p. 10). Automation of processes carried out in business process outsourcing centres has been taking place for a number of years. One of the notable examples is the conversion of old Lotus Notes databases to cloud-based web applications, finance dashboards, IT network security risk assessment portals, or earning release reports for their services units (Šipikal & Rafaj, 2020).

In the V4 countries, employees of centres providing accounting, financial, and banking services are at the highest risk of losing their jobs. Business process automation will most likely benefit centres that offer solutions and services for automating such processes and provide comprehensive and innovative services that are not easily algorithmised (IT, R&D, and hybrid types) and provide advanced as well as integrated services for internal clients (GBS).

Apart from changes in the employment structure, the automation of business processes will reduce the demand of BSCs for office space, and indirectly, will drive down rents. However, the latter do not differ much across cities of the region. In 2019–2020, they ranged from 11–13 euros/m^2/month in Brno, through 13.5–14.5 euros in Krakow, 14.8 euros in Budapest, and 17 euros in Bratislava (mean rents), and from 13–19.5 euros in Prague to 17–23.5 euros in Warsaw, which has the largest total area of modern office space in the region (5.4 million m^2). Budapest has 3.7 million m^2, Prague 3.2 million m^2, Bratislava 1.9 million m^2, Krakow 1.4 million m^2, and Brno 0.5 million m^2. A reduction in the demand for office space will also continue owing to the dynamic development of remote working, as a result of changes in work patterns due to restrictions caused by the COVID-19 epidemic.

The emergence of global business services

Since the intensive development of (internal and external) business process outsourcing, often accompanied by offshoring, the business process outsourcing sector is experiencing another profound transformation. This is the trend towards combining the services provided by numerous and dispersed SSCs operating within firms' structures, often operating according to the hybrid model (SSCs with BPO), into uniform global business services (GBS) centres. Wirtz et al. define the GBS model as "multifunction, multi-region, multisource and multi-business all the same time [with] a common leadership and governance structure that is closely tied to the firm's organisational objectives" (2015, p. 573). GBS are meant to integrate governance, location, and business practices, which have so far been dispersed across several centres and locations, in a single professional centre that supports all business processes of a given firm. These activities reflect the trend of developing services that will be enlarged and multidimensional due to an omnichannel and holistic approach (ABSL, 2019a). GBS are therefore a manifestation of a comprehensive and holistic 'end-to-end' process management approach for the firm and geared to provide added value in a partnership model with key executives (Piwowarczyk, 2017). Centres that embrace the GBS model are no longer focused on cost reduction and are moving away from being a service provider to a business partner (ABSL, 2019a).

GBS organisations have a chance to become the driving force behind the transformation of the firms they serve. They have accumulated the greatest knowledge of their parent firms' processes, possess a huge amount of data, and use technology more than do other parts of the organisation. GBS also often pioneer interdisciplinary cooperation. However, being the driving force behind a firm's transformation depends on the degree of maturity, performance, and scope of authority held by a given GBS centre (ABSL, 2019b).

It seems that those business centres in the V4 countries which already have SSCs or hybrid centres that support key global processes in their firms and provide integrated services have better prospects for creating and promoting the embeddedness of numerous GBS. Urban centres with the highest potential for transition to GBS, i.e. the strongest ones in terms of staffing, competencies, and technology use, also have greater opportunities. The spatial proximity of SSCs aspiring to the role of GBS to manufacturing and other SSCs should also be an advantage, since it is conducive to integrating key functions. Moreover, according to Micek et al., the coexistence of business centres with manufacturing may also promote embeddedness, as it means greater stability due to the high sunk costs and the existence of capital barriers to entry (2010).

The level of globalisation of services provided by centres in the V4 countries is similar and has increased from year to year. Fifty-nine percent of centres in the Czech Republic declare global coverage, 37% operate regionally (i.e. they serve clients from several countries in the region), whereas 4% locally (clients from a single country). In 2019, the share of services provided globally by centres located in the Czech Republic doubled in comparison with 2018 (ABSL, 2020). In Hungary, 59% of the BSCs also provided their services globally. Regional services are supplied by 36% of the centres, whereas 5% of them serve one customer (Drótos et al., 2019). In Poland, 53% of centres operate on a global scale, services for clients from several countries are provided by 44%, and a further 3% serve clients only from one country (ABSL, 2019b).

An important factor that stimulates the creation of GBS in specific locations is the size and potential of the local business environment, that is, the existence of a kind of 'business ecosystem' that promotes the exchange of ideas and experiences. In this respect, Krakow, Warsaw, Prague, Budapest, and Wroclaw offer the best conditions for the development of GBS. The establishment of GBS is also supported by membership in trade associations, including the largest ones in the region: ABSL in Poland, ABSL in Czech Republic, and the international ASPIRE based in Krakow.

It is worth noting that the establishment and development of GBS, which consists in increasing the range of services provided by the centres globally, may, but does not have to, lead to reduced local cooperative links, i.e. to the weakening of their territorial embeddedness. On the other hand, the development of GBS centres, if stimulated by interactions with the local business environment, will contribute not only to networking but also to the sector's territorial embeddedness in its current location. The development of integrated and advanced GBS in the region also means that these centres will adopt new functions that generate higher added value.

Competition for talent

The increasing complexity and integrity of business services generates demand for highly qualified employees and stimulates competition for the most talented ones. Indeed, changes in the sector create more value-added jobs, which means that employees will have to be upscaled in order to be able to handle more strategic and analytical work (ABSL, 2019a). Competition for talent in the region has been a fact for several years now. In order to attract and retain creative employees, employers devise Employee Value Propositions, which are attractively packaged communications explaining why it is worthwhile to work in a given firm and build one's career in it (Piwowarczyk, 2017), and expand as well as differentiate their offer of employee benefits.

Talent acquisition opportunities are greater in large cities, which have a positive migration rate, are large academic centres, and attractive places to live. In this respect, Warsaw, Budapest, Prague, Krakow, and Bratislava have the most favourable prospects for retaining and attracting service centres. For the same reasons, the possibilities of establishing business process outsourcing centres in medium-sized cities in the region are limited.

Note

1 The main source of data on the business process outsourcing sector in the V4 countries are reports published by The Association of Business Service Leaders (ABSL) in Poland (since 2009) and ABSL in the Czech Republic, established in 2013. The data in these reports come from surveys conducted among the operators in this sector and from publicly available information.

References

ABSL. (2016). *Europe's Business Services Destinations: A Journey Across 10 Countries and 20 Cities* [accessed from: https://absl.pl/pl/publikacje/default/2].

ABSL. (2019a). *Business Service Sector in the Czech Republic* [accessed from: www.absl.cz/report2019/].

ABSL. (2019b). *Business Services Sector in Poland 2019* [accessed from: https://absl.pl/en/publications/default/1].

ABSL. (2020). *Business Service Sector in the Czech Republic* [accessed from: www.absl.cz/report2020/].

Coe, N., & Yeung, H. (2015). *Global Production Networks: Theorizing Economic Development in an Interconnected World*. Oxford: Oxford University Press.

Csath, M. (2018). Competitiveness based on knowledge and innovation possibilities of increasing budget revenues in the era of digitalisation and robotisation. *Public Finance Quarterly*, 2018/1, pp. 64–79.

Drótos, G., Marciniak, R., & Ránki-Kovács, R. (2019). *Business Services Hungary 2019: Report on the Hungarian Business Services Industry*. Budapest: Hungarian Investment Promotion Agency, Hungarian Service and Outsourcing Association.

Gál, Z., & Marciniak, R. (2020). Budapest – The development and specific features of outsourcing, offshoring and the Global Business Services sector. In Ł. Mamica (Ed.), *Outsourcing in European Emerging Economies: Territorial Embeddedness and Global Business Services*. London: Routledge, pp. 98–113.

Górecki, J. (2020). Kraków vs. other Polish destinations of outsourcing, offshoring, and the Global Business Services sector. In Ł. Mamica (Ed.), *Outsourcing in European Emerging Economies: Territorial Embeddedness and Global Business Services*. London: Routledge, pp. 129–141.

Hess, M. (2004). Spatial relationships? Towards a reconceptualization of embeddedness. *Progress in Human Geography*, *28*(2), pp. 165–186.

Klazar, S., Ochrana, F., Plaček, M., & Vaceková, G. (2020). The development and specific features of outsourcing, offshoring, and knowledge intensive business services in the Czech Republic: The case of Prague and Brno. In Ł. Mamica (Ed.), *Outsourcing in European Emerging Economies: Territorial Embeddedness and Global Business Services*. London: Routledge, pp. 114–128.

McKinsey. (2017). *Jobs Lost, Jobs Gained: Workforce Transitions in a Time of Automation*. San Francisco, CA: McKinsey Global Institute.

Micek, G., Działek, J., & Górecki, J. (2010). *Centra usług w Krakowie i ich relacje z otoczeniem lokalnym*. Kraków: Wydawnictwo Uniwersytetu Jagiellońskiego.

Piwowarczyk, M. (2017). BPO i SSC od podstaw – o outsourcingu XXI w. *Business Services Magazine* [accessed from: http://business-services.pl/bpo-ssc-gbs/16/bpo-i-ssc-od-podstaw-o-outsourcingu-xxi-w/].

Polanyi, K. (1944). *The Great Transformation*. New York: Holt, Rinehart.

Roszkowska, D. (2019). Czy nowa generacja usług biznesowych z Polski podbije świat? *CXO* [accessed from: www.cxo.pl/news/Czy-nowa-generacja-uslug-biznesowych-z-Polski-podbije-swiat,412538.html].

SARIO. (2019). *Shared Services & Business Process Outsourcing Centers in Slovakia*. SARIO Slovak Investment and Trade Development Agency.

Schwab, K. (2016). *The Fourth Industrial Revolution*. Geneva: World Economic Forum.

Šipikal, M., & Rafaj, O. (2020). Bratislava – The development and specific features of outsourcing, offshoring and the Global Business Services sector. In Ł. Mamica (Ed.), *Outsourcing in European Emerging Economies: Territorial Embeddedness and Global Business Services*. London: Routledge, pp. 87–97.

Tholons. (2019). *Tholons Services Globalization Index* [accessed from: http://tholons.com/tholons-services-globalization-index/].

Wirtz, J., Tuzovic, S., & Ehret, M. (2015). Global business services. *Journal of Service Management*, *26*(4), pp. 565–587.

Zukin, S., & DiMaggio, P. (1990). *Introduction to Structures of Capital*. Cambridge: Cambridge University Press.

Part IIIa

Internal determinants of the embeddedness of the outsourcing and offshoring sector

12 The embeddedness of firms and employees in Central Europe

Krakow as an offshoring and outsourcing centre

Piotr Kopyciński

Introduction

A detailed theoretical discussion on the theory of embeddedness, the offshoring and outsourcing sector, as well as its operation in Krakow is presented in the previous chapters of this publication. For this reason, the author shall not consider them in more detail here but will instead focus on selected aspects of embeddedness of firms and employees of the offshoring and outsourcing sector in Krakow based on his research. This presentation will be preceded by theoretical remarks covering the issues of institutions and institutional context in Central European countries.

Institutions as a factor that fosters embeddedness

When deciding on their location, firms take into account not only the availability of suitable labour or its costs, but also such factors as the transparency of governance, corruption level, and the quality of institutions. Research on these issues in individual countries is regularly conducted for the purposes of compiling assorted indices and reports, to mention only the governance quality indicators prepared by Bertelsmann Stiftung (2018) or the Global Competitiveness Index (GCI) defined by the Global Economics Forum (with the partial GCI indicators on institutions). In these and similar rankings, the term *institution* deserves attention, since its colloquial understanding does not overlap with its denotation in science, for it is by no means synonymous with *organisation*.

Out of the many definitions of institutions in circulation, the one formulated by D. C. North appears to be the most appropriate in this context. In his view, "institutions are the humanly devised constraints that structure political, economic and social interaction" (North, 1991, p. 97). They include:

- Formal constraints (e.g. rules, laws, constitutions);
- Informal constraints (e.g. conventions, codes of conduct);
- Ways to impose and enforce them.

He further adds that institutions provide an incentive structure for the exchange processes in the political, social, and economic spheres (North, 1990, p. 3). Rules can be changed from day to day, whereas conventions/norms evolve gradually. Only changes in standards can bring success in terms of efficiency (i.e. ensure the desired direction of change) (North, 1991). In his view, institutions create the rules of the game, whereas organisations and their members are players.

Here we arrive at the distinction between institutions and organisations. As Ch. Edquist writes, organisations are consciously created formal structures (Edquist, 2005, p. 182). As such, they consist of groups and individuals who pursue or intend to pursue a common goal. They may constitute not only economic (e.g. enterprises), but also educational, political, and social bodies. According to D. C. North, the emergence of an organisation is sanctioned by its institutional structure. For example, if it rewards productive activity, organisations involved in it, such as enterprises, will be established (North, 1991). Thus, *institution* created by formal and informal conditions is a broader concept than *organisation* identified only with formal structures. An institution may consist of one or more organisations.

Creating and changing institutions are long-term processes, with their pace depending on specific local conditions. This issue was discussed by Fukuyama, who analysed the following four components of institutional potential: 1. designing and managing organisations; 2. designing political systems; 3. the basis of legitimacy; and 4. social and cultural factors in terms of susceptibility to change (Fukuyama, 2005, p. 47). According to Fukuyama, the design and management of organisations is the most susceptible (mobile), followed by designing political systems understood as institutions at the level of the state as a whole rather than its individual agencies. Both components are of interest to the science of economics. It is much more difficult to build the foundations of legitimacy, where institutions must not only be efficient but also reliable in the eyes of society. Whether or not these components succeed depends on cultural and structural factors that determine the kinds of institutions that can be created in a given society. As F. Fukuyama writes, cultural norms and values are susceptible to political intervention only to a limited extent. Conversely, cultural values can be shaped through education, authority, and cultural exchange with other countries. Although the latter two components do not tend to be directly addressed by economics scholars, they do influence economic processes and therefore must be taken into account in such studies (Fukuyama, 2005).

D. C. North also identified certain distinctive characteristics of institutional change in the economy, which, in his opinion, occurs through the evolution of institutions and organisations. He noted that transformations are possible in the process of mutual interaction between institutions and organisations (North, 1991). The emergence of organisations is determined by institutions; as was already mentioned, organisations that can be rewarded by existing institutional structures are established. Change takes place as long as individuals believe that modified versions of the latter will operate better. According to D. C. North, the primary source of change is the learning process of individuals and members of an organisation. Economic change takes place when it is necessary to modify the existing rules and standards of behaviour that govern the exchange processes. In other words, economic change, like the formation of an organisation, is determined by institutional change (North, 1991).

The brief discussion above is intended to emphasise the importance of institutions in economic processes, including specific location decisions taken by firms. Moreover, studies conducted in the spirit of institutions thus conceived are consistent with the concept of *path dependence*, where the dependence of present and future development directions on historical conditions is emphasised (cf. e.g. David, 2000), or the problem of *cultural lag*,[1] i.e. the failure of social change to keep pace with economic change. Institutional changes, especially those that affect rules and informal norms, generally take place over a longer period of time and should be reflected in the investors' decisions. Having a similar investment offer in different countries with similar labour costs and education of potential employees, the existing institutional conditions and prospects for their change may be crucial when choosing a given country as a place for outsourcing and offshoring activities.

Institutional conditions in Central Europe

Central Europe as a geographical concept can be understood in different ways. For the purposes of this chapter, it shall be taken to denote the Visegrad group countries (V4), namely the Czech Republic, Hungary, Poland, and Slovakia (cf. e.g. Tiersky, 2004). These countries share a common historical and cultural heritage and, in the case of prospective location decisions, are often put in a single investment basket. However, the Visegrad countries are burdened by their historical baggage, which for a long time prevented or at least significantly impeded independent decision-making on administrative and economic reforms. Suffice it to mention that from the early 19th century until 1989, these countries experienced only about 20 years of independence (in the interwar period). Before World War I, they were parts of other countries,[2] and in the mid-1940s, they became USSR's satellite countries. Throughout the 19th century, and the vast majority of the 20th century, reforms in the region were thus derived from those solutions pursued (or imposed) by the dominant countries. The implementation of Western socio-economic mechanisms in the V4 countries became possible only after 1989 (Kopyciński, 2020). Since then, the leaders of change have changed several times (initially, Hungary was perceived as such, then Slovakia, and eventually Poland). These countries often competed for the same investors, e.g. in the automotive industry.

Despite the significant differences, there is much to suggest that a distinct model of public governance has emerged (or is being consolidated) in the V4 countries, which shall be called the hesitant institutional convergence model (Kopyciński, 2020). This is a double hybrid model: on the one hand, it is an amalgam of institutions historically rooted in these countries, which include the legacy of socialism and the previous structures of other state organisations with elements of Western models (primarily new public management and, to some extent, public governance, which is particularly conspicuous at the local level); on the other, depending on the country, it is characterised by different proportions of the aforementioned features of Western and domestic models. In short, the characteristic features of the hesitant institutional convergence model include (Kopyciński, 2020):

1 Increasing Euro-scepticism and the superficial reforms carried out in connection with EU accession;
2 Sustainability of certain features inherited from the socialist system (and more broadly, from the Eastern-Byzantine tradition);
3 Attempts to put into practice the idea of illiberal democracy;
4 The fluidity of boundaries between the political and administrative spheres (impermanence of reforms originally intended to separate politics from administration or the relatively late adoption of civil service reforms);
5 Conflicts of interest between political and business activities;
6 Progressive centralisation and reducing local governments' range of responsibilities;
7 Higher levels of corruption than in the West;
8 Lower levels of trust than in the West.

As a result of a combination of historical and institutional factors, the Visegrad countries straddle East and West. Their levels of corruption are higher than in Northern European countries, but lower than in the East. Moreover, the level of trust in the state and its institutions also places them in the middle of Europe. Finally, the still existing remnants of the socialist (Byzantine) system mean that the presence of these countries in Western structures is not necessarily as permanent as it seemed until recently, and that their reform path may be reversed, as manifested by a range of authoritarian policy decisions, or the so-called illiberal democracy. Up to a point, such propensities may be considered as neutral from the investors' perspective. However, in the future, problems with the rule of law may affect corporate decisions about doing business in these countries.

Embeddedness the offshoring and outsourcing sector in Krakow – inspiration for research

Micek et al. (2010) noticed a lack of studies on services centres as embedded in their relevant socio-economic context. In response, they prepared a publication on the embeddedness of the offshoring and outsourcing sector in Krakow and its relations with the environment. In the introductory chapter, the authors refer, among other things, to relevant theories of embeddedness, understanding of outsourcing and offshoring, as well as the types of centres currently operating in Krakow. They draw on the institutional approach, which in the context under discussion refers to the impact of "the effects of various actors (foreign and domestic firms, local, regional, and state authorities, transnational organisations, trade unions, etc.) on local and regional development" (Micek et al., 2010, p. 11). It is worth emphasising that the cited research is comprehensive and includes such issues as reasons why particular services centres were established in Krakow, relations of these firms with the local environment, their employees' opinions

Table 12.1 Components of the local embeddedness indicator for offshoring and outsourcing firms

Component of embeddedness	*Measure*
Relations with suppliers and customers	Level of use of local suppliers
Relations with local actors	Relations with higher education institutions
	Relations with local authorities
	Relations with business environment institutions
Community activities	Community activities under corporate social responsibility (CSR) policy
Origin of employees, including managers	Share of Polish managers in managerial staff

Source: Own study based on Micek et al. (2010, s. 104).

about the studied sector, and finally, the embeddedness of firms in Krakow and the stability of their presence.

Micek et al. (2009, p. 15) defined the embeddedness of a firm as its participation "in a broad spectrum of socio-economic relations with the environment" and noted that the degree of embeddedness depends on the use of local supplies and services, as well as relations with local actors, i.e. public authorities, business environment institutions and universities, activities for the benefit of the local community, and the relations of their employees with the city. On this basis, they prepared a synthetic embeddedness index the components of which (without assigning individual weights) are presented in Table 12.1.

As a result, the authors identified the firms' durability understood as a low propensity to relocate, which is affected by the following factors (Micek et al., 2009, p. 15):

- Their degree of embeddedness in a given place;
- Their role (function) in the structure of the corporation as a whole;
- The characteristics of a given location that determine its attractiveness;
- The existence of other attractive locations;
- Capital commitment and financial performance of the company;
- The market situation related to doing business in the industry.

The findings of research on the embeddedness of firms and employees of the offshoring and outsourcing sector in Krakow

The cited publication (Micek et al., 2010) became one of the inspirations (apart from the significant growth of this sector in Krakow in the last decade) to conduct a study on the phenomenon of embeddedness of firms representing the offshoring and outsourcing sector and their employees in Krakow and Zabierzow near Krakow (for the sake of simplicity, we shall refer to both as Krakow).

The survey was conducted in 2019–2020 among the employees and management staff of firms representing the offshoring and outsourcing sector in the

Krakow agglomeration. The study consisted of two stages. In the first stage, 15 interviews with the CEOs of business services centres were conducted using a questionnaire. In the second stage, the survey covered 316 employees of the above-mentioned firms using an online questionnaire (CAWI).

Two aspects of embeddedness were studied:

1 Firms in Krakow;
2 Employees by type of embeddedness:

    a in Krakow (local embeddedness),
    b in the offshoring and outsourcing sector,
    c corporate embeddedness of a specific firm in the offshoring and outsourcing sector.

The comprehensive research concerned the firms' relations with a variety of actors (e.g. local suppliers, universities, public authorities, and relations with the environment in terms of corporate social responsibility [CSR] activities undertaken). This chapter discusses the findings on the embeddedness of firms and their employees in Krakow.

The findings of research on the embeddedness of employees of firms in the offshoring and outsourcing sector in Krakow

Employees were first asked about the legal title to their place of residence. In Poland, owning a house or a flat is considered to be one of the indicators of the strength of one's links with a given place. It turned out that almost 63% of respondents own their flats, whereas slightly over 37% live in rented premises (for Poland as a whole, the percentage of people living in houses or flats that they own is one of the highest in Europe and exceeded 84% in 2019). Then they were asked to assess the general quality of life in Krakow and their readiness to leave the city (Table 12.2). In general, Krakow was considered to be a good place to live (median close to 4.0), and the surveyed persons do not intend to move to another city in Poland (median = 1) or abroad (median = 1) in the coming years.

The next question was intended to assess specific aspects of life in Krakow. In this category, the highest scoring (median = 5) were attractiveness of the city centre, access to services, cultural and entertainment offer, and the situation of the labour

Table 12.2 General assessment of the quality of life in Krakow and potential mobility of employees in the offshoring and outsourcing sector

	Krakow is a good place to live	*I am planning to move out of Poland within the next year*	*Over the next year I am going to move to another city in Poland*
Median	4	1	1
Average	3.9	1.6	1.5

Assessed on a scale from 1 to 5, where 1 means "definitely no" and 5 means "definitely yes".

Source: Own study based on the survey findings.

market. The lowest scores were given to air quality in the city and availability of parking spaces (the city, as part of its policy of sustainable development and promotion of public transport, systematically reduces the number of parking spaces available for cars and limits the number of vehicles allowed in the centre, e.g. through a system of parking fees). Detailed evaluations are shown in Figure 12.1.

The findings of research on the embeddedness of offshoring and outsourcing firms in Krakow

Managers of Krakow's offshoring and outsourcing firms were asked about the scale of cooperation with selected local and regional entities (Table 12.3). In

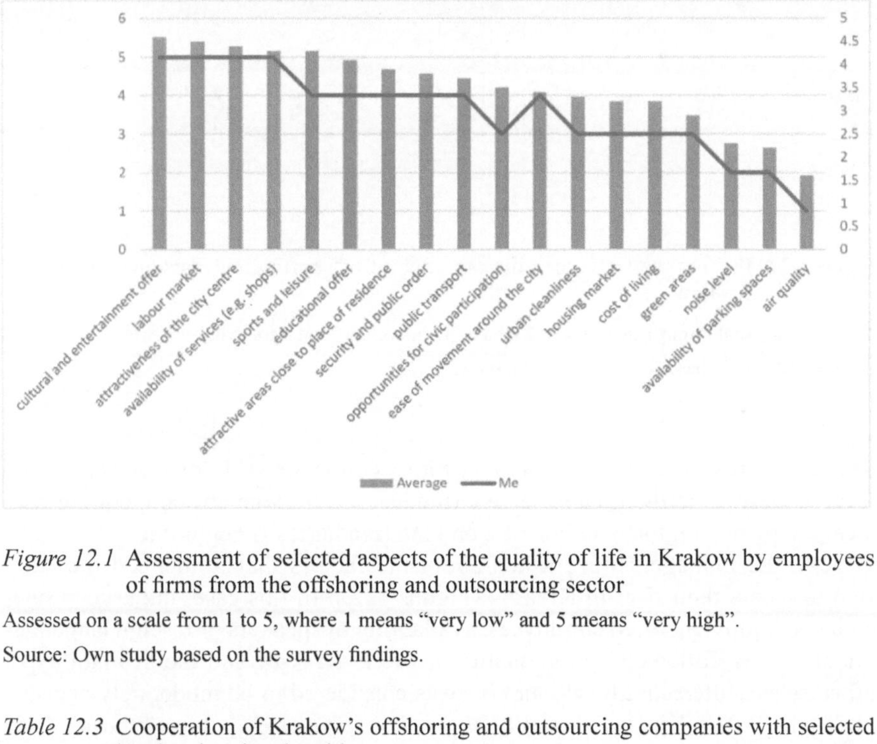

Figure 12.1 Assessment of selected aspects of the quality of life in Krakow by employees of firms from the offshoring and outsourcing sector

Assessed on a scale from 1 to 5, where 1 means "very low" and 5 means "very high".

Source: Own study based on the survey findings.

Table 12.3 Cooperation of Krakow's offshoring and outsourcing companies with selected local and regional entities

	Local suppliers	*Local authorities (incl. City of Krakow Office, Labour Offices)*	*Regional authorities (incl. Marshal's Office)*	*Local recipients*	*Intermediaries (e.g. technology park, financial institution)*
Median	3	3	2	2	2
Average	3.1	2.9	2.4	2.3	2.3

Assessed on a scale from 1 to 5, where 1 means "lack of cooperation" and 5 for "very active cooperation".

Source: Own study based on the survey findings.

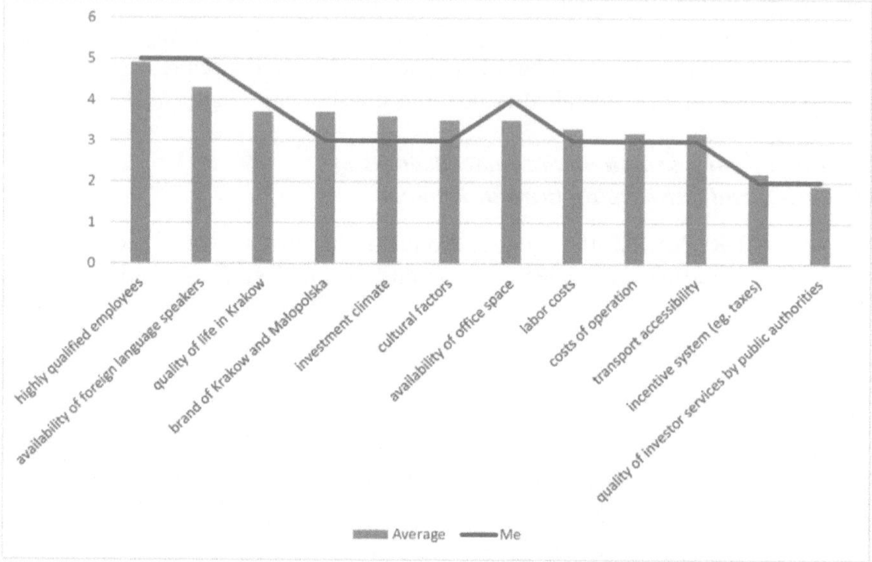

Figure 12.2 Factors that influence the presence of offshoring and outsourcing firms in Krakow

Assessed on a scale from 1 to 5, where 1 means "unimportant" and 5 for "very important".

Source: Own study based on the survey findings.

general, it proved to be fairly limited. Firms cooperate with local suppliers and local authorities to the greatest extent (median = 3.0), whereas cooperation with local recipients, regional authorities, and intermediaries is negligible.

Next, the managers were asked about the factors that influenced the decision to locate their firm in Krakow (Figure 12.2). In this case, the crucial ones included highly qualified employees, availability of speakers of foreign languages (median = 5), followed by the quality of life in Krakow and the availability of office space. Interestingly, labour cost was considered to be moderately decisive (median = 3.0), whereas the quality of investor services by public authorities and the incentive system were considered of minor importance.

However, the generally positive ratings of Krakow do not mean that the surveyed firms do not plan to relocate elsewhere. About half of them do consider moving some or all of their operations from Krakow to other locations.

Conclusions and summary

Since joining the European Union, the Central European countries have become an attractive place to invest in the offshoring and outsourcing sector. Especially, the decade after the 2007–2008 crisis marked a period of increased activity in this field. According to the latest Tholons Services Globalization City Index

2019, Krakow is the most attractive city in Central Europe and the second most attractive in Europe (after Dublin; in an earlier edition of the survey, Krakow ranked 1st in Europe) and 11th worldwide to locate such investment. From the firms' point of view, their presence in Krakow is not determined by the quality of investor services by public authorities or the incentive system, but by the presence of highly qualified employees, availability of speakers of foreign languages, and the quality of life in Krakow. Labour costs are moderately significant in their case. The embeddedness of these companies in Krakow as measured by their level of cooperation with local entities is limited to contacts with local suppliers and local authorities. On the other hand, the employees of these firms declare that Krakow is a good place to live; moreover, they do not intend to move elsewhere in Poland or abroad in the nearest future. They highly appreciate the attractive city centre, access to services, cultural and entertainment offerings, and the local situation on the labour market, which is clearly beneficial for them. What they consider to be a disadvantage is the low air quality in the city, even though it has recently improved thanks to the efforts of local activists and the city authorities (the ban on the use of solid fuels for heating purposes became effective in 2019). Further action is necessary in this respect, but this requires the involvement of neighbouring local governments as well as central government decision on a nationwide scale.

According to the cited research, the location of firms from the offshoring and outsourcing sector in Krakow is certainly influenced by institutional conditions, which include, among others, the aforementioned attractiveness of the city centre and rich cultural, entertainment, and culinary offerings, or the quality of life in Krakow, which all contribute to the kind of Krakow's genius loci – a city with a long-standing university and scientific traditions. Its tourism potential permits it to be considered on a par with other cities in the region, such as Budapest, Prague, and Vienna.

It is also worth noting that the arrival and growth of firms in the studied sector in Krakow is only to a small extent due to the quality of investor service provided by public authorities or the existence of an incentive system. The presence of the offshoring and outsourcing sector in Krakow is therefore largely independent of the efforts of public authorities, and for the most part depends on the situation in global markets as well as on its attractiveness as a location. Certainly, Poland's presence in the European Union helps, as it ensures a common economic and, to some extent, political space. However, this does not alter the fact that the surveyed firms are only moderately embedded in Krakow (as reflected by their limited cooperation with local actors and the anticipated relocation of at least part of their operations elsewhere). It transpires that public authorities do not have effective tools to prevent such transfers. What they can do is implement a long-term programme to develop Krakow as a brand in the world and to improve the attractiveness of Krakow as a place to live on an ongoing basis (e.g. by further improving the air quality). According to the research findings, this may prove to be more effective in retaining investors (and attracting new ones) than even the best investment service and/or tax exemptions.

Krakow directly competes with other Central European cities, including Bratislava, Budapest, and Prague for firms representing the offshoring and outsourcing sector. These cities have similar (or higher) standards of living and are equally attractive to tourists. They are also alike in terms of labour costs, staff education, and foreign language skills. Therefore, such phenomena as an unstable political situation or controversial institutional changes may translate into a decreased interest in investing in Krakow in favour of other Central European cities or may prompt these firms to relocate away from Krakow.

At the time of writing this text (first half of 2020), it is difficult to estimate the future impact of the coronavirus pandemic on the embeddedness of offshoring and outsourcing firms in Krakow. The situation has no precedent in recent history, in the modern era of globalisation. Certainly, at present, one cannot draw analogies between the 2007–2008 crisis, when a number of firms wanting to cut costs moved their selected operations to Krakow, thanks to which the city grew to be a significant player in the studied sector. Wages in the city are now much higher than a dozen or so years ago; besides, as was already pointed out, the wage pressure is no longer the basic factor in locating companies in Krakow. Moreover, many firms in the face of the pandemic have switched to remote working, where some employees can remain permanently even after the threat has subsided. The fact that the physical presence of employees in a given location may become gradually less important may adversely affect the development of the studied sector in Krakow or, in an extreme case, contribute to its shrinking.

Notes

1 The issue of social adjustment, including cultural lag, which means failure to keep up with the changes in culture in relation to the changes that occur e.g. in industry (nowadays, it could be technological change) was noted by W. F. Ogburn (1922, pp. 200–213).

2 Hungary was a co-equal kingdom in Austria-Hungary in 1867–1918.

References

Bertelsmann Stiftung. (2018). *Policy Performance and Governance Capacities in the OECD and EU: Sustainable Governance Indicators 2018*. Gütersloh: Bertelsmann Stiftung.

David, P. (2000). *Path Dependence, Its Critics and the Quest for 'Historical Economics'*. Working Paper. All Souls College, Oxford University.

Edquist, Ch. (2005). Systems of innovation. Perspectives and challenges. In J. Fegerberg, D.C. Mowery, & R.R. Nelson (Eds.), *The Oxford Handbook of Innovation*. New York: Oxford University Press.

Fukuyama, F. (2005). *Budowanie państwa. Władza i ład międzynarodowy w XXI wieku*. Poznań: Dom Wydawniczy Rebis.

Kopyciński, P. (2020). Modes of governance in the Visegrad countries: Towards the hesitant institutional convergence. In S. Mazur (Ed.), *Public Administration in Central Europe: Ideas as Causes of Reforms*. London and New York: Routledge.

Micek, G., Działek, J., & Górecki, J. (2009). *Centra usług w Krakowie i ich relacje z otoczeniem lokalnym* [accessed from: www.researchgate.net/publication/259008890].

Micek, G., Działek, J., & Górecki, J. (2010). *Centra usług w Krakowie i ich relacje z otoczeniem lokalnym*. Kraków: Wydawnictwo Uniwersytetu Jagiellońskiego.

North, D.C. (1990). *Institutions, Institutional Change and Economic Performance*. Cambridge: Cambridge University Press.

North, D.C. (1991). Institutions. *Journal of Economic Perspectives*, *5*(1), pp. 97–112.

Ogburn, W.F. (1922). *Social Change with Respect to Culture and Original Nature*. New York: University of California.

Tholons. (2019). *Tholons Services Globalization Index* [accessed from: http://tholons.com/tholons-services-globalization-index/].

Tiersky, R. (2004). *Europe Today*. Lanham: Rowman & Littlefield Publishers.

13 The importance of Fintech's development for the embeddedness of outsourcing and offshoring firms

Jakub Głowacki

Introduction

Currently, financial technology (Fintech) is a dynamically developing industry, which has changed the landscape of the financial sector in recent years. It has stirred up strong emotions around the world, both positive and negative ones, as Fintech solutions enter hitherto dominated markets, offering new customer-friendly solutions. Such trends are manifest not only in the financial markets of highly developed countries, but also in developing countries, including Central and Eastern Europe. The aim of this chapter is to assess the importance of Fintech for the embeddedness of outsourcing and offshoring firms operating in Krakow. It begins with a presentation of various definitions, history, and classifications of Fintech, and goes on to discuss the specific reasons for its popularity in Central and Eastern European countries. The chapter also explores a range of factors that determine Fintech's success and its impact on the financial sector. The final part of the chapter contains an analysis of a survey conducted among the employees of Krakow's branches of business services centres carried out in order to determine the importance of technological development (including Fintech) on the degree of embeddedness of outsourcing and offshoring firms.

Fintech – definitions and development history

Fintech can be defined in a variety of ways. On the one hand, the term is used in an instrumental sense to cover innovative solutions in the financial sector, and on the other, it denotes a firm (usually a start-up) that offers this kind of service. The latter approach is supported by Nicoletti (2017, p. 3), who describes Fintech as: "reshaping the financial services industry, offering customer-centric services capable of combining speed and flexibility, backed by forward-looking strategies, and cutting-edge business models". The sectoral approach is also present in the literature: Fintech is a "new financial industry that applies technology to improve financial activities" (Schueffel, 2017, p. 13).

Fintech is not a new phenomenon in the financial services industry. It can be described as a process that has been going on continuously for almost 200 years and is characterised by variable dynamics. Arner et al. (2015) identified three key stages in the development of Fintech, which resulted from specific technological breakthroughs. The first such breakthrough was the invention of the electromagnetic telegraph in 1833, which revolutionised the system of remote information transmission and had a considerable impact on the development of the financial sector (Du Boff, 1980; Winston, 1998). An extra factor that facilitated radiotelegraphic communication (not only in the financial sector) was the laying of a telegraphic cable across the floor of the Atlantic Ocean in 1866. It connected Europe with North America, and the scale of the subsequent revolution is reflected, among others, in the fact that it reduced the time needed to transmit a message between the two continents to a few minutes, while previously it used to take as many as 10 days by sea (Russell, 2011). Such a radically increased flow of information between the capital markets of New York and London led to a situation in which quotes on the then London Stock Exchange almost immediately reflected the newly available data from the New York Stock Exchange (Hoag, 2006). The dynamic development of communication via telegraph precisely coincided with the second industrial revolution (Kagermann et al., 2013), which extensively used electricity in the production process and provided the driving force for the world economy in the second half of the 19th century. The telegraphic link between Europe and North America was also the first harbinger of globalisation, which gradually began to take over the financial markets (and not only) in the 20th century. This era, until the outbreak of World War I, is known as Fintech 1.0.

The second technological breakthrough in the financial industry took place in 1967 with the introduction of ATMs by Barclays Bank. The world's first cash dispenser was installed in Enfield Town in North London and paid out cash upon insertion of a special perforated cheque with C14 stripes. This British innovation was quite quickly adapted by American (NCR) and German (Siemens-Wincor) manufacturers, who later came to dominate the world market. The evolution of this technology perfectly illustrates the change that took place in the organisation of financial institutions. Firstly, they started to digitalise and automate financial transactions in real time, which later made it possible to create electronic banking systems. Secondly, ATMs freed up a large proportion of the human resources (tellers) needed at bank branches to serve customers who wished to withdraw cash. These two trends, i.e. the beginnings of the process of digitalising services and the gradual transfer of employees to other areas of a firm's operations, are also characteristic of the third industrial revolution, which began in the late 1960s and involved the use of programmable controllers for further production automation (Kagermann et al., 2013). The period from 1967–2008 is called Fintech 2.0.

Today, Fintech is in its third stage of development and, unlike the first or the second ones, it was not a technological breakthrough that marked its beginning. It is widely acknowledged that the third era started in 2008 with the beginning of the global financial and economic crisis, which provided the trigger for a further development of this industry. Given the problems faced by large financial institutions all over the world, new start-ups and established technology firms began to provide financial products and services directly to the public, bypassing the major players in the field, mainly banks. This change was made possible by altering the way consumers think about who in the industry has the legitimacy and resources needed to provide financial services (Arner et al., 2015).

Fintech typology

A number of different Fintech classifications (Gimpel et al., 2018) can be found in the literature and industry reports. One of them (Deloitte, 2016) divides Fintech solutions into two parts:

1. **Established financial technologies**, which include banking, insurance, asset management and capital markets – in particular, they comprise information technology (IT) solutions developed directly by the employees of a given financial institution or by an external supplier in support of such primary areas of activity as CBS (capital budget system), CRM (customer relationship management), billing, online/mobile banking, trading, compliance, etc. Other solutions concern such aspects as: improving the offer, sales and service model, capabilities, or process efficiency of banking, insurance, and asset management players (e.g. application programming interface (API), alternative trading schemes, foreign exchange platforms).
2. **Emerging financial technologies**, which comprise:

    - **payments**, i.e. IT solutions supporting payments, money transfers, and cash handling, which may include e.g. mobile payment terminals (mPOS) or near-field communication (NFC) payments, software, and infrastructure for Internet and mobile payments, cryptographic, or prepaid and non-bank debit cards;
    - **capital raising and personal finance**, i.e. systems designed for non-banking capital raising and financial management, e.g. peer-to-peer (P2P) lending markets, micro-loans, social finance, mobile financial advice, and solutions intended to encourage saving habits;
    - **cybersecurity**, i.e. solutions to increase security at the level of the entire financial system (including data security, protection against fraud, and customer verification schemes) and at the level of individual users;
    - **data and analytics**, i.e. solutions enabling financial analysis based on large data sets, including analytical software, credit scores, and data-based market analyses for financial institutions;
    - **other software** – software not otherwise classified, including distributed ledger technologies (databases that can securely record financial, physical, and electronic assets for sharing across a network through entirely transparent updates of information) and systems and applications supporting the financial functions of companies (such as accounting, controlling, and debt collection).

Another convenient and up-to-date overview of Fintech's classification was presented by Chen et al. 2019. The Fintech industry was broken down into seven

Table 13.1 Fintech typology

Cybersecurity	**Category definitions:** Hardware or software used to protect financial privacy or safeguard against electronic theft or fraud **Key technologies:** Encryption, tokenization, authentication, and biometrics **Examples:** *Diebold iris-scanning ATM, Mastercard Biometric Card, USAA face recognition login, and Experian CreditLock*
Mobile Transactions	**Category definitions:** Technologies that facilitate payments via mobile wireless devices, such as smartphones, tablets, and wearables **Key technologies:** Smartphone wallets, digital wallets, and near-field communication **Examples:** *Apple Pay, Android Pay, PayPal, Mobile Express Checkout, Venmo, and Square*
Data Analytics	**Category definitions:** Technologies and algorithms that facilitate the analysis of transactions data or consumer financial data **Key technologies:** Big data, cloud computing, artificial intelligence, and machine learning **Examples:** *Equifax NeuroDecision credit scoring, JPMorgan Contract Intelligence (COiN), and Bloomberg Social Sentiment Analytics*
Blockchain	**Category definitions:** Distributed ledger technologies with a primary application to financial services **Key technologies:** Cryptocurrency, proof-of-work, smart contracts, and directed acyclic graphs **Examples:** *Bitcoin, Ripple Payment Network, Visa B2B Connect, and Nasdaq Linq asset trading platform*
Peer-to-peer (P2P)	**Category definitions:** Software, systems, or platforms that facilitate consumer-to-consumer financial transactions **Key technologies:** Crowdfunding, P2P lending, and customer-to-customer payments **Examples:** *GoFundMe, Kickstarter, Lending Club, Prosper Marketplace, and Zelle*
Robo-advising	**Category definitions:** Computer systems or programs that provide automated investment advice to customers or portfolio managers **Key technologies:** Artificial intelligence, big data, and machine learning **Examples:** *Betterment, E-Trade Core Portfolios, Schwab Intelligent Portfolios, and Vanguard Personal Advisor Services*
Internet of Things (IOT)	**Category definitions:** Technologies relating to smart devices that gather data in real time and communicate via the Internet **Key technologies:** Smart devices, near-field communication, wireless sensor networks, and actuators **Examples:** *UnitedHealthcare Motion F.I.T. tracker, Nationwide SmartRide telematics, and Travelers Insurance smart home sensors*

Source: Own study based on Chen et al. (2019).

areas: cybersecurity, mobile transactions, data analytics, blockchain, peer-to-peer (P2P), robo-advising, and the Internet of Things (IoT).

The development of Fintech in Central and Eastern Europe

The societies of Central and Eastern European countries quite readily accept various innovations in the area of finance. This provides a fertile ground for the development of assorted Fintech solutions; a trend supported by industry reports. For example, more than 90% of Slovenian firms issue and receive invoices in electronic format through their electronic banking systems (Deloitte, 2016). Data from MasterCard reveal that 50% of Slovak cardholders pay using contactless technology and 75% are willing to use (or will continue to use) it in the future. According to ING International Survey 2015 (ING, 2015), 60% of smartphone users in Poland have already used or expect to use mobile banking apps, which is the third best result in Europe, just behind the Netherlands (67%), the United Kingdom (63%), and on a par with Spain. Another example of consumers' readiness to use financial innovations in the Polish banking sector is the use of contactless debit cards. Almost 80% of all the cards issued in Poland have dedicated chips, compared to 54% in the UK.

According to Deloitte's calculations (2016), the value of the Fintech sector in nine Central and Eastern European (CEE) countries totals 2.2 billion euros. Poland emerges as a clear leader in the region, ahead of Austria and the Czech Republic.

In recent years, Fintech firms have shown a particular interest in payments, since in the era of numerous breakthrough solutions and the growing popularity of e-commerce, this area has become remarkably profitable. Poland and the Czech Republic have emerged as regional leaders thanks to the development of sophisticated payment solutions where transactions are processed by robots, which enables rapid order execution.

Table 13.2 Fintech market in CEE countries

Country	*Fintech market size (in million euros)*
Poland	856
Austria	588
Czech Republic	190
Slovenia	121
Romania	119
Croatia	92
Hungary	83
Slovakia	73
Bulgaria	39

Source: Own study based on Deloitte (2016, p. 75).

The main barriers to further development of the CEE markets are posed by regulatory issues. Public institutions quite often introduce special requirements or restrictions which hinder the implementation of innovative financial solutions. Countries with less-developed economies and limited internal demand are usually less attractive for the Fintech industry. The favourable features of business environments, such as low tax rates and competitive labour costs, attract young start-ups intent on succeeding in the CEE countries (Deloitte, 2016).

Development factors and impacts on the financial sector

Puschmann (2017) identifies a range of factors conducive to the development of Fintech in the traditional banking and insurance industry over the past several years. First is the internal digitalisation of financial institutions. The first attempts to use the IT potential focused on internal processes, such as payment transactions or portfolio management. In the initial stages, banks and insurers embarked on the automation of financial services processes mainly with a view to increasing their efficiency. Firms offered only one or two customer service channels (branch/consultant or insurance agent + ATM) and focused on support, mostly through back-office services. The integration of IT systems at the time did not exist or was only partial. It emerged and developed in the third stage, in which the first multi-channel approaches were adopted.

Chronologically speaking, the next development factor was provider-oriented digitalisation. In this stage, financial institutions began to integrate their suppliers. To that end, they introduced uniform rules for the standardisation of processes and software functions. The outsourcing of business processes began with support areas such as IT, and only later did it involve the back-office areas such as payments, investments, and credit service. Currently, the degree of utilisation of own resources in business processes is relatively high in the German-speaking countries, such as Germany (73.8% in-house production), Austria (77.5%), and Switzerland (90%). Other European countries usually display lower rates, e.g. Luxembourg 50.7% or Sweden 53.8% (Alt, 2016).

The latest Fintech development factor involved customer-oriented digitalisation processes. This area focuses on the needs and expectations of clients and redefines the existing product-oriented logic towards creating new solutions. Early examples of this approach comprised electronic wallets, including not only payments but also the ability to collect, store, and issue loyalty points and other personal data. These new services also take advantage of the development of peer-to-peer (P2P) business models. In Poland, this development is perhaps best exemplified by the Internet exchange offices, which entered the market quite quickly and continue to operate successfully largely due to the demand for this kind of service on the part of people who pay off foreign currency loans. The scale of operations of these entities, thanks to the automation of currency exchange processes, makes the currency spreads much more competitive than those offered by traditional exchange offices. In this case, Fintech's solution has, on the one hand, reduced the required human resources and on the other, solved the problem of building expensive infrastructure needed to secure the premises of an exchange office.

The development of Fintech provoked a discussion on its potential threats to the traditional financial sector. In the literature and industry reports, opinions are divided. Although the innovations created by Fintech are considered to have a destructive impact on the financial services sector (Waupsh, 2017; Zalan & Toufaily, 2017; PwC, 2017), some analysts assert that both sectors will find their market niches and their services will prove to be complementary (Vives, 2017). Fintech often provides the same services as banks, probably even more efficiently due to the technology used. However, it does this in a slightly different way. For example, even though social funding platforms, like banks, transform savings into loans and investments, the former rely heavily on big data to process information. In contrast, banks use long-term customer relations for this purpose. It is also difficult for platforms to offer diverse investment opportunities without keeping part of the risk on their books. Thus, Fintech solutions providers undoubtedly increase competition in financial markets, provide services that traditional financial institutions do less efficiently or not at all, and expand the pool of users of such services. Yet they cannot replace banks in most of their key functions. Fintech solutions devise ever more efficient ways of delivering traditional financial services, but banks are also well prepared to accept technological innovations and provide these traditional services themselves (Vives, 2017).

Fintech and the embeddedness of the business process outsourcing sector in Krakow

For many years, the level of embeddedness of Krakow's business process outsourcing centres (BPOCs) has been discussed by the industry's representatives and local government. In 2005, when a regular inflow of such firms to Krakow began and employment in the sector grew very dynamically (20–30% per annum on average; Aspire, 2019), more and more concerns were raised about the stability of employment for a large proportion of the city's population in the event of a further increase in labour costs and potential relocation to other parts of the world (e.g. India). Nevertheless, the Krakow business services centres (BSC) environment believes that recent years have seen a steady increase in the complexity of services provided by them. The aim of the discussion below is therefore, firstly, to verify this opinion and, secondly, to identify the links between the change in the nature of services and the technological changes in the area of finance and the embeddedness of business process outsourcing centres (BPOCs) in Krakow. The following are the findings of research conducted in 2019 and 2020 among the CEOs (15) – branch managers of firms operating in Krakow (interviews based on questionnaire), and their employees (316) using an online questionnaire (CAWI). In the part covering technological change, the survey contained questions about the complexity and uniqueness of the services provided. The respondents rated the current characteristics of the processes (on a 1–5 scale, where 1 meant 'not complex/unique at all' and 5 meant 'highly complex'), and the change in complexity/

uniqueness that has taken place over the last 5 years (1 – 'significantly decreased', 3 – 'no change', 5 – 'significantly increased').

Employees were also asked to evaluate the technological changes in the last five years (on a 1–5 scale, where 1 meant 'no change', 5 – 'very big change', and 0 – 'don't know') that have taken place in the main areas of their firms' activity: finance, human resources, IT, research and development, supply chain management, help desk, information security, technology tools, cloud platforms, and others.

It was assumed that the complexity and uniqueness of the services provided are positively correlated with the embeddedness of Krakow's BPOCs. The research, therefore, verified the following hypotheses:

1 The last five years have seen profound changes in the complexity and uniqueness of services provided by BPOCs in Krakow.
2 Changes in complexity and uniqueness of the services provided are associated with the process of technological change.

In order to verify the first hypothesis, a simple frequency analysis was used (Table 13.3), which shows that more than 70% of the employees believe that the complexity of their services is high or very high; only less than 8% responded that the services are 'not complex at all' or 'complex to a very small extent'. As far as uniqueness is concerned, the distribution of responses almost perfectly follows normal distribution. This means that according to the employees of Krakow's BPOCs, the services that they provide are characterised by an average level of uniqueness.

When analysing the changes in complexity and uniqueness that have occurred in the last five years, one can see a clear increasing trend in complexity (almost 73% of respondents believe that the positive change in this respect was large or very

Table 13.3 Current complexity and uniqueness of processes performed by BPOCs operating in Krakow in the opinion of their employees (N = 316)

Complexity			*Uniqueness*		
Rating	*No. of responses*	*Percentage*	*Rating*	*No. of responses*	*Percentage*
1	2	0.65%	1	43	13.92%
2	22	7.12%	2	67	21.68%
3	65	21.04%	3	98	31.72%
4	130	42.07%	4	70	22.65%
5	90	29.13%	5	31	10.03%

Mean	*Median*	*Mode*	*Standard deviation*	*Mean*	*Median*	*Mode*	*Standard deviation*
3.9191	4	4	0.91697	2.932	3	3	1.1837

Source: Own study.

large, whereas only 6.5% say that the change was negative) and a slight increase in uniqueness (almost 45% of respondents believe that the positive change was large or very large in this respect, whereas less than 9% think that it was negative). However, it is worth noting that a large group of respondents (46.5%) reported no change in uniqueness.

Surveys conducted among the CEOs support the conclusions drawn from the employee survey. The distribution of answers concerning complexity is very

Table 13.4 Changes in the complexity and uniqueness of processes performed by BPOCs operating in Krakow in the last five years in the opinion of their employees (N = 316)

Change in Complexity in the Last Five Years				*Change in Uniqueness in the Last Five Years*			
Rating	*No. of responses*	*Percentage*		*Rating*	*No. of responses*	*Percentage*	
1	4	1.30%		1	9	2.93%	
2	16	5.19%		2	18	5.86%	
3	64	20.78%		3	143	46.58%	
4	147	47.73%		4	96	31.27%	
5	77	25.00%		5	41	13.36%	
Mean	*Median*	*Mode*	*Standard deviation*	*Mean*	*Median*	*Mode*	*Standard deviation*
3.8994	4	4	0.88026	3.4625	3	3	0.90083

Source: Own study.

Table 13.5 Current relative complexity and uniqueness of processes performed by BPOCs operating in Krakow in the opinion of their CEOs (N = 15)

Complexity			*Uniqueness*		
Rating	*No. of responses*	*Percentage*	*Rating*	*No. of responses*	*Percentage*
1	0	0.00%	1	0	0.00%
2	2	15.38%	2	0	0.00%
3	1	7.69%	3	3	21.43%
4	5	38.46%	4	6	42.86%
5	5	38.46%	5	5	35.71%
Mean	*Median*	*Standard deviation*	*Mean*	*Median*	*Standard deviation*
4.1429	4	0.7703	4.0000	4	1.0801

Source: Own study.

similar. In terms of uniqueness, the answers of the surveyed CEOs suggest that it is indeed above average in comparison with other branches of their firms.

As regards the change in complexity which has occurred over the last five years, the CEOs considered it to be large or very large. No one reported a downward trend in this parameter in recent years. The CEOs also considered the change in uniqueness to be rather positive (71%), and the extent of this change does not differ much from the extent of change in complexity.

Table 13.6 Change in the relative complexity and uniqueness of processes performed by BPOCs operating in Krakow in the last five years in the opinion of their CEOs (N = 15)

Change in Complexity in the Last Five Years			*Change in Uniqueness in the Last Five Years*		
Rating	*No. of responses*	*Percentage*	*Rating*	*No. of responses*	*Percentage*
1	0	0.00%	1	0	0.00%
2	0	0.00%	2	0	0.00%
3	2	15.38%	3	4	28.57%
4	9	69.23%	4	7	50.00%
5	2	15.38%	5	3	21.43%
Mean	*Median*	*Standard deviation*	*Mean*	*Median*	*Standard deviation*
4.0000	4	0.5774	3.9286	4	0.7300

Source: Own study.

Table 13.7 Correlations between complexity/uniqueness of processes performed by BPOCs operating in Krakow and technological changes in the opinion of their employees

		Change in complexity in the last five years	*Change in uniqueness in the last five years*
Technological changes in the last five years in . . .	finance	**0.2250**	**0.2182**
	human resources	0.1429	0.0677
	IT	0.1159	–0.0037
	research & development	0.1150	0.0555
	supply chain management	0.1225	0.0305
	help desk	0.0629	0.0823
	information security	**0.2503**	0.0877
	technology tools	0.1394	0.0944
	cloud platforms	0.1483	0.0568
	other	0.0656	0.0118

Source: Own study.

The process of verification of the second hypothesis consisted in calculating the correlation between changes that occurred in complexity and uniqueness of the services provided, and technological changes in specific areas of operation. The analysis shows that even though the correlations are positive, they are mostly very small. However, it is worth noting that finance (both in comparison with complexity and uniqueness) is characterised by a much higher level of correlation than other areas of operation. Moreover, a slightly higher correlation is noticeable between technological changes and complexity.

Conclusion

Fintech is one of the main beneficiaries of the fourth industrial revolution in the services sector. Its success is primarily due to the specific features of the products offered, which mostly involve data collection and processing with no physical element necessary in the process of service provision. Consequently, the vast majority of processes can be automated using algorithms, which offers a huge potential to the IT industry, especially if this is done by strong established financial institutions such as banks and insurance firms. However, the picture of the industry is diverse, since alongside the traditional financial institutions, small start-ups appeared immediately after the 2008 crisis and tried to take over part of the profitable market from banks. They have succeeded to a considerable extent, although the size advantage of the traditional financial institutions, which used their potential through the effect of scale, their own client base, or legal lobbying, endured this attack and are trying to work out a scheme under which their relations with Fintech start-ups will be symbiotic rather than competitive. The analysis of employee surveys shows that in recent years, the complexity of services provided by the BPOCs in Krakow has appreciably increased, whereas their uniqueness remains average and has only slightly changed. This may mean that in the employees' opinion, Krakow's BPOCs have recorded a major change in complexity, but the global financial industry has also significantly changed and has benefited from automation and robotisation of the simplest processes, with human labour being needed to carry out increasingly sophisticated tasks. These conclusions are supported by the findings of a survey conducted among the CEOs, who opine that both complexity and uniqueness of services are high or very high in Krakow; moreover, the change in both parameters in the last five years has been positive. Assuming that CEOs usually have more experience and have a broader view of the context of outsourcing and offshoring activities, their responses can be considered as somewhat more reflective of the facts.

References

Alt. (2016). *Digitalisierung der Finanzindustrie: Grundlagen der Fintech-Evolution*. Berlin and Heidelberg: Springer Berlin Heidelberg. https://doi.org/10.1007/978-3-662-50542-7.

Arner, D.W., Barberis, J.N., & Buckley, R.P. (2015). *The Evolution of Fintech: A New Post-crisis Paradigm*? University of Hong Kong Faculty of Law Research Paper No. 2015/047; UNSW Law Research Paper No. 2016-62. https://doi.org/10.2139/ssrn.2676553.

Aspire. (2019). *Aspire Headcount Tracker* [accessed from: www.aspire.org.pl/wp-content/uploads/The-ASPIRE-Headcount-Tracker-2019-Executive-Summary.pdf].

Chen, M.A., Wu, Q., & Yang, B. (2019). How valuable is FinTech innovation? *The Review of Financial Studies*, *32*(5), pp. 2062–2106. https://doi.org/10.1093/rfs/hhy130.

Deloitte. (2016). *Fintech in CEE: Charting the Course for Innovation in Financial Services Technology* [accessed from: www2.deloitte.com/content/dam/Deloitte/global/Documents/About-Deloitte/central-europe/ce-fintech-in-cee-region-2016.pdf].

Du Boff, R.B. (1980). Business demand and the development of the telegraph in the United States, 1844–1860. *Business History Review*, *54*(4), pp. 459–479. https://doi.org/10.2307/3114215.

Gimpel, H., Rau, D., & Röglinger, M. (2018). Understanding FinTech start-ups: A taxonomy of consumer-oriented service offerings. *Electronic Markets*, *28*(3), pp. 245–264. https://doi.org/10.1007/s12525-017-0275-0.

Hoag, C. (2006). The Atlantic telegraph cable and capital market information flows. *The Journal of Economic History*, *66*(2), pp. 342–353.

ING. (2015). *ING International Survey: Mobile Banking, New Technologies and Financial Behaviour. The Rise of Mobile Banking and the Changing Face of Payments in the Digital Age* [accessed from: https://think.ing.com/uploads/reports/ING_International_Survey_Mobile_Banking_2015.pdf].

Kagermann, H., Helbig, J., Hellinger, A., & Wahlster, W. (2013). *Recommendations for Implementing the Strategic Initiative INDUSTRIE 4.0: Securing the Future of German Manufacturing Industry; Final Report of the Industrie 4.0 Working Group*. Forschungsunion [accessed from: https://books.google.pl/books?id=AsfOoAEACAAJ].

Nicoletti, B. (2017). *The Future of FinTech*. Cham: Springer International Publishing.

Puschmann, T. (2017). Fintech. *Business & Information Systems Engineering*, *59*(1), pp. 69–76. https://doi.org/10.1007/s12599-017-0464-6.

PwC. (2017). *Global FinTech Report 2017: Redrawing the Lines: FinTech's Growing Influence on Financial Services* [accessed from: www.pwc.com/jg/en/publications/pwc-global-fintech-report-17.3.17-final.pdf].

Russell, W.H. (2011). *The Atlantic Telegraph*. Cambridge: Cambridge University Press.

Schueffel, P. (2017). Taming the beast: A scientific definition of FinTech. *Journal of Innovation Management*, *4*(4), pp. 32–54. https://doi.org/10.24840/2183-0606_004.004_0004.

Vives, X. (2017). The impact of Fintech on banking. *European Economy*, *2*, pp. 97–105.

Waupsh, J. (2017). *Bankruption: How Community Banking Can Survive Fintech*. Hoboken, NJ: Wiley.

Winston, B. (1998). *Media Technology and Society: A History: From the Telegraph to the Internet*. London: Routledge.

Zalan, T., & Toufaily, E. (2017). The promise of Fintech in emerging markets: Not as disruptive. *Contemporary Economics*, *11*(4), pp. 415–430.

Part IIIb

External determinants of the embeddedness of the outsourcing and offshoring sector

14 The importance of corporate social responsibility in the embedding of the offshore services industry in Krakow

Agnieszka Pacut

Introduction

As a result of globalisation, growing stakeholder expectations, the changing legal environment, changes in the way societies function, environmental problems, and a host of other factors, both domestic and international firms are expected to demonstrate socially responsible attitudes and behaviours. Corporate social responsibility (CSR) is a multidimensional concept which reflects the response of firms to the expectations of a broad range of stakeholders (Dahlsrud, 2008; Joyner & Payne, 2002). In recent years, the concept has gained in importance and became not only an element of corporate strategy but also the object of research (Aguinis & Glavas, 2012; De Bakker et al., 2005; Wang et al., 2016; McWilliams & Siegel, 2001). Studies on CSR are used to analyse the results obtained by firms, including their relations with the environment.

This chapter examines the role of CSR in the embeddedness of firms in the offshoring and outsourcing sector in Krakow. The case of this city, one of the most attractive locations for the offshore services industry in Europe (cf. Chapter 1), prompted us to reflect on the factors and conditions that influence the decisions to select and maintain offshored and outsourced operations in a given place. The concept of embeddedness (cf. Chapter 3) is used to explain the durability and lower propensity to relocate of the industry from Krakow. It was assumed that local embeddedness consisted in "a company's efforts to interact and build relationships with local actors in order to exchange resources, knowledge and information" (Wright, 2010, p. 127). In other words, what is examined is "the firm's participation in a broad spectrum of socio-economic relations with its environment" (Micek et al., 2010).

The objects of empirical research in this book are the relations established by the offshore services industry with various stakeholder groups, such as employees, universities, public authorities, the local community, non-profit organisations, and other local actors. The analysis of the scope, quality, and intensity of these relations is used to describe and discuss the factors that affect embeddedness understood as the sustainability of the offshoring and outsourcing firms in Krakow.

The aim of the survey discussed in this chapter was to analyse the importance of CSR practices in offshoring and outsourcing firms in Krakow, including their impact on the embeddedness of employees – the main stakeholders of the firms in the sector. Although activities in the field of CSR constitute an important element of a strategy pursued by transnational corporations, there is a knowledge gap in the literature on CSR as practised by multinational firms in Central and Eastern Europe (Szanto, 2019). For this reason, the analysis covers the identification of CSR practices applied in the offshoring and outsourcing sector in Krakow and the prerequisites for involvement or lack of involvement in them. This informs our reflection on the activities (factors) which contribute to building relations with the employees in the host country.

This chapter consists of three parts. It opens with an outline of the analytic approach and presents the concept of CSR and its significance for the activities of multinational firms. This introduction is followed by a presentation of the strategy of empirical research based on quantitative analysis, which covered employees and managers of business services centres operating in the Krakow agglomeration. Finally, the findings of the empirical research are presented, discussed, and summarized.

Definitions of corporate social responsibility

The concept of corporate social responsibility has been the object of scientific interest since the mid-20th century, although its origins date much further back (Carroll & Shabana, 2010; Okoye, 2009). CSR is an umbrella term for a variety of theories and practices (Blowfield & Frynas, 2005) which recognise the need for a broader view of the activities of firms, taking into account their relations with the environment and society, as well the importance of values and ethics in managing them.

Definitions of the concept of CSR in the literature differ both in their essence and types (dimensions, aspects, levels) of responsibility assumed by firms. The literature identifies five dimensions of CSR (Dahlsrud, 2008): 1. stakeholders (interaction between business and their stakeholders: employees, suppliers, customers, and communities); 2. social (the relationship between business and society and its contribution to a better society); 3. economic (socio-economic or financial aspects including CSR in terms of a business operation and preserving the profitability); 4. voluntariness (actions not prescribed by law, based on ethical values); and 5. environmental (environmental concerns in business operations, environmental stewardship). These dimensions are reflected in the numerous definitions of the term and discussed in different configurations. They illustrate the variety of requirements and expectations from firms formulated by their shareholders and society (Aguinis & Glavas, 2012). One of the prominent researchers in this area, A.B. Carroll (1999), defined the concept of CSR with reference to four levels of corporate responsibility. His pyramid of responsibility includes the following dimensions: economic (providing profit); legal (acting in accordance with the law, avoiding possible disputes, and anticipating the law); ethical (doing what is right, fair, and honest); and philanthropic (improving community life). The economic and legal responsibility is mandatory, whereas the others are voluntary. On the other hand, the European Commission promotes the triple bottom line approach by pointing to economic, social, and especially environmental dimensions of CSR. Being a responsible firm entails not only fulfilling legal obligations but also going beyond them by investing more in human capital, the environment, and its relations with stakeholders (Green Paper, 2001).

The concept of CSR emphasises the voluntary nature of such efforts and their inseparable links with stakeholder dialogue, sustainability reporting, and transparency (Marrewijk, 2003). Analyses of this concept reflect its evolution and changes in the approach to its understanding and implementation (Visser, 2010; Frederick, 1986, 1994, 1998). It is not only the definition of the term that poses a challenge to researchers. The issue of operationalisation and measurement of CSR standards in a firm is similar. So far, a number of different ways and tools have been developed in order to clarify and measure the level of corporate responsibility (cf. Gallardo-Vázquez & Sanchez-Hernandez, 2014).

Studies on corporate social responsibility are conducted by researchers in various fields and represent many theoretical currents. D. Secchi focuses on utilitarian, managerial, and relational theories of the phenomenon (Secchi, 2007), whereas E. Garriga and D. Melé (2004) singled out instrumental theories, political theories, integrated theories, and ethical theories as the most helpful in explaining the actions taken by firms to achieve commercial success in a way that respects ethical values, people, communities, and the environment (Aguinis & Glavas, 2012).

R. E. Freeman's stakeholder theory occupies a special place in this classification. It assumes that the modern approach to business management requires taking into account the interests of the largest possible stakeholders group present both inside and outside the firm. Stakeholders are defined as groups with vested interests or claims on the firm (suppliers, clients, employees, shareholders, and the local community) (Freeman, 1984). In other words, stakeholders are individuals or groups that have a legitimate interest in procedural and/or substantive aspects of corporate activity (whether or not the corporation actually has any corresponding functional interest in them), and the interests of all the stakeholders are of intrinsic value (Donaldson & Preston, 1995). Owing to the specificities of offshoring and outsourcing firms, the primary group of stakeholders are their employees who constitute their primary development resource and capital.

Corporate social responsibility in multinational firms

Today, the demands for social responsibility and ethical behaviour of firms and their leaders are stronger than ever before, especially in relation to multinational corporations (Joyner & Payne, 2002; Husted & Allen, 2006). In Poland, the CSR concept was readily embraced by large enterprises, especially multinational firms, rather than small and medium-sized enterprises, which often lack the financial, organisational, and knowledge resources in this respect (Szczęsna, 2010). The growing importance of CSR among transnational or multinational corporations corresponds to the growing scope of activities undertaken by them in the contemporary global economy (OECD, 2017; The Social Responsibility, 1999). Their interest in this practice also results from the fear of criticism of their way of doing business, the need to preserve a good image, as well as the risk of negative effects of corporate actions on local communities (The Social Responsibility, 1999). Other factors that generally promote CSR activities involve increased expectations of citizens, consumers, public authorities, and investors in association with economic and civilisational changes, as well as the intensification of various environmental problems and pressure on the transparency of business activities, which is intensified by the media and modern information/communication technologies (Green Paper, 2001). CSR activities are treated by firms not only as a response to the needs of various stakeholder groups but also as a business opportunity, a way of improving their attractiveness, credibility, and building their brands on the domestic and international market (Mark-Herbert & Von Schantz, 2007). The implementation of this concept by international firms is also encouraged by building an organisational culture based on general ethical principles shared by society. The CSR idea is a set of principles and values that bind together an internally diverse and geographically dispersed organisation (Rozkwitalska, 2006).

The available studies demonstrate that multinational firms, including those that offshore and outsource, tend to engage in CSR activities in a variety of ways, depending on the country and region. They pursue a wide range of activities, from ethical through environmental to sustainable development (Kolk, 2016). There are numerous similarities and differences in such activities worldwide (Jamali & Neville, 2011). CSR ensures global integration and local responsiveness (da Cunha et al., 2016).

Research method

Quantitative methods based on a diagnostic survey were used to achieve the research objectives. The survey was conducted in 2019–2020 among the employees and management staff of firms representing the offshoring and outsourcing sector in the Krakow agglomeration. The sample selection was deliberate. The survey was carried out among the staff of partner firms in an educational project carried out by the Cracow University of Economics. Four kinds of firms participated in the study: shared services centres (SSC); business process outsourcing (BPO); information technology outsourcing (ITO); and research and development (R&D).

The study consisted of two stages. In the first stage, 15 interviews with the CEOs of business services centres were conducted using a questionnaire. In the second step, the survey covered 316 employees of the above-mentioned firms using an online questionnaire (CAWI).

The questionnaire consisted of a range of introductory issues (reasons for taking up a job in a given firm, assessment of current job satisfaction, etc.) and four thematic blocks, which covered technological changes, corporate social responsibility, relations of the firm's employees with Krakow, the relations of firms representing the offshore services industry with the environment, and respondent details. Apart from closed questions, filtering and Likert scale questions were also used (where 1 meant the least significant and 5 the most significant). The questionnaire was anonymous; respondents were informed that their answers would be presented only as collective generalisations.

In the surveyed group, 84% of employees came from Poland. Most of them held expert positions in their firms, 24% were managers, whereas 3% were board members. Thirty percent of the participants were people whose total work experience was 6–10 years, whereas 29% were starting their professional career (0–5 years). Experienced employees (11–15 years) constituted 19% of the sample, whereas the most experienced employees (over 15 years) made up the remaining 9%. The question concerning work experience was answered by 72% of the respondents.

Activity and characteristics of CSR activities of Krakow's offshoring and outsourcing firms

In the subsequent part of the survey, employees of the offshore services industry were asked about the extent to which they are satisfied with the selected employment-related parameters. Generally, when analysing the mean ratings on a five-point scale, the respondents are most satisfied with the co called 'soft' aspects of their work, such as relations with co-workers and superiors (mean rating almost 4.5). They equally highly appreciate the flexible working hours, which allows them to reconcile work and private life. On the other hand, the respondents are least satisfied with salaries and bonuses offered by the employers and promotion opportunities (mean approx. 3.5). Employers' involvement in CSR ranks in the middle. The average rating of 3.8 suggests that this is not a fundamental aspect of fulfilment in their professional lives, but it is not irrelevant either. It is worth noting that CSR finished ahead of the remuneration system in the ranking.

Based on the responses of employees to the question concerning their firm's activities in the area of CSR, it can be concluded that the latter usually comprise programmes that directly involve the employees in activities for the benefit of local communities, e.g. through cooperation with non-governmental organisations, which was mentioned by four out of five respondents. On the other hand, the least frequently mentioned was the firms' involvement in pro-environmental projects. The organisation and internal processes – governance and management systems, including the issue of ethics in relations with business partners – were rated equally low. Consequently, the findings in this part of the survey imply that offshoring and outsourcing firms emphasise human resources development and identify the needs and problems of local communities, but in the perception of their employees, they pay less attention to processes within the organisation.

A fairly high percentage of those surveyed declared that their firms are involved in CSR activities. Regardless of the category of response, at least 25% of employees sometimes or regularly participate in such undertakings. The most frequently given answer was the simplest option – direct financial support of organisations or individuals (every fourth respondent does it regularly, whereas almost a half

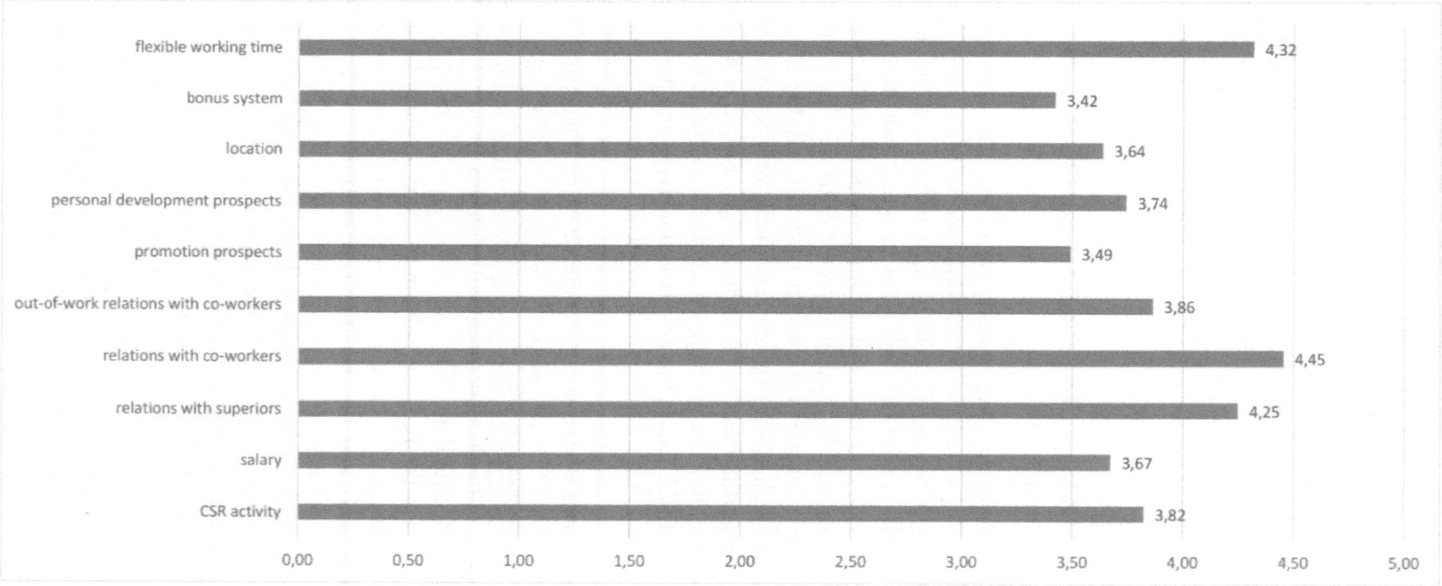

Figure 14.1 Employee satisfaction with selected aspects of work in Krakow's offshoring and outsourcing firms

Source: Own calculation on the survey findings.

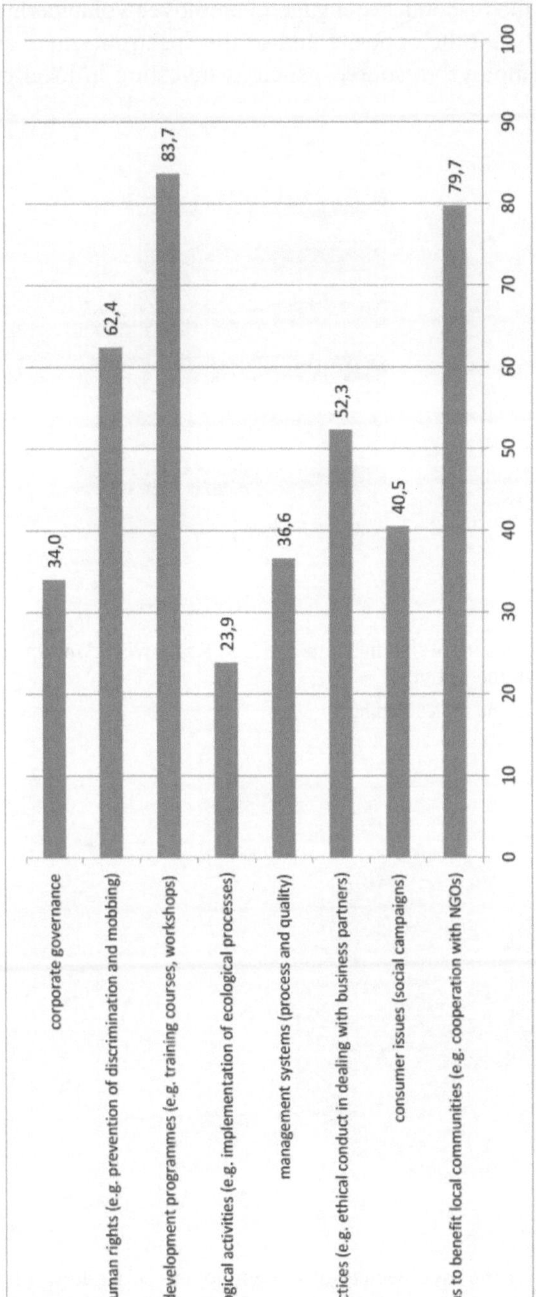

Figure 14.2 Activities in the area of corporate social responsibility undertaken by Krakow's offshoring and outsourcing firms

Source: Own calculation on the survey findings.

sometimes), or a direct purchase of products or services from social enterprises. More than a half of the respondents engage in employee volunteering, and every fifth does it regularly. At the opposite end of the spectrum, there are activities that require fewer employee resources, such as investing in local communities

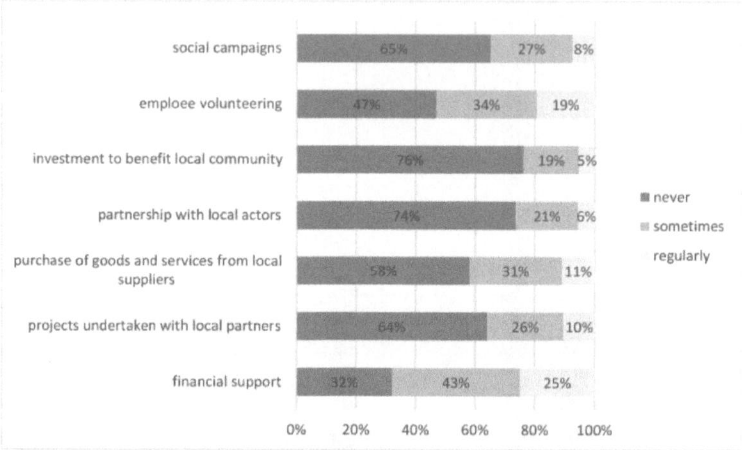

Figure 14.3 CSR activities involving the employees of Krakow's offshoring and outsourcing firms in the last year

Source: Own calculation on the survey findings.

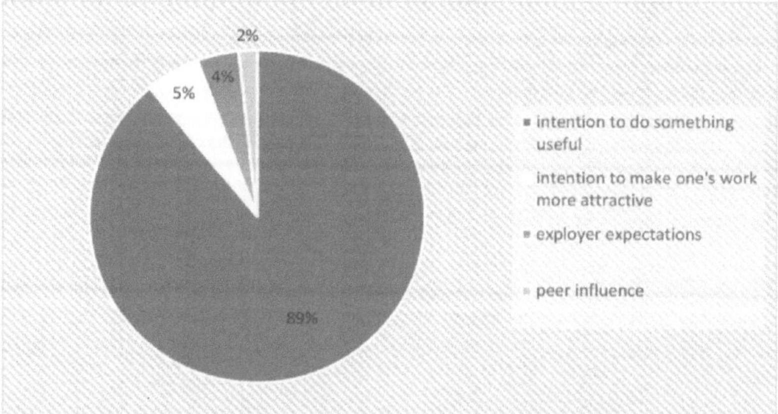

Figure 14.4 Reasons for the involvement of the employees of Krakow's offshoring and outsourcing firms in CSR activities

Source: Own calculation on the survey findings.

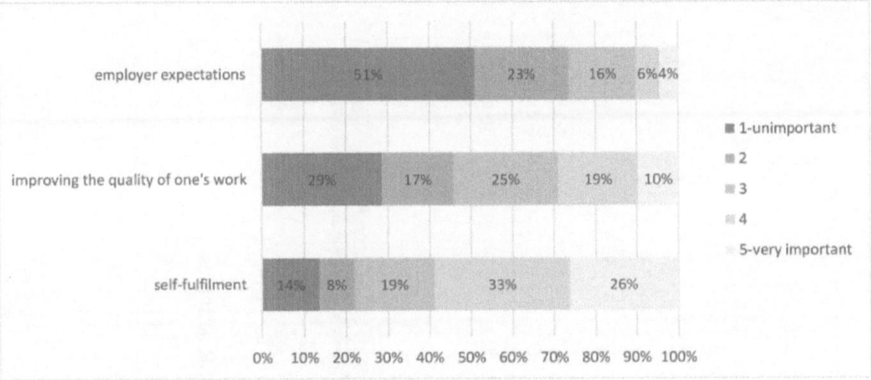

Figure 14.5 The importance of involvement in CSR activities of employees of Krakow's offshoring and outsourcing firms for their professional work

Source: Own calculation on the survey findings.

or creating partnerships with local entities. A few percent are involved here on a permanent basis, whereas 20% do it occasionally.

In the next part of the survey, employees were asked to provide the reasons why they got involved in the CSR activities undertaken by their employers. Responses were quite uniform. The vast majority of people wanted to do something useful on their own. Very few people mentioned employer expectations or the influence of their peers.

Employees of the offshore services industry were also asked to answer the question of the importance of engaging in CSR activities in their professional work. The results obtained correlate with the responses to the previous question: self-fulfilment is much more important for employees than what their employers may expect from them. Therefore, they do not feel pressure on the part of their own organisation; moreover, they do not associate participation in CSR projects directly with their professional development. Half of them stated that such activities have no impact on improving the quality of their work.

Individuals who declared that their employers are not involved in CSR activities in the previous questions were then asked to choose the reasons for such a decision (more than one could be given). The most frequent response (nearly 60%) was lack of time, which explained many discontinued or uninitiated activities. In part, it may be due to the large number of areas of non-professional involvement of the respondents, but it may also be due to psychological reasons. At the same time, every fifth respondent openly mentioned their lack of interest in such activities.

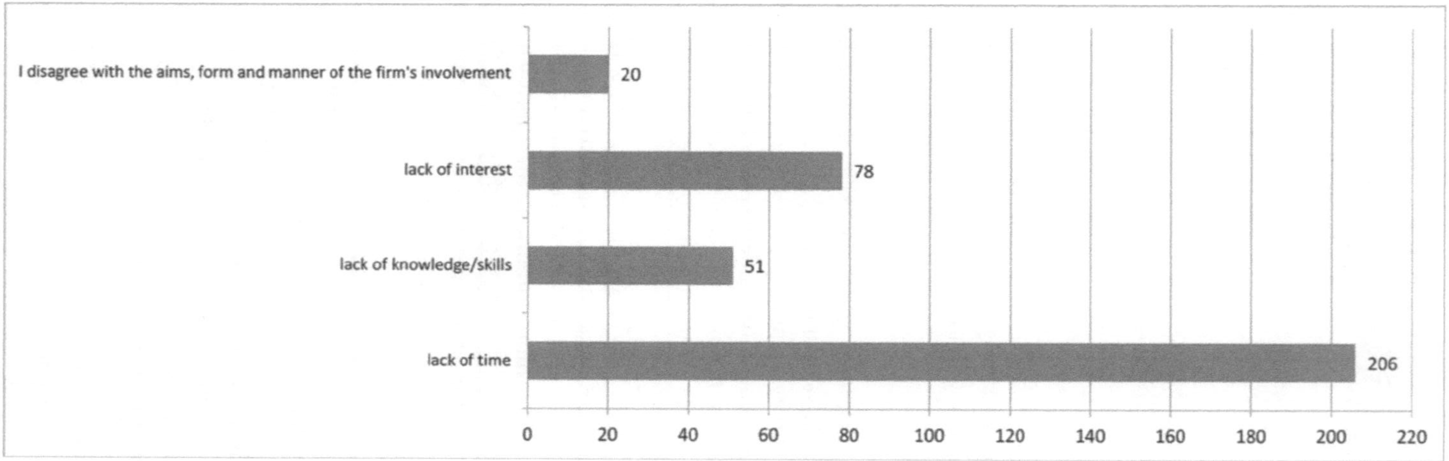

Figure 14.6 Reasons for lack of involvement of employees of Krakow's offshoring and outsourcing firms in CSR activities

Source: Own calculation on the survey findings.

Conclusion

CSR is often described as an eclectic, multifaceted, and multidimensional field with loose boundaries (Carroll, 1991). Its exact scope depends on the adopted definition and interpretation of the term. However, by and large, a socially responsible firm is one that achieves its business objectives while taking into account the social, environmental, employee, and other expectations (Rowley & Berman, 2000). The definitions of CSR formulated so far exemplify the multiplicity and complexity of variables that make up the phenomenon as well as the difficulties inherent in measuring it. The current discourse on CSR also reveals a certain contradiction – on the one hand, the issue has taken root in the management sciences, and on the other, a multitude of new terms and approaches keep emerging (de Bakker et al., 2005; Aguinis & Glavas, 2012; Dionisio & de Vargas, 2020). Apart from the definitional and terminological issues, it should be noted that the role of CSR in contemporary society and economy will grow (Filek, 2018).

Research on CSR is dominated by two currents: the impact of CSR on building a competitive advantage and promoting social responsibility by defining the value created by firms in their relations with stakeholders in a novel way (Stefańska, 2013). The findings discussed in this chapter represent the latter current. The survey findings show that the firms representing the offshore services industry in Krakow engage in CSR activities in a variety of ways. Their employees most frequently mentioned programmes addressed to them, activities for the benefit of the local community, and human rights. These activities were viewed more positively than others mentioned in the survey (i.e. salary, bonus system). The vast majority of the employees surveyed said that they were autotelically motivated rather than by implicit or explicit employer expectations; moreover, self-fulfilment was definitely more important than any obligation arising from the CSR strategy implemented in their firm. They neither felt pressured by their organisation nor directly associated participation in CSR projects with their professional development. Nevertheless, this kind of activity contributed to improving the quality of work in the surveyed group of firms.

The analysis of the collected data warrants the conclusion that CSR activity conducted by offshoring and outsourcing firms may earn them recognition as quality workplaces. Voluntary CSR activity creates opportunities for broadly understood employee development. The adoption of CSR strategies means in practice the implementation of solutions, which at the meso (local branch) level contributes to linking the use of resources and productivity to the improvement in the quality of life and work of individuals (employees). The CSR concept reflects the social needs of employees and the social consequences of business success (Matten & Moon, 2008), and above all, it contributes to building relationships (vertical embeddedness) with the host country's employees, who are the main internal stakeholder group for companies in the offshore services industry.

The significance of CSR practices undertaken by the offshore services industry can be analysed in the context of both the expectations formulated towards employers (multinational firms) as well as the needs of their employees. Research conducted at the macro level increasingly more often supports the observation that productivity determines efficiency (Hausner, 2018). The productivity of a firm and ways of increasing it depend to a large extent on institutions other than the market, namely those that are based on cooperation and partnership rather than on competition; in other words, on institutions which are more relational than transactional in nature (Hausner, 2018). This approach emphasises the importance of firms using the available resources in such a way that they are multiplied and renewed, as well as the role of cooperation, which promotes the use of collective knowledge and skills dispersed within an organisation or society. This process must be accompanied by the recognition of the needs of different stakeholder groups (individuals and communities) and their empowerment in the management process. At the same time, the discourse on employees' competencies and resources emphasises the importance of the quality of the working environment (Jelonek, 2019). Apart from having a well-paid job, social or 'soft' issues, i.e. the sense of doing meaningful work, relations with co-workers, and ethical and responsible action of the employer are becoming increasingly important (CEDEFOP, 2018; The World Bank, 2019).

References

Aguinis, H., & Glavas, A. (2012). What we know and don't know about corporate social responsibility: A review and research agenda. *Journal of Management, 38*(4), pp. 932–968. https://doi.org/10.1177/0149206311436079.

Blowfield, M., & Frynas, J.G. (2005). Critical perspectives on corporate social responsibility. *International Affairs, 81*(3), pp. 499–513.

Carroll, A.B. (1991). The pyramid of corporate social responsibility: Toward the moral management of organizational stakeholders. *Business Horizons*, July–August, pp. 39–48.

Carroll, A.B. (1999). Corporate social responsibility: Evolution of a definitional construction. *Business and Society, 38*(3), 268–295.

Carroll, A.B., & Shabana, K.M. (2010). The business case for corporate social responsibility: A review of concepts, research and practice. *International Journal of Management Reviews, 12*(1), pp. 85–105.

CEDEFOP. (2018). *The Changing Nature and Role of Vocational Education and Training in Europe. Volume 3: The Responsiveness of European VET Systems to External Change (1995–2015).* Cedefop Research Paper, No 67. Luxembourg: Publications Office.

da Cunha, C.H., dos Santos Parisotto, I.R., Carpes, Dani, A., & Siewert, V. (2016). CSR, local embeddedness and the performance of MNCs in Brazil during the 2008 financial crisis. *Revista de Negócios, 21*(3–4), pp. 25–38.

Dahlsrud, A. (2008). How corporate social responsibility is defined: An analysis of 37 definitions. *Corporate Social Responsibility and Environmental Management, 15*(1), pp. 1–13.

De Bakker, F.G.A., Groenewegen, P., & Den Hond, F. (2005). A bibliometric analysis of 30 years of research and theory on corporate social responsibility and corporate social performance. *Business & Society, 44*(3), pp. 283–317. https://doi.org/10.1177/0007650305278086.

Dionisio, M., & de Vargas, E.R. (2020). Corporate social innovation: A systematic literature review. *International Business Review, 29*(2). https://doi.org/10.1016/j.ibusrev.2019.101641.

Donaldson, T., & Preston, L.E. (1995). The stakeholder theory of the corporation: Concepts, evidence, and implications. *Academy of Management Review*, *20*(1), pp. 65–91.

Filek, J. (2018). Społeczna odpowiedzialność biznesu jako nowa forma dialogu w obszarze działań gospodarczych. *Zeszyty Naukowe Uniwersytet Ekonomiczny w Krakowie*, *5*(977), pp. 97–113.

Frederick, W.C. (1986). Toward CSR3: Why ethical analysis is indispensable and unavoidable in corporate affairs. *California Management Review*, *28*(2), pp. 126–141. https://doi.org/10.2307/41165190.

Frederick, W.C. (1994). From CSR1 to CSR2: The maturing of business-and-society thought. *Business & Society*, *33*(2), pp. 150–164.

Frederick, W.C. (1998). Moving to CSR4: What to pack for the trip. *Business and Society*, *37*(1), pp. 40–59.

Freeman, R.E. (1984). *Strategic Management: A Stakeholder Perspective*. Boston: Pitman Publishing Inc.

Gallardo-Vázquez, D., & Sanchez-Hernandez, M.I. (2014). Measuring Corporate Social Responsibility for competitive success at a regional level. *Journal of Cleaner Production*, *72*, pp. 14–22. https://doi.org/10.1016/j.jclepro.2014.02.051.

Garriga, E., & Melé, D. (2004). Corporate social responsibilities theories: Mapping the territory. *Journal of Business Ethics*, *53*, pp. 51–71.

Green Paper. (2001). *Promoting a European Framework for Corporate Social Responsibility*. COM (2001) 366 final, Brussels.

Hausner, J. (2018). Społeczna czasoprzestrzeń wytwarzania wartości ekonomicznych. In *Open Eyes Book 3*. Kraków: Kraków: Fundacja Gospodarki i Administracji Publicznej.

Husted, B.W., & Allen, D.B. (2006). Corporate social responsibility in the multinational enterprise: Strategic and institutional approaches. *Journal of International Business Studies*, *37*(6), pp. 838–849. https://doi.org/10.1057/palgrave.jibs.8400227.

Jamali, D., & Neville, B. (2011). Convergence versus divergence of CSR in developing countries: An embedded multi-layered institutional lens. *Journal of Business Ethics*, *102*, pp. 599–621. https://doi.org/10.1007/s10551-011-0830-0.

Jelonek, M. (2019). Kompetencje, potrzeby pracodawców a współodpowiedzialność za zasoby kompetencyjne regionów. In *Open Eyes Book 4*. Kraków: Fundacja Gospodarki i Administracji Publicznej.

Joyner, B.E., & Payne, D. (2002). Evolution and implementation: A study of values, business ethics and corporate social responsibility. *Journal of Business Ethics*, *41*(4), pp. 297–311. https://doi.org/10.1023/A:1021237420663.

Kolk, A. (2016). The social responsibility of international business: From ethics and the environment to CSR and sustainable development, *Journal of World Business*, *51*(1), pp. 23–34.

Mark-Herbert, C., & Von Schantz, C. (2007). Communicating corporate social responsibility: Brand management. *Electronic Journal of Business Ethics and Organization Studies*, *12*(2), pp. 4–11.

Matten, D., & Moon, J. (2008). Implicit and explicit CSR: A conceptual framework for a comparative understanding of corporate social responsibility. *The Academy of Management Review*, *33*(2), pp. 404–424.

McWilliams, A., & Siegel, D. (2001). Corporate social responsibility: A theory of the firm perspective. *Academy of Management Review*, *26*(1), pp. 117–127.

Micek, G., Górecki, J., & Działek, J. (2010). *Centra usług w Krakowie i ich relacje z otoczeniem lokalnym*. Kraków: Wydawnictwo Uniwersytetu Jagiellońskiego.

OECD. (2017). *Annual Report on the OECD Guidelines for Multinational Enterprises 2016* [accessed from: www.oecd.org/daf/inv/mne/2016-Annual-Report-MNE-Guidelines-EN.pdf, 23 April 2020].

Okoye, A. (2009). Theorising corporate social responsibility as an essentially contested concept: Is a definition necessary? *Journal of Business Ethics*, *89*(4), pp. 613–627.

Rowley, T.J., & Berman, S. (2000). A brand new brand of corporate social performance. *Business & Society*, *39*(4), pp. 397–418.

Rozkwitalska, M. (2006). Kultura organizacyjna korporacji transnarodowych oparta o społeczną odpowiedzialność. *Organizacja i Kierowanie*, *2*(124), pp. 33–47.

Secchi, D. (2007). Utilitarian, managerial and relational theories of corporate social responsibility. *International Journal of Management Reviews*, *9*(4), pp. 347–373.

The Social Responsibility. (1999). *The Social Responsibility of Transnational Corporations*. United Nations Conference on Trade and Development. New York and Geneva: United Nations [accessed from: https://unctad.org/en/Docs/poiteiitm21_en.pdf].

Stefańska, M. (2013). Podstawy teoretyczne i ewolucja pojęcia społeczna odpowiedzialność biznesu (CSR). *Prace Naukowe Uniwersytetu Ekonomicznego we Wrocławiu*, *288*, pp. 198–211.

Szanto, R. (2019). CSR dilemmas at multinational companies: Global pressures vs. local expectations in the lights of the hungarian evidence. *Marketing and Management of Innovations*, *2*, pp. 217–227. https://doi.org/10.21272/mmi.2019.2–19.

Szczęsna, B. (Ed.). (2010). *CSR w Polsce – Menedżerowie/menedżerki 500. Lider/liderka CSR*. Warszawa: GoodBrand & Company Polska [accessed from: http://odpowiedzialnybiznes.pl/wpcontent/uploads/2014/03/Raport_Menedzerowie500_LiderCSR_2010.pdf, 5.11.2019].

van Marrewijk, M. (2003). Concepts and definitions of CSR and corporate sustainability: Between agency and communion. *Journal of Business Ethics*, *44*, pp. 95–105.

Visser, W. (2010). The age of responsibility: CSR 2.0 and the new DNA of business. *Journal of Business Systems, Governance and Ethics*, *5*(3), pp. 7–22.

Wang, Q., Dou, J., & Jia, S. (2016). A meta-analytic review of corporate social responsibility and corporate financial performance: The moderating effect of contextual factors. *Business & Society*, *55*(8), pp. 1083–1121.

The World Bank. (2019). *The Changing Nature of Work*. Washington, DC: The World Bank.

Wright, R. (2010). Competitiveness and changing patterns of embeddedness in Romania. *Competitiveness Review: An International Business Journal*, *20*(2), pp. 126–138.

15 The role of universities in the embeddedness of business process outsourcing

Łukasz Mamica

The value of university

It is widely believed that universities have a positive impact on economic development (Fotea & Gutu, 2016; Sarkar & Perényi, 2017). The value of universities as publicly financed (or co-financed) institutions reflects their individual and social dimensions. In this context, individual or private value can be defined as that part of income and job satisfaction of a former student achieved thanks to the qualifications obtained at university as compared to other individuals with lower qualifications. The social dimension of university value covers a wide range of benefits, such as the rate of economic growth (especially innovation-based) and the quality of life. The value of university treated as an economic return can be discussed from the perspective of institutions in regard of new technologies or other innovations adopted by them and the return on the human capital employed. The growing perception of the higher education system as a creator of economic value led to its restructuring into a market-driven arrangement (John & Fanghanel, 2016). However, the economisation of universities is associated with the risk that their financial performance will be emphasised over the broader social benefits, which are notoriously difficult to measure. At the outset of the 2008 financial crisis, Skidelsky pointed to the moral failure of an approach whereby money "was worshipped for its own sake, rather than as a way of to achieve the 'good life'" (Skidelsky, 2009, p. 169). According to Barnett, an *ecological university* should "put its resources into play such that they serve the world" (2013, p. 137). The visible costs of the global temperature increase, which must be covered from public sources, mean that investment in universities, where solutions can be developed, appear to be more profitable from the national point of view. Thus, the value of universities must not be perceived exclusively from the perspective of their capacity to generate income or to minimise the necessary public subsidies.

The discussion about the sources of funding for higher education was substantially influenced by the World Bank, which stated that private benefits of higher education exceeded the public benefits (Psacharopoulos, 1994). This argument was later used as a pretext for increasing student fees and led to a phenomenon known as university customisation. Some sectors benefit more than others from universities, the business process outsourcing (BPO) sector being one of them.

Any discussion of the value of university must take into account the costs of alternative sources of delivery of similar products and services. The global Internet network and e-learning solutions permit a number of traditional outputs to be delivered at a much lower cost and with a higher quality than that offered by most universities. Such a pressure should lead to the modification of the traditional educational process with a special emphasis on mentored group work and experiments. The development of e-learning platforms may therefore, in the long term, have a negative impact on the attachment of the BPO sector to university cities, assuming of course that a significant proportion of education were to be obtainable online. Difficulties with estimating the value of university are also associated with the more popular and effective "commons-based peer production" (Benkler, 2006, p. 60), which enables people at different ages, with different skills and interests, and based in various locations to work together thanks to social media. However, the fact that within such a framework anyone can contribute and access the resource just by being online makes the created value unfocused, unpredictable, and difficult to control.

The primary sector where graduates decide to seek jobs also affects the discussion about the value of university in the context of funding available from public sources. Public opinion accepts that training staff for the public sector should be financed from the state budget. Interestingly, indicating the public sector as a preferable place of employment may have a negative impact on economic growth. This was found to be the case in India, where the public sector paid above-market wages and employed a disproportionately large proportion of university-educated people, which, in effect, significantly reduced the country's economic growth (Schündeln & Playforth, 2014). A similar problem can potentially be recognised from the BPO perspective. The value of university may also be analysed from the perspective of its impact on local development. The empirical analysis of technology transfer office (TTO) managers at European universities reveal that low-prestige, generalist universities tend to focus mainly on local development strategies, while high-prestige, specialist ones are more income oriented (Giuri et al., 2019).

The university as a supplier of education

The development of new social media and technologies makes it easier to share ideas and collaborate. At the same time, access to the best lectures and training materials, which can be picked by users from the global resource base, exerts extra pressure on universities in terms of what they can offer their students. Users of online educational platforms receive a space that enables them to exchange virtual contents and to co-create and co-produce new knowledge beyond the traditional institutions.

All this shifts the traditional role of individual entrepreneur as a development driver into the more collective dimension, which is possible thanks to new technologies. Owing to the interactive nature of social media, instead of vertical communication from one content provider to several recipients, participants interact on an equal footing according to the many-to-many formula. Universities with their traditional knowledge transfer based on the one-to-many formula find themselves subject to the pressure of the changing communication habits characteristic of the new generation of students.

Although the vast majority of universities are publicly funded, the process of education is increasingly perceived as a private good to be purchased by students (Besley & Peters, 2007). The imposition of student fees or their increases, often associated with the funding cuts in the wake of the 2008 global financial crisis, only serve to spread such a perception amongst students and their parents. The consequences of the current crisis caused by the coronavirus in 2020 are difficult to predict at this stage, although they are likely to be at least as significant. The decreasing proportion of university graduates capable of finding satisfactory employment has a negative impact on the perception of universities as effective suppliers of competencies expected by the market. On the other hand, the wide range of relatively well-paid job opportunities offered by the BPO sector in Krakow, especially those addressed to IT professionals, means that some students do not continue to study at the master's level as this is not required in their current positions.

From the point of view of BPO sector managers, the education process is of crucial importance in their relations with universities, as the quality of research conducted by the latter plays a key role in whether they are sufficiently attractive to most talented individuals to be subsequently recruited by firms (Mansfield & Lee, 1996).

Factors with a negative impact on the quality of university education

As a result of decreasing public subsidies caused by budgetary constraints in the wake of the 2008 global financial crisis, many universities increased their tuition fees which, in turn, had to be covered by parents whose incomes had decreased because of the crisis. This had a negative impact on the social makeup of candidates, which had been a serious problem even before the crisis. According to an analysis conducted by Sutton Trust (2008), which covered over a million university student admissions in 2002–2006, schools with the highest admissions rates to universities were highly socially selective: out of 30 schools with the highest admission rates, 28 were independent (i.e. provided fee-based education). The expectation formulated by Peter Lampl that "universities should be about nurturing and developing talent, not honing a finished product" (Sutton Trust, 2008, p. 2) provides a good illustration of the problem of preferences in a system of education for students whose families are rich enough to pay university tuition fees.

Increasing student fees strengthened the process of university marketisation. The implementation of the student-as-customer model increased the pressure on the academic institutions to put students' satisfaction first. According to Furedi (2011, p. 3), "feedback is often used as a vehicle for validating the efforts of a student instead of pointing out weaknesses in presentation and argument". In some cases, a literal interpretation of teacher evaluation forms leads to conformist behaviours.

The focus on satisfying students' needs as customers is indeed in line with consumerist attitudes but is likely to lead to a host of undesirable consequences.

A factor which has a decidedly negative impact on the quality of the education process is the limited time spent by lecturers in contact with their students. Research involving undergraduate students revealed that those who reported having acquired skills from interaction with their supervisors were considerably more satisfied (Del Río et al., 2018). Project work devoted to solving actual problems identified by BPO sector managers as part of a pilot project carried out by Cracow University of Economics (GAP, 2020) naturally requires greater involvement on the part of supervisors, but has a major positive effect on the entire educational process. Since industry-university collaboration is seen as a win-win situation (Chandraseakaran et al., 2015), the lack of contacts between the two entities or their insufficient intensity may significantly reduce the effectiveness of the teaching process.

Teaching focused on the development of creativity as a form of industry-university relations

One of the ways in which students can effectively familiarise themselves with business issues are case studies, generally considered to be a good practice-oriented teaching tool (Rodríguez et al., 2019; Dorta-Afonso, 2019). A more advanced form of relations with companies involves solving specific problems reported by company managers, by students who prepare dedicated bachelor's and master's theses. The participation of students in tackling problems identified by companies is reflected by the indicators of success in student activity as defined by Shaw et al. (2013). They include approach to learning, research self-efficacy, familiarity with the research environment, and positive orientation towards research. This type of work, where the students themselves decide on the choice of the problem reported by their potential employees, also fulfils the essential requirement of education, which, according to Lillo-Bañuls et al. (2016), consists in adapting teaching methodologies to student learning preferences. This kind of student involvement in relations with companies does not necessarily mean that the former participate in research during their studies, although naturally, such participation is desirable and increases the likelihood that the acquired knowledge will be productively applied in a future job (Brennan et al., 2019).

Students' involvement in solving actual problems, if carried out in interdisciplinary groups composed of several members, also contributes to the intensification of interdisciplinary research, which, according to Bentley et al. (2015) constitutes an important response to the expectations of university stakeholders. This kind of so-called commissioned student graduation work scheme, when pursued by interdisciplinary teams, does a lot to shape the key competencies needed in a knowledge-based economy, where "workers not only need to cultivate specialised skills, but they must be creative, work in teams, and adapt to rapidly-evolving technologies and innovations" (Tierney & Lanford, 2016, pp. 4–5). Even if the proposals put forward by the student or their group are eventually not implemented by the firm, the students benefit from an invaluable opportunity to undertake an in-depth actual case study, which is one of the key milestones in the process of action learning (Smith, 2017). The relations between universities and firms create an opportunity not only to validate the research findings, but also to confront the curricula with employer expectations. As the research demonstrated (Jorre de St Jorre & Oliver, 2018), students themselves also expect greater involvement of employers in determining the learning outcomes of individual courses or modules, which should contribute to the improvement of the graduates' employment prospects.

What senior managers primarily expect from their potential employees is creativity, defined as an ability to combine a variety of growth-oriented factors (Baumol, 1968). Research conducted among the CEOs (IBM, 2010) showed that creativity was selected as the key factor for the future success of leaders operating in an economically complex and volatile environment. In a World Economic Forum report (2016), creativity ranked second among the top employability characteristics under abilities, next to cognitive flexibility. Creativity as a skill is especially often analysed in the context of workplace and education (Adobe, 2016) and is also perceived as an aspect of innovation (Tang, 2017). The technological changes which are taking place in today's economy, including, in particular, the automation and computerisation of numerous processes, also put unrelenting pressure on the BPO sector, which must adapt to the changes as they occur. The process of creative destruction described years ago by Schumpeter (1942) requires readiness to respond to changes in the environment. This, in turn, requires creativity, which constitutes one of the most important competencies that universities should be able to foster in their students. Their role in this context is also important, because research shows a clear link between creativity and openness to take risks and independent thinking (Simonton, 2003).

The 18th century ushered in a recognition that all individuals are endowed with a creative potential, which underscored the relevance of the university mission to the economy (Runco & Albert, 2010). Thus, an appropriately designed and implemented education process may stimulate creative behaviours in individuals, which, in turn, allow them to gain a competitive advantage. Universities may foster the level of creativity in a number of ways, among which Caroff et al. (2018) identify cognitive, conative, affective, and environmental factors. The development of creativity requires a favourable external environment, such as academic freedom and an atmosphere of intellectual excitement, which, according to Altbach (2003), is central to every world-class university.

Evaluation of industry-university cooperation by CEOs of Krakow's BPO firms

The issue of relations of the BPO with universities was raised in direct interviews with the Chief Executive Officers of 15 firms representing this sector based in Krakow. The mean score for such relations on a five-point scale (where 1 – no relations; 5 – very strong relations) was 3.8. The intensity of these relations along individual dimensions was evaluated using a similar five-point scale (Figure 15.1).

The most intensive cooperation (mean score 4.14) was observed in the area of joint implementation of educational projects. Such a high score reflected the fact that these companies participated in the implementation of accredited degree specialisation The Future of global business services at the Cracow University of Economics (GAP, 2020). The activity in the field of joint recruitment was also rated quite highly – in the respondents' opinion, it was a particularly important aspect of cooperation. Likewise, the aforementioned joint implementation of educational projects is not only a quality-oriented aspect of cooperation, but also facilitates the recruitment of qualified candidates. In contrast, cooperation on the joint implementation of research projects and commissioning expert reviews was rated as very low. Six interviewees reported a complete absence of such cooperation in the former area and seven in the latter. It can be thus concluded that the main area of interest for BPO firms in their relations with universities is employee recruitment. However, it should be remembered that as shown by the research conducted by Chandraseakaran et al. (2015), cooperation with universities brings the industry indirect benefits in the form of increased graduate recruitment rate and a wider recognition as desirable workplaces.

The CEOs' interest in particular areas of potential cooperation with universities is higher than its current level (Figure 15.1). What is noteworthy is that the rating

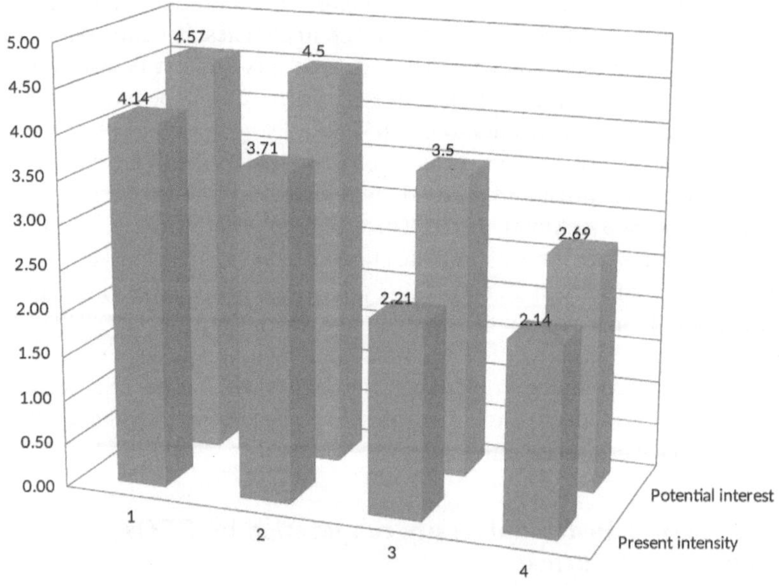

Figure 15.1 Average intensity of relations between the surveyed BPO companies and universities vs. interest in such relations in specific areas in the opinion of CEOs

(1 = lack of cooperation/lack of interest in cooperation; 5 = intensive cooperation/very high interest in cooperation; n = 15)

Source: Own research.

of interest in cooperation in particular fields corresponds to the current intensity of cooperation. The greatest potential for the development of cooperation is to be found in a joint implementation of research projects, where the potential interest scores on average 1.29 points (on a five-point scale) higher than the evaluation of the current level of cooperation.

The importance of specific competencies in professional work vs. the extent to which they were fostered at university in the opinion of BPO employees

The 316 surveyed employees (an online questionnaire [CAWI] was used) of BPO firms in Krakow were asked to evaluate the importance of six competence/knowledge areas in their professional work in comparison with the level of relevant support obtained while at university (Figure 15.2). Practical knowledge was considered to be the most important and scored 4.34 on a five-point scale (where 1 = unimportant and 5 = very important). At the same time, the level of support obtained in this area from the university was rated the lowest in comparison with other types of competencies and knowledge (only 2.34 on a five-point scale). Group work came second (mean score 3.93), whereas the extent to which it was fostered at university was rated as 3.39. They were followed by the ability to establish personal contacts (mean score 3.85), but the university's capacity to develop this competence was rated much lower (2.93). The second largest gap between the perceived importance of a competence in professional work and the actual support provided by the university was found to occur in leadership (mean scores 3.63 and 2.81, respectively). Only the provision of theoretical knowledge was rated slightly higher than what was deemed necessary for professional work (3.37 vs. 3.05). Apart from theoretical knowledge, every other type of competence and knowledge obtained during the study was rated lower than the actual level needed for professional work. Consequently, the research findings can be interpreted as a starting point for the modification of university curricula. A better match between the key desirable competencies and level of support offered by higher education institutions should contribute to a greater embeddedness of BPO sector companies in the region.

Men ranked the importance of personal contacts and leadership in their professional work higher than women. As regards creativity, the average rating for both genders is almost identical. Women, on the other hand, attached a greater importance to group work, theoretical knowledge, and practical knowledge (Figure 15.3).

The average rating of the level of support in the area of establishment of personal contacts was the same among the surveyed men and women. In other cases, women tended to rate the support for the development of specific competencies and knowledge obtained at university slightly higher than men (Figure 15.4). The largest difference, although only 0.25 points on the five-point scale, concerned the evaluation of group work.

The interviewed employees were also asked to evaluate the usefulness of internships from the perspective of their current employment. The mean score in this

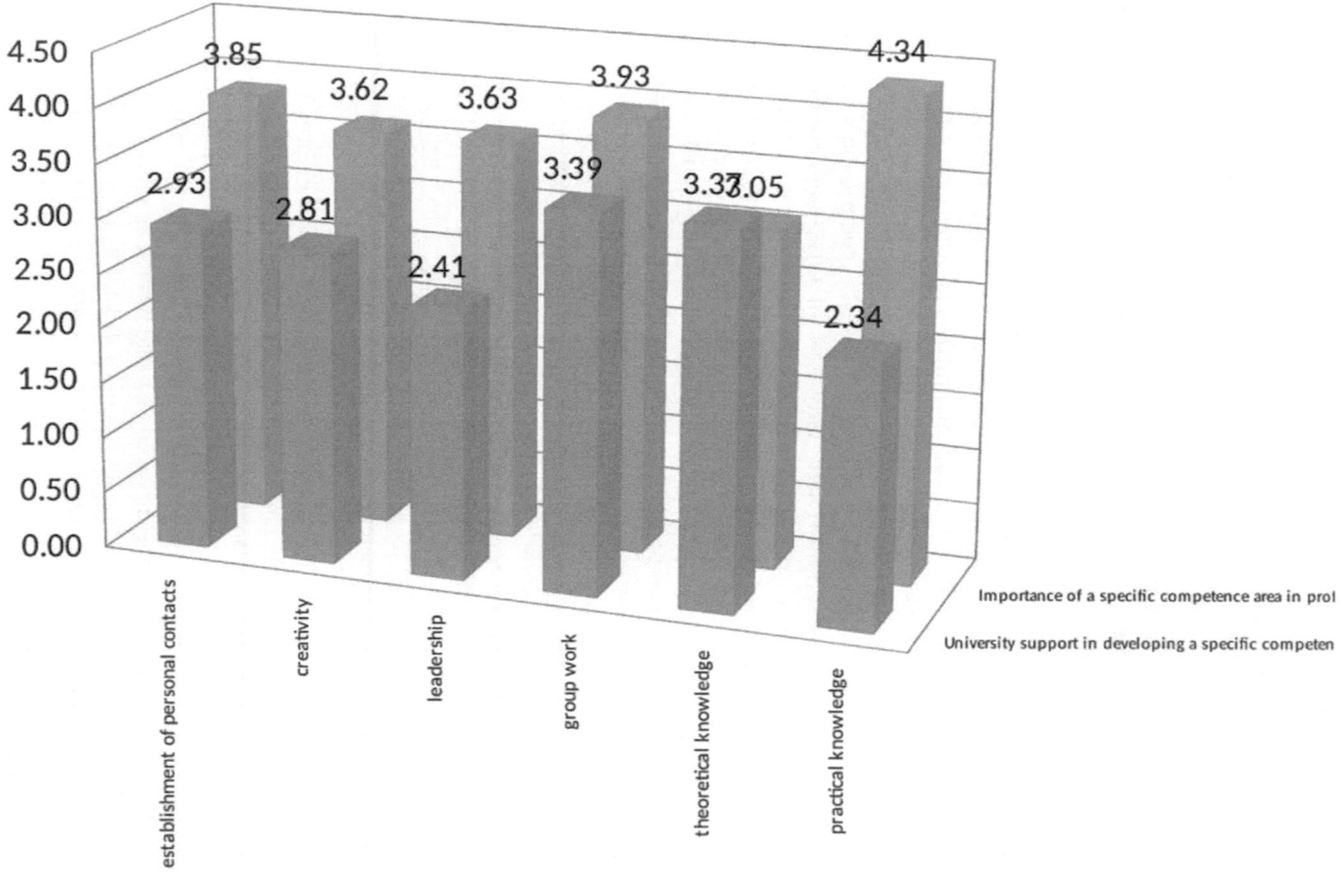

Figure 15.2 The importance of specific types of competencies and knowledge in professional work vs. the level of support offered by university

(1 – not important/no support at all; 5 – very important/excellent support; n = 316).

Source: Own research.

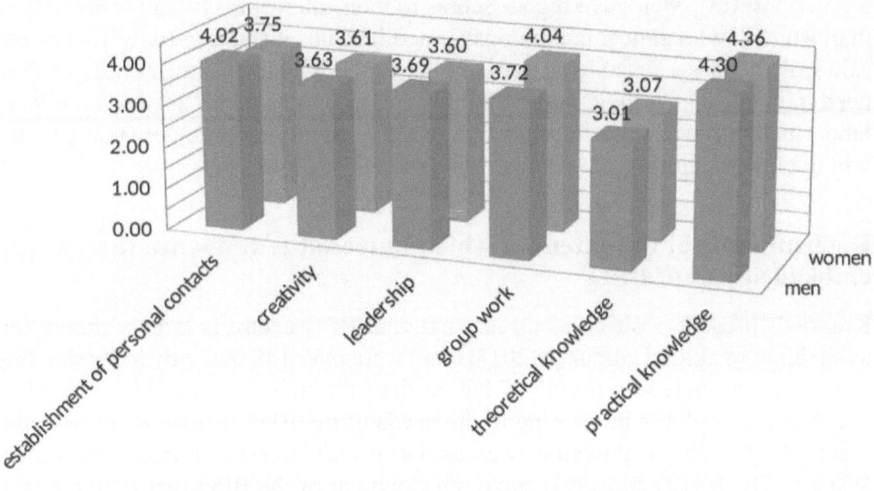

Figure 15.3 The importance of individual types of competencies and knowledge in professional work by gender

(1 – not important at all; 5 – very important; n = 316)

Source: Own research.

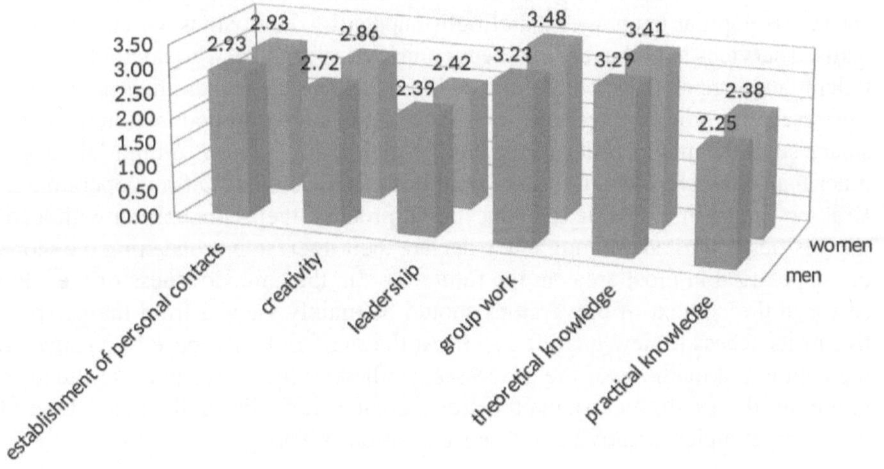

Figure 15.4 Evaluation of the level of support for the development of specific types of competencies and knowledge during higher education by gender

(1 – no support; 5 – very high support; n = 316)

Source: Own research.

category was only 2.08 points on a five-point scale (where 1 – not useful at all; 5 – very useful). Men gave higher scores to their internships (mean score of 2.1) than women, who almost unanimously rated it as unsatisfactory (only 1.1) on the said scale. This is a clear signal to the authorities of Krakow's universities that they need to better match their student internship systems with the needs of the local labour market, even though it must be borne in mind that the internship profiles will not always closely reflect the eventually chosen jobs.

Determinants of the extent to which universities influence the embeddedness of BPO

Krakow's present position as an international BPO centre is largely due to the availability of skilled labour (in 2018, there were over 148,000 university students in the region, including nearly 15,000 at the Cracow University of Economics, which is a key player in catering to the needs of the BPO sector). Krakow is the second largest city in Poland as well as the second largest academic centre after Warsaw. The barrier to further rapid development of the BPO sector may be the declining number of students in the country (over the last 10 years, it has systematically decreased from 1.92 million in the academic year 2008–2009 to 1.23 million in the academic year 2018–2019; at the end of 2018, there were over 61,000 fewer students than in the previous year).

The fairly wide range of foreign language courses available, including the tuition provided as part of university curricula, also serves to increase the attractiveness of Krakow as an outsourcing centre. The availability of employable people who speak less popular languages than English appeals to companies which offer specialised services to end users in other countries, i.e. to those who do not have sufficient language skills to communicate in a language other than their native one. The research findings reveal that most corporations offer attractive monthly basic salary supplements in order to encourage their staff to learn foreign languages other than English. The analysis of opinions of CEOs of BPO firms operating in Krakow shows that outside the educational process, their cooperation with local universities is limited, although they declare their interest in broadening the scope of cooperation in most areas in the future. So far, the embeddedness of the BPO sector in the context of universities should be mainly viewed from the perspective of its access to new qualified staff. At the same time, the pace of changes in the nature and methods of the processes handled by the sector point to the need to modify the existing curricula towards a greater flexibility in the acquisition of new competencies, creativity, and self-education skills.

References

Adobe. (2016). *State of Create 2016* [accessed from: www. adobe.com/content/dam/acom/en/max/pdfs/AdobeStateofCreate_2016_Report_ Final.pdf].

Altbach, Ph.G. (2003). The costs and benefits of world-class universities. *International Higher Education*, *33*, pp. 5–8.

Baumol, W.J. (1968). Entrepreneurship in economic theory. *The American Economic Review*, *58*(2), pp. 64–71.

Barnett, R. (2013). *Imagining the University.* London and New York: Routledge.

Benkler, Y. (2006). *The Wealth of Networks, How Social Production Transforms Markets and Freedom*. New Haven and London: Yale University Press.

Bentley, P.J., Gulbrandsen, M., & Kyvik, S. (2015). The relationship between basic and applied research in universities. *Higher Education, 70*(4), pp. 689–709. https://doi.org/10.1007/S10734-015-9861-2.

Besley, T.A., & Peters, M.A. (2007). *Subjectivity & Truth: Foucault, Education and the Culture of Self.* New York: Peter Lang.

Brennan, L., Cusack, T., Delahunt, E., Kuznesof, Sh., & Donnelly, S. (2019). Academics' conceptualisations of the research-teaching nexus in a research-intensive Irish university: A dynamic framework for growth & development. *Learning and Instruction, 60*, pp. 301–309. https://doi.org/10.1016/j.learninstruc.2017.10.005.

Caroff, X., Massu, J., & Lubart, T. (2018). Measuring Creativity at Work. In M. Lee & N. Wilson (Eds.), *The Palgrave Handbook of Creativity at Work.* Cham: Springer International Publishing, pp. 3–22.

Chandraseakaran, S., Littlefair, G., & Stojcevski, A. (2015). Staff and students views on industry-university collaboration in engineering. *International Journal of Advanced Corporate Learning*, *8*(2), pp. 13. https://doi.org/10.3991/ijac.v8i2.4408.

Del Río, M.L., Díaz-Vázquez, R., & Maside Sanfiz, J.M. (2018). Satisfaction with the supervision of undergraduate dissertations. *Active Learning in Higher Education, 19*(2), pp. 159–172. https://doi.org/10.1177/1469787417721365.

Dorta-Afonso, D. (2019). Teaching organizational behavior in the bachelor of tourism through the case study method. *Journal of Hospitality, Leisure, Sport & Tourism Education, 25*, pp. 100–204. https://doi.org/10.1016/j.jhlste.2019.100204.

Fotea, A.C., & Gutu, C. (2016). Historical and theoretical framework of the relation between higher education institutions and the process of regional economic development. *EBER*, *4*(1), pp. 23–42. https://doi.org/10.15678/EBER.2016.040103.

Furedi, F. (2011). Introduction to the marketisation of higher education and the student as consumer. In M. Molesworth, R. Scullion, & E. Nixon (Eds.), *The Marketisation of Higher Education and the Student as Consumer*. London and New York: Routledge, pp. 1–8.

GAP. (2020). *The Future of Global Business Services* [accessed from: https://gap.uek.krakow.pl/the-future-of-global-business-services/, 24 March 2020].

Giuri, P., Munari, F., Scandura, A., & Toschi, L. (2019). The strategic orientation of universities in knowledge transfer activities. *Technological Forecasting and Social Change*, *138*, pp. 261–278. https://doi.org/10.1016/j.techfore.2018.09.030.

IBM. (2010). *2010 Global CEO Study: Creativity Selected as Most Crucial Factor for Future Success* [accessed from: Available online at: www03.ibm.com/press/us/en/pressrelease/31670.wss].

John, P., & Fanghanel, J. (2016). *Dimensions of Marketisation in Higher Education*. London: Routledge.

Jorre de St Jorre, T., & Oliver, B. (2018). Want students to engage? Contextualise graduate learning outcomes and assess for employability. *Higher Education Research & Development, 37*(1), pp. 44–57. https://doi.org/10.1080/07294360.2017.1339183.

Lillo-Bañuls, A., Perles-Ribes, J.F. & Fuentes, R. (2016). Wiki and blog as teaching tools in tourism higher education. *Journal of Teaching in Travel & Tourism*, *16*(2), pp. 81–100. https://doi.org/10.1080/15313220.2015.1118367.

Mansfield, E., & Lee, J.-Y. (1996). The modern university: Contributor to industrial innovation and recipient of industrial R&D support. *Research Policy, 25*(7), pp. 1047–1058. https://doi.org/10.1016/S0048-7333(96)00893-1.

Psacharopoulos, G. (1994). Returns to investment in education: A global update. *World Development, 22*(9), pp. 1325–1343.

Rodríguez, G., Díez, J., Pérez, N., Baños, J.E., & Carrió, M. (2019). Flipped classroom: Fostering creative skills in undergraduate students of health sciences. *Thinking Skills and Creativity, 33*, pp. 100575. https://doi.org/10.1016/j.tsc.2019.100575.

Runco, M.A., Albert, R.S. (2010). Creativity Research. A Historical View. In J.C. Kaufman & R.J. Sternberg (Eds.), *The Cambridge Handbook of Creativity*. New York: Cambridge University Press, pp. 3–19.

Sarkar, A., & Perényi, Á. (2017). Education agents as competitiveness enhancers of Australian universities by internationalisation facilitation. *EBER, 5*(4), pp. 61–89. https://doi.org/10.15678/EBER.2017.050403.

Schumpeter, J.A. (1942). *Capitalism, Socialism, and Democracy*. New York: Harper & Brothers.

Schündeln, M., & Playforth, J. (2014). Private versus social returns to human capital: Education and economic growth in India. *European Economic Review, 66*, pp. 266–283.

Shaw, K., Holbrook, A., & Bourke, S. (2013). Student experience of final-year undergraduate research projects: An exploration of "research preparedness". *Studies in Higher Education, 38*(5), pp. 711–727. https://doi.org/10.1080/03075079.2011.592937.

Simonton, D.K. (2003). Scientific creativity as constrained stochastic behavior: The integration of product, person, and process perspectives. *Psychological Bulletin, 129*(4), pp. 475–494. https://doi.org/10.1037/0033-2909.129.4.475.

Skidelsky, R. (2009). *Keynes: The Return of the Master*. London: Allen Lane Penguin.

Smith, S. (2017). Reflections for postgraduate students on writing an action research thesis. *IUP Journal of Operations Management, 23*(1), pp. 61–76.

Sutton Trust (2008). *University Admissions by Individual Schools*. London: The Sutton Trust.

Tang, Min (2017). Creativity and Innovation: Basic Concepts and Approaches. In Min Tang & Ch.H. Werner (Eds.), *Handbook of the Management of Creativity and Innovation*. Singapore: World Scientific, pp. 3–32.

Tierney, W.G., & Lanford, M. (2016). Conceptualizing Innovation in Higher Education. In M.B. Paulsen (Ed.), *Higher Education: Handbook of Theory and Research*. Cham: Springer International Publishing (t. 31), pp. 1–40.

World Economic Forum. (2016). *The Future of Jobs: Employment, Skills, and Workforce Strategy for the Fourth Industrial Revolution* [accessed from: www3. weforum.org/docs/WEF_Future_of_Jobs.pdf].

16 The role of public authorities and other business environment institutions in the territorial embedding of offshore firms in Krakow

Paweł Białynicki-Birula

Determinants of territorial embeddedness of offshoring and outsourcing firms

Offshoring and outsourcing should be considered as part of a wider phenomenon, i.e. foreign direct investment (FDI), which serves as a tool for transferring physical capital, advanced technology, managerial skills, and/or innovative products from developed to developing countries (Wang, 2009). It is believed that such a diffusion of knowledge and technology results in tangible benefits for the host countries, among others, by promoting their economic development. Consequently, according to numerous governments, FDI makes it possible to overcome economic stagnation and combat poverty (Brooks et al., 2010). From this point of view, a detailed analysis of the conditions for attracting FDI is likely to provide a basis for effective public action intended to stimulate economic development.

Since the 1960s, various theories have been developed to explain the determinants of FDI, both at the microeconomic level and the macroeconomic one. The forces that influence location-specific decisions are perceived as the resultant of a number of pushing and pulling factors (Dunning, 2001). Since the late 1990s, in the context of FDI, the focus has been on institutional issues as the main factor that purports to explain the differences in both development and levels of corruption or political instability between countries. Institutional reforms are thought to be particularly important, because they make for a greater transparency in the activities of public authorities and thus ensure the security of economic turnover (Bénassy-Quéré et al., 2007).

The most frequently discussed determinants of FDI location belong to the so-called ownership, location, and internalisation (OLI) model and include: infrastructure, human capital, economic stability of the country, production costs, and institutional factors (corruption, political stability, quality of public institutions, and tax and financial incentives) as well as the parameters introduced by the new trade theory (market size, market growth, open economy, and capital equipment) (Dunning, 2001, Assuncao et al., 2011). Empirical research shows that in less-developed countries, the key to attracting investment is the fundamental factors rather than public incentives (Dorozynski et al., 2014; Morisset & Pirnia, 2000).

Currently the economic effects of FDI inflows are being studied not so much from a national but from a regional perspective. Foreign capital is thought to contribute to the socio-economic development of a number of regions by promoting production growth and improving people's living standards. Economic geographers recognise that regional public actors play a key role in attracting foreign investment, which, as part of the 'strategic interconnection' processes, ensures the integration of national actors into global production networks (GPNs) and stimulates regional development (Coe et al., 2008; Kleibert, 2014). As a result, attracting FDI to a considerable extent depends on the efforts of regional or local authorities, and thus the capacity to create new jobs, increase incomes, and improve the residents' living conditions.

Many instruments, including financial ones, such as grants and tax breaks, serve to attract foreign investors. The literature shows that investors appreciate preferential access to public services or grants for setting up and developing a business (Harding & Javorcik, 2011). They also welcome information, promotional support, and business consulting services provided by public authorities. Although such aid is somewhat less important than investment support, in developing economies with certain market distortions, it may be one of the factors that will ultimately determine the location decision. A special role is played by investment incentives which affect the size, location, or sector of the economy in which the investment is planned and which are generally not available to comparable domestic investor projects (OECD, 2003, Dorozynski et al., 2014).

The literature indicates that an important factor in FDI location decisions is a specific cost category referred to in business literature as *liability of foreignness* (LOF) and in economic geography as *border effects* or *frictions of distance*. These include extra coordination and communication costs incurred due to the distance from the home country, mistakes due to ignorance of the local conditions or cultural norms, and discrimination against foreign firms. A significant role in reducing these costs is attributed to the so-called global cities, although the operation of these centres is usually associated with congestion costs and the risk of reducing multinational enterprises' (MNE) competitive advantage over local entrepreneurs thanks to favourable conditions for generating knowledge (Goerzen et al., 2013).

Taking into account the specificity of the outsourcing sector, the literature underscores its apparent 'footlooseness', which means that it is fairly easy to attract firms to a given location, but it may prove difficult to keep them there (Kleibert, 2014). Such firms are generally characterised by relatively low investment outlays, which implies ease of relocation. On the other hand, due to the nature of the business, i.e. the provision of services, the availability of human capital is considered to be the most important factor in choosing location, followed by the quality of telecommunications infrastructure, the quality of institutions, and a proactive public policy, but with the provision that the actual importance of the last one is difficult to estimate (Kleibert, 2014).

The literature highlights the dynamic development of new forms of offshoring in recent years, namely knowledge-based offshoring. This kind of activity aims not so much to reduce the costs borne by parent firms (MNEs) as to create high added value in benefit chains. In this context, researchers focus on knowledge clusters or a similar concept of knowledge hub, duly emphasising the organisational aspects related to agglomerations and proximity or the effects of concentration, sharing, and dissemination of knowledge. They are considered in terms of local innovation systems and analysed through the prism of using intangible resources to create innovation and diffusion of knowledge (Przygrodzki, 2019).

In the context of MNEs, the issue of political embeddedness, understood as a specific form of integration of these firms with political actors and institutions in the host country, is widely discussed in the literature. The political embeddedness of a business network within the framework of IMP research takes four forms: political institutions, political entities, political activities of firms, and political resources (Welch & Wilkinson, 2004). Traditionally, there has been a positive correlation between political embeddedness and the organisational performance of firms in both developed and emerging economies. It is therefore argued that relations with the political sphere legitimise MNEs' status and provide access to valuable resources and information, while the rents generated by political resources provide an advantage over rivals. It should be noted, however, that the significance of political networks is now increasingly being questioned, which implies that in the face of unexpected changes in government policy or political regimes, political capital may quickly turn into a liability (Sun et al., 2010). Moreover, liberalisation is generally associated with the idea of equality of economic actors, which, by definition, limits the space for more or less informal endeavours.

Economic theories tend to take politics into account when analysing economic activity, a good example being institutionalism with its emphasis on the role of public choice theory (Wilkin, 2012). In the context of embeddedness, the IMP approach is of particular importance – the third generation of research focuses on business networks, namely the existence of relationships with two kinds of public actors (political and administrative). In the opinion of IMP researchers, removing political actors from business transactions leads to conclusions which are far removed from the economic reality, as exchange relationships are essentially influenced by political relations (Welch & Wilkinson, 2004).

The issue of the role of national actors in attracting investment in services remains an important element of the debate. While many governments are aware of the potential for economic development offered by foreign investment, the scientific literature on the effectiveness of their efforts to attract FDI is quite sceptical. It is often pointed out that the capacity of countries to negotiate with multinational corporations is limited due to the difference in potential between these two classes of actors (Phelps, 2008). Moreover, competition between countries often leads to location tournaments (Mytelka, 2000). Research in this area focuses primarily on the role of governments and national institutions in negotiations, while ignoring the regional and local actors.

A different perspective is offered by economic geography, where the importance of such factors as human and social capital or local laws and regulations for local development is emphasised (Przygrodzki, 2019). The process starts with a foreign investor declaring interest in a specific space where they plan to pursue their projects. Therefore, at the first stage, even if eligible countries have been shortlisted, ultimately the part of their territories that offers the best conditions for starting a business is chosen. As a result, it is the regions or smaller territorial entities that compete for the final location decision. It is emphasised that MNEs now prospect for optimal locations in almost every region worldwide provided they can ensure a minimum of business security.

It is recognised that local authorities have a wide range of instruments at their disposal to directly or indirectly influence the social, economic, and territorial features of individual areas, using the available legal tools, administrative procedures, and financial resources. Five main areas of local government action affect the investment climate in a given area: regulation, information and promotion, investment and organisation, finance, and coordination and mediation. At the same time, it is observed that foreign operators supply resources unavailable in the local economy or better use of the available ones, regardless of the political will or capabilities of the central government (Dorozynski et al., 2014).

The role of public authorities and other business institutions in embedding offshore outsourcing firms in Krakow

This section presents the research findings on the conditions of embeddedness of firms from the outsourcing and offshoring sector in Krakow from the point of view of the activity of public entities and mutual interactions. The study was based on interviews in 2019–2020. In the first stage, 15 interviews with the CEOs of business services centres were conducted using a questionnaire. Other interviews were carried out with representatives of key local/regional policy actors and a representative of ASPIRE – an association of offshoring and outsourcing firms based in Krakow. Public bodies participating in the interview included the Krakow City Hall (former and current Deputy Mayor and director of the relevant department of the City Hall), the Marshal's Office of the Małopolska Region (management and employees of the relevant departments), and the Krakow Technology Park (member of the board).

In order to better grasp the implications of the research findings, the issue of empowering policy actors in Poland to create conditions conducive for the development of business by foreign firms should be briefly clarified. In general, the responsibility for attracting and supporting foreign investors is shared between central and local administrations at the regional and local level. The central level has institutional and financial resources to coordinate national economic policy towards operators partly owned by foreign capital. An important role in this respect is played by the Ministries of the Economy and Finance, as well as central agencies for information and foreign investment or entrepreneurship development, which have the budgetary resources and EU funds for various investment programmes. Another support instrument is the Special Economic Zones (SEZ), which offer preferential operating conditions, investment areas, and qualified staff. After Poland's accession to the EU in 2004, the importance of the local government in providing assistance to foreign investors significantly increased. Currently, regional and local authorities have the organisational and financial capacity to create favourable conditions for business at the regional level. The European funds, which are distributed by the self-governing voivodeships, are of particular importance. Local authorities not only offer economic incentives, but also invest in hard and soft infrastructure (Dorozynski et al., 2014).

As regards the survey, the questions asked of CEOs were divided into three groups: 1. the non-economic factors determining the choice of Krakow as a location; 2. the key factors that may induce a firm to relocate from Krakow; and 3. an evaluation of the intensity of relations between offshoring and outsourcing firms and public bodies. Responses to the first group of questions are summarized in Table 16.1.

From the CEOs' point of view, the most important factor that influenced the location decisions was the brand of Krakow and Malopolska (3.67), followed by the investment climate (3.60) and cultural factors (3.53). The quality of life in Krakow (3.40), the availability of office space (3.33), and transport accessibility (3.20) were the next most important factors. The system of incentives for entrepreneurs (2.20) and the quality of investor service (1.87) come at the bottom of the table. These results suggest that the key factors in attracting firms from this sector to Krakow are best described as indirect and long-term outcomes of the efforts of public authorities, namely Krakow as a brand, the investment climate, and the quality of life. It is worth noting that the respondents attach relatively little importance to direct public actions, such as the incentive system or the quality of investor service.

The respondents were then asked to rank the factors that might conceivably persuade them to relocate from Krakow (Table 16.2). The most important in this respect is access to a highly qualified workforce (2.31) and labour cost (1.31). The respondents considered the operating costs (0.69) and foreign language skills of

Table 16.1 Factors determining the choice of Krakow as a business location in the opinion of CEOs of Krakow-based outsourcing and offshoring firms

Factors	*Importance*					
	Very important (5)	*(4)*	*(3)*	*(2)*	*Unimportant (1)*	*Weighted mean*
Krakow and Malopolska as brands	5	2	7	0	1	3.67
Investment climate	3	4	7	1	0	3.60
Cultural factors	4	1	9	1	0	3.53
Quality of life in Krakow	4	4	4	1	1	3.40
Availability of office space	2	6	4	2	0	3.33
Transport accessibility	2	3	7	2	1	3.20
Incentive system	0	1	4	7	3	2.20
Quality of investor service (public authorities)	0	0	5	3	7	1.87

Source: Own study.

potential employees (0.46) as less important. The lowest scoring was the investment climate (0.31), political stability (0.23), the quality of life (0.15), and the existence of an incentive system (0.08). Thus, the main considerations in a decision to relocate mainly reflect the operational side of a firm's activity, whereas the factors determined by the political/public side play a relatively minor role.

The last group of questions concerned the intensity of relations between business services firms and public local and regional bodies (Table 16.3). Three categories of actors were taken into account: municipal authorities (Krakow City Hall), regional authorities (Marshal's Office of the Małopolska Region), and local business support institutions (Krakow Technology Park). Respondents were asked to score the intensity on a scale from 1 (none) to 4 (strong). The table presents the number of responses and the weighted mean for each partner category.

Table 16.2 The most important factors taken into consideration in a potential decision to relocate a Krakow-based subsidiary in the opinion of CEOs of local outsourcing and offshoring firms

Factors	*First (3)*	*Second (2)*	*Third (1)*	*Weighted mean*
Supply of highly qualified employees	10	–	–	2.31
Labour costs	2	4	3	1.31
Operating costs	–	4	1	0.69
Availability of foreign language speakers	–	3	–	0.46
Investment climate	–	1	2	0.31
Political stability	–	–	3	0.23
Quality of life in Krakow	–	–	2	0.15
Incentive system (e.g. taxes)	–	–	1	0.08

Source: Own study.

Table 16.3 The intensity of relations between offshoring/outsourcing firms and public bodies in the opinion of CEOs of Krakow's outsourcing and offshoring firms

Relationship partner	*Intensity of relations with partners*				*Weighted mean*
	Strong (4)	*(3)*	*(2)*	*None (1)*	
Local authorities (Krakow City Hall)	5	4	6	0	2.93
Regional authorities (Marshal's Office)	4	2	5	4	2.40
Local intermediaries (Krakow Technology Park)	3	4	3	5	2.33
Other bodies	–	–	–	–	0

Source: Own study.

The relations between offshoring and outsourcing firms and the city of Krakow (2.93) proved to be the strongest, followed by relations with the Marshal's Office (2.40) and the Krakow Technology Park (2.33). The results suggest that local authorities play a major role in contacts with the surveyed firms. It is noteworthy that none of the respondents mentioned government administration institutions or central departments/agencies responsible for dealing with foreign investors.

Moving on to the analysis of the interviews, the topics covered and the subsequent analysis focus on the following problem areas:

1 The role of public authorities in bringing offshore outsourcing firms to Krakow;
2 The efforts of public authorities to attract and promote the embeddedness of firms from this sector;
3 Cooperation of public authorities with offshoring and outsourcing firms.

The role of public authorities in bringing offshoring and outsourcing firms to Krakow

Efforts to include Krakow in the processes of globalisation and European integration were started by the first local government in the transformation period, which, drawing on the city's brand and its academic profile, set out to attract high-tech industry firms inspired by the success of California's Silicon Valley, Ireland's Silicon Docks, and Scotland's Silicon Glen. The city authorities turned to consultants – experts from banking institutions and aid donors (World Bank, USAID, UNDP, Know-How Fund) and began to actively seek investors (participation in international fairs, contacts with experts), all the while preparing suitable locations. They signed letters of intent with the rectors of Krakow's universities, committing themselves to bringing the necessary infrastructure to potential investment sites (Ruczaj, Pychowice). The organisation of the Conference on Security and Cooperation in Europe in 1993 proved to be a success in promoting the city in the international arena.

Motorola was the first major company to invest in Krakow in 1994. The city authorities showed a great determination in making it happen, aided by one of Motorola's managers of Polish descent. The negotiations, which took several months to complete, were characterised not only by frequent meetings but also by dramatic twists of the plot since at the time, Krakow competed with Warsaw, Wroclaw, and Prague. Originally, Motorola was looking for a place/laboratory to test mobile phone parts (SDRs). After preliminary agreements had been reached, however, due to a change in the market situation (global overproduction), the company abandoned its original project, and thanks to efforts on the part of the city (favourable conditions for the acquisition of the site, creation of the special economic zone in 1997, making the premises of Przegorzały Castle available by the Jagiellonian University as a temporary premises), decided to establish a software centre in Krakow. In 1998, the Motorola Software Centre started its operations, and in 2002, it moved to its newly built premises in the economic zone.

Public authorities' efforts to attract and improve the embeddedness of firms in the outsourcing and offshoring sector

Encouraged by Motorola's successful project, other firms started to arrive in Krakow mostly to previously prepared sites, until the process became increasingly self-perpetuating. An important role in this respect was played by the already present firms, which, on various occasions, 'unwittingly' provided good publicity at conferences and business meetings. Naturally, both the municipal and provincial authorities continue to promote the city at various industry events. Nevertheless, operators that intend to locate their activity in Krakow rely mainly on commercial intermediaries (e.g. Cushman) for investment preparation. For that reason, they have excellent ex-ante knowledge and do not seek special support from public bodies – either government institutions providing FDI services or local public authorities.

From the point of view of the firms' representatives, the issue of providing convenient living conditions for employees and their families seems to be very significant for their embeddedness in the city and its agglomeration. This applies, in particular, to public transport, social infrastructure (education, health care), and public spaces (green areas). The interviewed representative of ASPIRE particularly emphasised two issues: the need to ensure convenient commuting for employees and educational institutions providing tuition in foreign languages. The former is a prerequisite for an adequate inflow of local staff, while the latter directly translates into the possibility to recruit specialists unavailable in Poland. For example, one interviewee said that he could immediately employ several dozen engineers from abroad with unique qualifications, but the limited availability of schools with English as a teaching language closed further discussion. The representatives of public authorities interviewed also see their role in promoting the embeddedness of firms primarily in providing more convenient living conditions for local residents/employees. Moreover, the latter underscore the need to encourage diversity and balance in economic development to prevent overdependence on a single sector.

Cooperation of public authorities with firms from the offshoring outsourcing sector

In the interviews, the sector's representatives generally expressed positive opinions on their cooperation with public authorities, even though they consider it to be mostly routine in nature. Generally speaking, they are never denied support or assistance in organising various activities (annual conferences, exchange of information, ongoing contacts), but they do not feel they are treated in any special way. Although the CEOs appreciate the benefits resulting from attractive conditions for doing business (technology park, economic zone), they see the key role of public bodies primarily in promoting Krakow globally. They perceive the development and embeddedness of the services sector as dependent on creating a favourable image and ensuring brand recognition. The interlocutors emphasised that strong competition from other centres allows no room for complacency.

From the perspective of public actors, the sector develops in a self-sustaining manner, and hence they do not have to undertake any special activities apart from promotion, such as participation in fairs. It was pointed out that since 2008, an innovation committee has been operating in the city council (as the first one in the local government in Poland), which provides a forum for exchanging ideas and initiates actions to support the sector's development. Both sides – firms and public authorities – recognise the advantages of having an association representing business services entities in Krakow, the only such organisation in Poland.

Conclusion

Outsourcing and offshoring firms do not expect any special direct action on the part of the city/public authorities targeted at their sector, consequently, the quality of investor service and incentive systems are to be found at the bottom of the hierarchy of factors that affect Krakow's attractiveness. The basic determinants of the firms' embeddedness are the availability of highly qualified employees and their salaries. In other words, the city and public authorities cannot significantly influence the main potential relocation drivers and conversely, the factors that they can partly control have little or no weight in relocation decisions. From this point of view, the activities of public decision-makers generally have a limited impact on the embeddedness of outsourcing and offshoring firms. What remains is international promotion of the city/region directed at two categories of recipients: firms and potential candidates for employees who would like to live here.

The most important factor in how successful offshoring and outsourcing firms are in a certain location is human resources. From this point of view, the city's task is not only to attract investors by improving the overall quality of life for employees but also to provide the necessary services (schools, health care) at the expected level. Bringing in firms and fostering their development/embeddedness has a primarily social aspect and cannot exclusively rely on technical aspects. From the respondents' point of view, the key issue is ensuring appropriate living conditions for employees. Therefore, the task of the authorities is to create a friendly environment (ecology, greenery, taking actions, creating the image of an open good-for-living city).

In recent years, the business services sector in Krakow has developed spontaneously, but it must not lull the city authorities into a false sense of security owing to intense worldwide competition. From this point of view, the key issue is the promotion of the city and further investment in its brand. Otherwise, Krakow's economic boom may rapidly wane – in this respect, the 2019 Tholons ranking should be taken as a warning, since after a period of stability, the city dropped by four places (from sixth to eleventh). While the outsourcing and offshoring firms do not expect special treatment from public authorities, they would like the administrative procedures regarding city transport and infrastructure to be completed within reasonable timeframes.

From the point of view of the territorial embeddedness of offshoring and outsourcing firms, the human factor, understood in terms of access to appropriate personnel, is of paramount importance. In view of this fact, the role of local authorities cannot be reduced only to promoting the city as a convenient place to do business but must also involve efforts to ensure convenient living conditions for employees as city residents. Attracting foreign investments and fostering their development/embeddedness is therefore not only a strictly technical or economic issue; it also has a social dimension. Consequently, public authorities should both enhance the image of the city and do their utmost to make it people-friendly so that the employees of offshoring and outsourcing firms want to live there permanently.

References

Assuncao, S., Forte, R., & Teixeira, A. (2011). *Location Determinants of FDI: A Literature Review*. FEP Working Papers, No. 433, pp. 1–23.

Bénassy-Quéré, A., Coupet, M., & Mayer, Th. (2007). *Institutional Determinants of Foreign Direct Investment*. CEPII Working Paper, No. 2005–05.

Brooks, D.H., Hasan, R., Lee, J.-W., Son, H.H., & Zhuang, J. (2010). *Closing Development Gaps: Challenges and Policy Options*. ADB Economics Working Paper, Series 209, Manila: Asian Development Bank.

Coe, N.M., Dicken, P., & Hess, M. (2008). Global production networks: Realizing the potential. *Journal of Economic Geography*, *8*(3), pp. 271–295.

Dorozynski, T., Dorozynska, A., & Urbaniak, W. (2014). The role of local government units in attracting FDI: The case of the Lodz Region. *Business and Economic Horizons*, *10*(4), |pp. 281–304.

Dunning, J.H. (2001). The eclectic (OLI) paradigm of international production: Past, present and future. *International Journal of the Economics of Business*, *8*(2), pp. 173–190.

Goerzen, A., Asmussen, Ch.G., & Nielsen, B. (2013). Global cities and multinational enterprise location strategy. *Journal of International Business Studies*, *44*, pp. 427–450.

Harding, T., & Javorcik, B.S. (2011). Roll out the red carpet and they will come: Investment promotion and FDI inflows. *The Economic Journal*, *121*(557), pp. 1445–1476.

Kleibert, J.M. (2014). Strategic coupling in "next wave cities": Local institutional actors and the offshore service sector in the Philippines, *Singapore Journal of Tropical Geography*, *35*, pp. 245–260.

Morisset, J., & Pirnia, N. (2000). *How Tax Policy and Incentives Affect Foreign Direct Investment: A Review*. Policy Research Working Paper, No. 2509, World Bank.

Mytelka, L. (2000). Locational tournaments for FDI: Inward investment into Europe in a global world. In N. Hood & S. Young (Eds.), *The Globalization of Multinational Enterprise Activity and Economic Development*. London: Palgrave Macmillan.

OECD. (2003). *Checklist for Foreign Direct Investment Incentive Policies*.

Phelps, N.A. (2008). Cluster or capture? Manufacturing foreign direct investment, external economies and agglomeration. *Regional Studies*, *42*(4), pp. 457–473.

Przygrodzki, Z. (2019). Territorial dimension of human capital. *Gospodarka Narodowa*, *300*(4), pp. 105–130.

Sun, P., Mellahi, K., & Thun, E. (2010). The dynamic value of MNE political embeddedness: The case of the Chinese automobile industry. *Journal of International Business Studies*, *41*, pp. 1161–1182.

Wang, M. (2009). *Manufacturing FDI and Economic Growth: Evidence from Asian Economies* [accessed from: https://ssrn.com/abstract=440440 or http://doi.org/10.2139/ssrn.440440].

Welch, C., & Wilkinson, I. (2004). The political embeddedness of international business networks. *International Marketing Review*, *21*(2), pp. 216–231.

Wilkin, J. (2012). *Teoria wyboru publicznego. Główne nurty i zastosowania*. Warszawa: Wydawnictwo Naukowe Scholar.

Afterword

Łukasz Mamica

Over the last decade, the business process outsourcing and offshoring sector has become one of the most important players creating relatively well-paid jobs in the Visegrad group cities selected for analysis in this monograph, such as Budapest, Bratislava, Prague, Brno, and Krakow. In the last city, the broadly understood business process outsourcing (BPO) sector employs over 70,000 people and well over 520,000 people (2019) in the above-mentioned group of countries as a whole. Large agglomerations constitute natural spaces for locating offshoring and outsourcing services, especially more advanced global business ones. In times of crisis, answering the question about the stability of jobs and the sustainable presence of firms offering them in specific locations becomes all the more important. However, it is not easy to determine the degree of embeddedness (understood as the likelihood of relocation) of multinational corporations in the outsourcing and offshoring business for a number of reasons, one of them being changes resulting from various pressures from both the external and the internal environment. External factors, such as increased relative attractiveness of other locations due to the resources available there, the level of security, or technological changes that lead to the replacement of human labour, may lead to the decision to relocate or increase the likelihood of relocation. At the peak of the coronavirus pandemic in spring 2020, it is also difficult to predict the exact course of further economic globalisation processes and how they will be affected by remote work on an unprecedented scale.

The findings of the research conducted among the CEOs of firms representing the business process outsourcing and offshoring sector operating in Krakow warrant the conclusion that these firms are embedded in the city to a fairly high degree. Despite the increasing salaries, but thanks to the improving workforce qualifications, these firms are capable of performing ever more advanced processes. Consequently, their CEOs expect to be able to maintain their competitive advantage and further increase employment. When asked about the change in the complexity of processes implemented in their firms, which have taken place in the last five years, they consider it to be large or very large. In their opinion, the period in question has also seen increased uniqueness of the processes implemented.

Despite the fact that international contacts decidedly prevail in the sector studied, the degree of its embeddedness in the cities selected for the study is fairly high and results mainly from the availability of a well-qualified labour force with a good command of foreign languages, which is still less expensive than its Western European counterpart. On the other hand, the employees appreciate the quality of life in the main metropolitan cities of this part of Europe. For these reasons, the situation can be described as 'ripple-effect embeddedness', where global corporations from the business process outsourcing and offshoring sector develop ties with locations that provide creative employees with a desirable ratio of value added to wages paid. Their employees in Krakow declare that the city is a good place to live and that they do not intend to move elsewhere in Poland or abroad in the nearest future. They highly appreciate the attractive centre, the cultural milieu and entertainment opportunities, access to services, as well as the situation on the local labour market.

The perception of the city as highly attractive by the employees of firms operating in Krakow means that the latter can count on a stable access to a qualified workforce, which has a positive impact on their embeddedness. Thus, thanks to the ability to attract (or retain, as in the case of university graduates) qualified staff, metropolises, and specifically their social fabric, are becoming the key factors in the embeddedness of the analysed sector, which is looking for dispersed knowledge-based resources. The quality of life is influenced not only by the broadly conceived working conditions, but also by such parameters as the quality of health care, cultural milieu, opportunities for leisure activities, or the quality of the natural environment. All these areas require appropriate regulation on the part of institutions, especially public ones. Therefore, the institutional set-up and its capacity to regulate are particularly important for the embeddedness of the business process outsourcing and offshoring sector. However, mainly thanks to its high-quality human capital, this sector in European emerging economies is undergoing a qualitative transformation towards more advanced global business services processes and increasing the level of embeddedness of its constituent firms in the region.

Index